AN INTRODUCT
THOUGHT OF KARL POPPER

Sir Karl Popper is widely acclaimed as one of the most influential thinkers of our time. Born in Vienna in 1902, he fled the Nazis in 1937 and took up a university post in New Zealand. He followed a distinguished academic career, teaching and lecturing all over Europe, Australasia, India, Japan and the USA. He has written numerous books, articles and essays. His publications have appeared in some thirty languages.

This study offers an accessible introduction to the life and work of this extraordinary thinker, including his often-neglected *Postscript* on scientific method published in three volumes in the 1980s. It charts the development of Popper's philosophy and shows his unfailing political commitment to humanism and enlightenment. At the centre of Popper's thought stands rationality and a strong belief in the power of the human mind to change things for the better. Rationality thus serves as a guide both in his philosophical considerations and for his political views.

Approved by Karl Popper himself as a careful and comprehensive study, *An Introduction to the Thought of Karl Popper* will be ideal to meet the increasing demand for a summary introduction to his work. It has been translated into English by Patrick Camiller.

Roberta Corvi is a Lecturer of Philosophy at the Catholic University of Milan. She is the author of *La filosofia di P.F. Strawson* (1979) and *I fraintendimenti della ragione* (1992), a monograph about Paul Feyerabend.

AN INTRODUCTION TO THE THOUGHT OF KARL POPPER

Roberta Corvi

Translated by Patrick Camiller

London and New York

First published 1997
by Routledge
11 New Fetter Lane, London EC4P 4EE

Simultaneously published in the USA and Canada
by Routledge
29 West 35th Street, New York, NY 10001

© 1993 Gruppo Ugo Mursia Editore S.p.A.
English translation © 1997 Patrick Camiller

Phototypeset in Garamond by Intype London Ltd
Printed and bound in Great Britain by
Clays Ltd, St. Ives PLC

British Library Cataloguing in Publication Data
A catalogue record for this book is available from the British Library

Library of Congress Cataloguing in Publication Data
Corvi, Roberta.
[Invito al pensiero di Karl Popper. English]
Introduction to the thought of Karl Popper / Roberta Corvi;
translated by Patrick Camiller.
p. cm.
Includes bibliographical references and index.
1. Popper, Karl Raimund, Sir, 1902–1994. 2. Social sciences—
Philosophy. 3. Knowledge, Theory of. I. Title.
B1649.P64C66613 1996
192—dc20 96–7922

ISBN 0–415–12956–7 (hbk)
ISBN 0–415–12957–5 (pbk)

CONTENTS

FOREWORD TO THE
ENGLISH EDITION

This book was conceived, written and published in Italian at a time when Sir Karl Popper was still alive and active. It therefore seemed fitting, for the English translation, to update the biographical information as well as the bibliography. I did not think it necessary to make any major changes, because the aim of this work is to draw out the main lines of Popper's thought and to show that they remained constant through the evolution of his huge body of writings.

The Italian text was, however, intended for a public familiar with a cultural context that is not exactly the same as that of the English-speaking countries, and so the present edition differs at certain points from the original. I have also adopted a number of suggestions made by Professor Pieranna Garavaso of Minnesota University, who very kindly read the text and commented on it in detail. I would like to thank her most warmly for her invaluable remarks, which helped me in no small measure to improve the book and to make it more suitable for English-speaking readers. I am well aware that my survey of Popper's thought is not free from gaps, and probably also misunderstandings, but for these I am, of course, alone responsible.

ABBREVIATIONS OF POPPER'S WORKS

BG   *Die beiden Grundprobleme der Erkenntnistheorie*, J.C.B. Mohr, Tübingen, 1979.

CR   *Conjectures and Refutations: The Growth of Scientific Knowledge*, Routledge & Kegan Paul, London, 1963.

EE   'Die erkenntnistheoretische Position der evolutionären Erkenntnistheorie', in R. Riedl and F.M. Wuketits (eds), *Die evolutionäre Erkenntnistheorie. Bedingungen, Lösungen, Kontroversen*, Parey, Berlin and Hamburg, 1987, pp. 29ff.

ISBW   *In Search of a Better World*, Routledge, London, 1992.

LSD   *The Logic of Scientific Discovery*, Hutchinson, London, 1959.

MF   *The Myth of the Framework*, Routledge, London, 1994.

NS   'Normal Science and Its Dangers', in I. Lakatos and A. Musgrave, (eds), *Criticism and the Growth of Knowledge*, Cambridge University Press, Cambridge, 1974, pp. 51–58.

NSEM   'Natural Selection and the Emergence of Mind', *Dialectica* 32/3–4, (1978), pp. 339–355.

OK   *Objective Knowledge: An Evolutionary Approach*, Clarendon Press, Oxford, 1972.

OGOU   *Offene Gesellschaft, offenes Universum*, Franz Deuticke, Vienna, 1982.

OS I   *The Open Society and Its Enemies; Part One*, one-volume edition, Routledge, London, 1995.

OS II   *The Open Society and Its Enemies; Part Two*, one-volume edition, Routledge, London, 1995.

P1   *Postscript to the Logic of Scientific Discovery*, vol. 1:

	Realism and the Aim of Science, Routledge, London, 1985.
P2	*Postscript to the Logic of Scientific Discovery*, vol. 2: *The Open Universe: Arguments for Indeterminism*, Routledge, London, 1988.
P3	*Postscript to the Logic of Scientific Discovery*, vol. 3: *Quantum Theory and the Schism in Physics*, Routledge, London, 1992.
PH	*The Poverty of Historicism*, Routledge, London, 1991.
RC	'Replies to My Critics', in P.A. Schilpp (ed.), *The Philosophy of Karl Popper*, Open Court, La Salle, 1974, vol. 2, pp. 961–1197.
RR	*Revolution oder Reform? Herbert Marcuse und Karl Popper – Eine Konfrontation*, Kösel, Munich, 1971.
SB	*The Self and Its Brain* (written with Sir John Eccles), Routledge, London, 1993.
TIR	'Toleration and Intellectual Responsibility', in S. Medus and D. Edwards (eds), *On Toleration*, Clarendon Press, Oxford, 1987, pp. 17–34.
UQ	*Unended Quest: an Intellectual Biography*, Routledge, London, 1992.
WP	*A World of Propensities*, Thoemmes, Bristol, 1990.
ZO	*Die Zukunft ist offen. Das Altenberger Gespräch. Mit den Texten des Wiener Popper-Symposiums*, Piper, Munich, 1985.

A CHRONOLOGY OF POPPER'S LIFE

1902   Karl Raimund Popper born 28 July at Himmelhof (Vienna).

1914   First contacts with socialism.

1917   'Key year' in which a lengthy illness keeps him away from school.

1918   Leaves school to attend university, but without taking the entrance exam (*Matura*).

1919   In spring, joins the Association of Socialist School Students, but leaves it for good a few months later. Discovers Adler's 'individual psychology' and Freudian psychoanalysis. Studies Einstein and hears a lecture of his in Vienna.

1920   Leaves home in the winter to live in student accommodation and does various jobs to become independent.

1922–4 Passes the *Matura* as an external candidate. Serves a cabinetmaker's apprenticeship.

1924–5 Obtains a primary school teaching diploma. Does social work with abandoned children.

1925   Registers at the newly founded Pedagogical Institute in Vienna. Leaves his job as a social worker. Meets his future wife.

1928   Successfully submits a doctoral thesis in philosophy.

1929   Qualifies to teach mathematics and physics in lower secondary schools.

1930   Teaching in a secondary school. Marries Josefine Anna Henninger. Meets Feigl, who encourages him to write a book.

1932	Completes *The Two Fundamental Problems of the Theory of Knowledge*. Stays in the Tyrol with Carnap and Feigl.
1934	His book, revised and shortened, appears as the *Logik der Forschung*. Meets Tarski for the first time at a congress in Prague.
1935–6	Makes two long lecture trips to England.
1937	Accepts a post at University College in New Zealand, and moves there with his wife.
1938	Starts to work on his political texts.
1939–42	Devotes himself to political reflection, in addition to teaching duties.
1943	Finishes *The Open Society and Its Enemies*.
1944	Publishes *The Poverty of Historicism*.
1945	Publishes *The Open Society*. The University of London offers him a readership.
1946–7	Returns to Europe and settles in London. Begins work at the London School of Economics, where he takes charge of the Department of Philosophy, Logic and Scientific Method. Wittgenstein and others hear him lecture in Cambridge. Frequent meetings with Schrödinger.
1949	Becomes professor of logic and scientific methodology at the University of London.
1950	Moves to Penn, Buckinghamshire. First trip to America and first meeting with Einstein.
1951–3	Resumes work on a book that will be called *Postscript: Twenty Years After*. Summarizes his ideas on the philosophy of science at a lecture in Cambridge: 'Philosophy of Science: a Personal Report'.
1956–8	Finishes a draft of the first part of the *Postscript*, but further work is prevented by an operation on both eyes.
1959	Publication of *The Logic of Scientific Discovery*, an expanded English edition of the 1934 original.
1961	'Methodological dispute' between Popper's critical rationalism and the Frankfurt School at the German Sociological Congress in Heidelberg.
1962–3	Publishes a major collection of articles as *Conjectures and Refutations*.
1965	Knighted Sir Karl Popper in 1965.

1967   Gives a lecture in Amsterdam, 'Epistemology without a Knowing Subject', in which he formulates for the first time the theory of World 3.

1969   Gives up teaching at the University of London, but continues his writing and lecturing activity.

1971   Bavarian Radio broadcasts a long-distance debate between Popper and Marcuse later published as *Revolution oder Reform?*

1972   Publishes *Objective Knowledge*, in which he develops his theory of the objective mind (Worlds 1, 2 and 3).

1974   Two volumes in the *Library of Living Philosophers* series are devoted to his thought – including his *Intellectual Autobiography* (later republished as *Unended Quest*) and 'Replies to My Critics'.

1977   Publishes a book jointly written with John Eccles, *The Self and Its Brain*.

1979   Popper's first work, *Die beiden Grundprobleme der Erkenntnistheorie*, is finally published in its original form. On 8 July he is awarded an *ad honorem* degree of Frankfurt University, and on 27 July an *honoris causa* degree of Salzburg University.

1981   The first French conference on Popper's thought.

1983   Between 24 and 26 May a Popper Symposium is held in Vienna.

1985   Death of his wife. Moves from Penn to London.

1986   Visiting professor at the University of Vienna.

1987   A conference, entitled 'The Philosophy of Critical Rationalism', is organized for his 85th birthday in Dubrovnik, between 28 September and 9 October. It is attended by scholars from various countries.

1988   On 24 August he gives a lecture, 'A World of Propensities', at the World Congress of Philosophy in Brighton.

1989   On 9 June he gives a lecture, 'Towards an Evolutionary Theory of Knowledge', at the London School of Economics.

1990   Publishes *A World of Propensities*.

1991   Gives press and television interviews about major political events such as the Gulf War and the break-up of the Soviet Union.

1992   His views on recent events that have changed the shape of world politics are published as a book-interview in Italian (*The Lesson of This Century*). Publishes an article on Parmenides in *The Classical Quarterly*.

1994   His last essay, *Una patente per fare TV*, appears in Italian. Dies in London on 17 September.

Part I

Part I

1

THE LIFE

Karl Popper was born at Himmelhof, in the district of Vienna, on 28 July 1902, the last of three children after two sisters. His family was of Jewish origin, and the atmosphere in which he grew up was, as he put it, 'decidedly bookish' (UQ: 10): his father, Simon, was a lawyer and his mother, Jenny Schiff, came from a family in which music was enthusiastically cultivated. The personalities of both parents made their mark on the child's development. The father, 'more of a scholar than a lawyer' (UQ: 11), translated the classics, greatly appreciated philosophy, and took a keen interest in social problems. He gave the young Karl numerous opportunities to channel his precocious intelligence: for example, the portraits of Schopenhauer and Darwin hanging in his father's studio aroused in him a questioning curiosity, 'even before [he] had learned to read' (NSEM: 339). His mother, on the other hand, passed on to him such a passion for music that between 1920 and 1922 he seriously thought of taking it up as a career. Even after this idea was abandoned, his love for music did not diminish and indeed was fundamental in the development of his philosophical thinking.

This stimulating climate favoured a spontaneous interest in books, but also in the political events that marked his early adolescence and culminated in the First World War and the ensuing collapse of the Austro-Hungarian Empire. Meanwhile Karl attended the *Realgymnasium*, but he was not satisfied with the instruction he received there. After a long illness that kept him at home for more than two months, he became convinced that his class no longer offered any scope for significant progress. He therefore left in late 1918 and enrolled at the University of Vienna, but it was only in 1922 that he finally sat the entrance examination

3

THE LIFE

(the *Matura*) and became a properly matriculated student. He later recalled that he wanted to study not in order to start a career, but for the pleasure of learning and for the opportunity it gave him of exchanging political views with his friends. He had in fact joined a Socialist association, and for a few months in 1919 considered himself a Communist. But soon a clash between demonstrators and police in the Hörlgasse led him to think more critically about Marxism, which could justify the spilling of blood for the sake of the revolution on the grounds that one day of capitalism took a heavier toll of lives than the whole social revolution would do (OGOU: 9). Karl felt sure that when it came to sacrificing human lives, it was necessary to act with extreme prudence. Disillusioned with the dogmatic character of Marxism, he moved away from it but continued to call himself a socialist for a number of years. Socialism was then for him no more than 'an ethical postulate: nothing other than the idea of justice' (RR: 10). Only later did he realize that state socialism was merely oppression and could not be reconciled with freedom; that 'freedom is more important than equality' because 'if freedom is lost, there will not even be equality among the unfree' (UQ: 36).

Of minor importance, though still crucial, was the young Karl's discovery – also in 1919 – of Freud's psychoanalysis and Alfred Adler's 'individual psychology'. As we shall see, he thought of these as lacking scientific status, unlike Einstein's theories that made such a strong impression on him during that critical year. He managed to attend a lecture in Vienna at which Einstein unfolded before a 'dazed' Popper (UQ: 37) a new cosmology which challenged Newtonian mechanics and Maxwellian electrodynamics, both hitherto accepted as true beyond all doubt.

This decisive encounter revealed to the young physics student the difference between the positions of Marx, Freud and Adler, on the one hand, and those of Einstein on the other: the former were dogmatic attitudes that went looking for verifications, whereas the latter constituted a critical approach seeking not confirmation but crucial tests. By late 1919, then, Popper was convinced that what distinguished the scientist was the critical attitude (UQ: 38). Though showing some interest in philosophy, which led him to read Kant's *Critique of Pure Reason* and *Prolegomena*, he was mainly captivated by mathematics and theoretical physics. In the winter of 1919–20, when he left the parental home to live in modest student accommodation, he tried to become

4

independent by doing various kinds of work, so as not to burden a family whose economic situation was anything but flourishing in the runaway post-war inflation. Besides, he was eager to do some manual activity and avoid becoming an isolated intellectual remote from the social reality he was supposed to interpret and influence (OGOU: 10). His first jobs were irregular, but later he served an apprenticeship as a cabinetmaker and did social work with neglected children. Meanwhile he obtained a qualification to teach mathematics, physics and chemistry in secondary schools, and above all developed his own ideas on the demarcation between science and pseudo-science (UQ: 41). (As he later admitted, however, the first stimulus here came from his interest in political philosophy, which subsequently broadened out into a more general conception of philosophy (OGOU: 24).)

The 1920s were thus a watershed in Popper's formation, enriching it not only with intellectual discoveries but also with experience of life that wove together varied human and cultural interests. In 1925 he started to attend the Pedagogic Institute, where he met, among others, the woman who would become his wife in 1930 and always be close to him in his work (UQ: 73). To this period, too, belong his first unofficial academic experiments in the holding of seminars to help other students prepare for their exams. Although he had not yet published anything, he read and wrote a great deal, identified problems and outlined the solutions that would later be fleshed out in his most famous works. In particular, he was very keen on the ideas of Karl Bühler, a Gestalt psychologist who, as his professor, taught him that language was capable of serving different functions – to which Popper later added the argumentative function, as the basis of all critical thought (UQ: 74).

Around this time Popper got to know Heinrich Gomperz, son of the Hellenist Theodor Gomperz, with whom he often discussed problems of the psychology of knowledge and discovery. But then it became clear that what really interested Popper was the logic of discovery, and that his belief in a real world to be discovered and known made it impossible for him to accept Gomperz's very different 'psychological' approach. This option in favour of realism, one of the cornerstones of Popper's epistemology, would become stronger in later years and eventually lead to his theory of three worlds in which the realism applies even to creations of the human mind. If knowledge has an objective dimension beyond the subjective one, there is for Popper no choice but to reject the associationist psychology of the English empiricists; the study of logic – that is, of the objective aspects of knowledge – takes priority over the study of subjective thought processes. This view shows an affinity with the ideas of the Würzburg School, according to which human beings think not in pictures but in terms of problems (UQ: 76). It is not surprising, then, that Popper's PhD thesis, 'On the Problem of Method in the Psychology of Thinking', marked his final move away from psychology and towards philosophy or, to be more precise, a consideration of methodology.

It was in 1928, in the city where Popper had so far lived and studied, that the Vienna Circle was officially born with its 'scientific conception of the world' better known as logical positivism. Previously called the *Verein Ernst Mach*, the Circle had already been meeting for some time around the figure of Moritz Schlick, and its main exponents included Rudolf Carnap, Otto Neurath (who first brought the group to Popper's attention through an article and a lecture), Hans Hahn (his former mathematics professor), Viktor Kraft and Herbert Feigl (both of whom Popper knew personally). It was Feigl who, after a 'nightlong' discussion, had a major influence on Popper's philosophical future by encouraging him to write up his ideas in book form (UQ: 82).

Early in 1932, after a couple of years' work, Popper finished what he considered at the time to be the first volume of *The Two Fundamental Problems of the Theory of Knowledge*. It was read first by Feigl and then by other members of the Circle, including Carnap and Schlick, who thought highly of it despite its open criticism of the theories held by the logical positivists. The Springer publishing house, however, insisted that it had to be 'radically shortened' (UQ: 85) to no more than 240 pages. The version that finally appeared in 1934, under the title *Logik der Forschung*, was widely reviewed in the press, including by Circle members – Carnap and Hempel were quite favourable, while Reichenbach and Neurath were more critical.

Popper was certainly inclined to be polemical in relation to the Wiener Kreis, but he shared its members' Enlightenment attitude and critical view of philosophy (UQ: 89), so much so that many people identified him with the Circle. In fact, although Popper maintained contact with many of its leading members, he was never invited to the meetings organized by Schlick (OGOU:

39–41). Later he claimed that the objections contained in his first work actually killed off logical positivism (UQ: 88), but that it was at most a question of manslaughter rather than premeditated murder (OGOU: 39). Whatever the author's responsibilities, it certainly had a greater success than he had expected, and this brought him numerous invitations to lecture abroad. Because of the new commitments, he took a period of leave from the secondary school teaching in which he had been employed since 1930. Then, apart from a brief spell back in Austria, he spent almost nine months in England between 1935 and 1936, having the opportunity to put forward his anti-inductionist theory in a discussion following a lecture by Russell. (According to Popper, those present 'took this for a joke ... and laughed' (UQ: 110).) Altogether the time Popper spent in England was very profitable, both scientifically and in personal terms, because he was able to make new contacts with representatives of British culture that would prove invaluable during the difficult years of Nazi dictatorship and war.

Popper's interests soon extended to the quantum theory formulated by Heisenberg in 1925, whose interpretation he saw as closely bound up with the calculus of probability (UQ: 92). He had the chance to go more deeply into the problem at a congress in Copenhagen in 1936, where he discussed with Bohr some aspects of the theory that struck him as less than convincing – especially the Danish physicist's view that quantum mechanics, unlike classical physics, could not really be understood. This encounter led Popper to investigate the idea of understanding, not in terms of pictures but by focusing on the logical force of a theory. This problem, together with that of corroboration and truth, kept him busy immediately after the publication of the *Logik*. In fact, between 1934 and 1935 he had met Tarski successively in Prague, Vienna and Paris and realized that 'he had finally rehabilitated the much maligned correspondence theory of truth which, I suggest, is and always has been the commonsense idea of truth' (UQ: 98). Popper attached so much importance to this that in the autumn of 1935 his first two lectures at Bedford College, London were devoted to Tarski, at that time unknown in England.

Europe was meanwhile passing through difficult years as a result of the totalitarian regimes that had been imposed in various countries. Austria itself was the object of Hitler's barely concealed appetites, as well as having many Nazi sympathizers among its own citizens. Members of the Vienna Circle were moving to Britain or the United States, and Schlick was assassinated in 1936 by a Nazi student. Given his Jewish origins, Popper also finally decided to leave the country and applied for a position teaching philosophy at the University of Canterbury in New Zealand. Towards the end of 1936 Cambridge University offered him its hospitality, but as he had meanwhile obtained the post in New Zealand he declined the offer in favour of Fritz Waismann, a follower of Schlick's, who was also seeking a secure refuge from racial and political persecution.

And so Popper and his wife left for their new destination and arrived in March 1937. They spent the whole of the war there in a climate of exceptional calm, though at the price of a certain isolation from the rest of the world; Britain, with which they had the easiest and most frequent contact, was five weeks away by sea. Nevertheless, and despite his heavy teaching load, Popper found the time and concentration to immerse himself in study: he resumed his reflections on probability theory and quantum physics, and investigated more systematically the methodology of the social sciences which had begun to interest him at the time of his break from Marxism. Already in England he had given a lecture 'The Poverty of Historicism' in which he tried to apply the ideas of the *Logik* to the social sciences. In 1938 Hitler's annexation of Austria induced the philosopher to collect and publish his political reflections that had been maturing since 1919. He naturally had difficulty in writing in a language which, however much practised, was not his own. But during his time in New Zealand he completed two works of a political character: *The Poverty of Historicism* (which argues that historicism inspired both Marxism and fascism), and *The Open Society and Its Enemies*, which started as a spin-off from the historicism essay but soon acquired a dimension of its own. The problems of composition were followed by still more wearisome ones of publication: the journal *Mind* turned down *The Poverty of Historicism*, and *The Open Society* was judged too irreverent towards Aristotle (not Plato, as it would be more logical to think in view of the book's contents) (UQ: 119). Thus, the acquaintances to whom Popper had turned in America did not even submit the book for consideration by publishers, and it was only a year later, thanks to the intervention of Gombrich and Hayek, that an edition finally appeared. Soon afterwards, it was Hayek who 'saved [Popper's] life once more' (UQ: 120) by offering him a readership at the London School of Economics and so enabled him to leave New Zealand for Europe.

Popper returned to London with his wife at the beginning of 1946 and began to teach at the LSE. Among his many students was a former Navy officer, John Watkins, who later succeeded him at the LSE. Popper did not conceal his preference for the natural sciences, but he adjusted to his new academic environment by concentrating more on problems of method in the social sciences, though trying at the same time to compare and contrast the two fields. Nor did this prevent him from composing articles between 1946 and 1948 on formal logic or – as he preferred to call it – metalogic.

The Open Society had been well received in England, and so Popper was invited to attend various symposia and to deliver a number of lectures. Especially worthy of note was the one he gave at Cambridge in October 1946 in the presence of Wittgenstein, when he posed the question 'Are There Philosophical Problems?' His somewhat provocative tone of argument soon angered Wittgenstein, who walked out of the room and slammed the door (UQ: 123). But less stormy minds were also present, including Bertrand Russell, and he moved on to argue that there are genu- inely philosophical problems which cannot all be reduced to lan- guage mistakes. Popper's relations with Wittgenstein were always rather argumentative – indeed, one writer has seen in his work an attempt to refute the thought of his fellow-Austrian. But according to Sir Karl himself, he had formulated all his major problems by the fateful year of 1919, long before he became acquainted with Wittgenstein and his doctrines around 1925 (OGOU: 37–38). On the other hand, he was quite willing to recognize the influence exerted on him not only by members of the Vienna Circle, but also by leading figures of the previous generation: he even regarded Boltzmann as an intellectual father because of his clash with Mach over the question of realism (OGOU: 64). Despite this admiration for two 'Titans' of Viennese philosophy, we shall see that Popper distanced himself from both to keep faith with his own realist commitment (OGOU: 45–47, 51–54).

In 1949 Popper became professor of logic and scientific method in the University of London. The next year he stopped living in the capital, of which he was never very fond, and moved to Penn, Buckinghamshire where he lived until his wife's death in 1985. Also in 1950 he made his first trip to the United States, where he met a number of old friends, such as Kurt Gödel, whom he had not seen since 1936. America made a good impression on him for the 'feeling of freedom, of personal independence, which did not exist in Europe; (UQ: 128), but the real highlight was at Princeton where Einstein attended one of his lectures together with Bohr. He had three meetings with the great scientist, all mainly focused on Popper's theory of indeterminism. Against Einstein's view that 'the world was a four-dimensional Parmenidean block universe in which change was a human illusion, or very nearly so' (UQ: 129), Popper argued that if it was possible to experience change and temporal succession, they could not be just an illusion. (In the years to come he would never give up his realism even when it meant quarrels not only with Einstein or Gödel but also with his friend Schrödinger, with whom he regularly corresponded after they met again in England in the late 1940s.) Thomas Kuhn also attended Popper's lectures in America, and not long afterwards he went to visit him in England. Subsequently, of course, Kuhn became famous for his critique of Popper's methodology, in his book published in 1962, *The Structure of Scientific Revolutions*.

From 1951 to 1956 Popper worked on revisions 'to correct, expand and develop the ideas of his first published book' (P1: xi). Little by little, however, what were supposed to be mere appendices became autonomous of the whole and acquired the dimensions of a single, homogeneous work, much longer than the original *Logik der Forschung*. It was therefore decided to publish it as a kind of companion volume to the first English translation of the *Logic*, with the title *Postscript: After Twenty Years*. But early in 1957, when the galleys were ready for correction, a serious eye complaint forced the author to postpone the proofreading and to undergo a difficult operation on both retinas that kept him from working for a considerable time. In the end *The Logic of Scientific Discovery* only came out in 1959; and by the time his eyes had returned to normal, other projects had become more pressing and the *Postscript* was set aside.

In 1963 a collection of Popper's major articles and lectures from a dazzling fifteen-year period appeared under the title *Conjectures and Refutations*. The next decade or so then saw the publication of *Objective Knowledge* (1972), an intellectual autobiography *Unended Quest* (1974) and a joint work with Sir John Eccles, *The Self and Its Brain* (1977). In the late sixties and early 1970s, Popper developed and refined his theory of objective mind, according to which three real and distinct worlds coexist within the single world perceived and accepted by common sense. It thus strayed into cosmological and ontological questions that were the province of metaphysics, in Popper's use of the term: that is, such theories were not open to empirical refutation yet made it possible to provide arguments, and without them it would be difficult to see science as having the significance that is normally attributed to it.

From 1950 on, as he once confessed during a lecture (ISBW: 223), Popper led quite a secluded life in the Chiltern Hills, completely absorbed in his work. From time to time, however, it took him to America, Australia or Japan, as well as his own country of birth and various European cities, to give the kind of lecture series that was in ever greater demand as his fame as a philosopher continued to grow. After his wife's death, he preferred to leave the home they had shared for so many years and moved to Kenley, near London, where he was assisted by his loyal secretary Melitta Mew up to his death on 17 September 1994.

Popper's intellectual activity continued, at least as strongly as before, even after his retirement in 1969. And as old age crept up on him, he went on contributing interviews and articles to the press and television, especially in connection with the burning issues of the day. Although his health worsened with the passing years, he never abandoned his struggle against irrationalism and his faith in science, even as an antidote, for example, to environmental disasters. Indeed, he thought that such problems could only be solved through scientific and technological effort, and not – as the ecologists maintained – by renouncing science and industry.[1] He also insisted that it would be impossible to protect the environment if the demographic explosion was not brought under control: 5 billion human beings with a tendency to double themselves had become a dangerous species, and Popper argued in favour of birth control by all non-authoritarian means.

These were not, in his view, the only reasons for humanity to feel anxious about the contemporary world. Popper was also very concerned about the mass media, especially television, which exercised 'unlimited power without responsibility'.[2] Indeed, the last text he published before his death was a pamphlet called *Una patente per fare TV* (A Licence to Make TV), which, far from being just a sterile denunciation, proposed a solution for the safeguarding of democracy and, above all, for the protection of young children and those least able to defend themselves from the aggressiveness of images and messages appearing on the small screen. What he suggested was to establish an organization similar to a professional body, which would train its members in certain values and have the power to issue reprimands for breaches of the rules.

Popper also saw a continuing threat from the Russian nuclear arsenal, which Yeltsin promised to dismantle but without offering effective guarantees. Immediately after the failed putsch of August 1991 in Moscow, he expressed a harsh judgement both of Gorbachev (whom he accused of having neither ideas nor projects) and of Yeltsin ('a man obsessed with his own ego').[3] He did not hide his satisfaction that he had witnessed not only the revolution which brought communism to power in Russia, but also the one which defeated it and exposed the flimsy basis of Marxism. But Popper did not assume a triumphalist tone, being well aware of all the problems crowding the world arena that have still to be resolved.

As Popper reached his 90th birthday, he published a long article on Parmenides in *The Classical Quarterly* and brought out a new book of interviews in Italy[4] – two signs of a will and vitality undiminished by the objective hurdles of old age and failing health. At the same time, they expressed the worries of this great old man without progeny concerning the future of the new generations. He knew that 'we have a duty towards our children: to educate them, to teach them to construct a better world. A less violent world. For the goal of civilization is precisely the elimination of violence.'[5] Popper did not flinch from this duty as long as he still had the strength.

Part II

2

THE EPISTEMOLOGICAL
WORKS

A LAYERED STRUCTURE

As we have seen, Popper's first book was written in the early
1930s at the urging of Herbert Feigl. Only after years of work on
the manuscript, however, did Troels Eggers Hansen succeed in
preparing a text for publication, a text which was then revised by
Popper in 1975 and finally brought out by Mohr's of Tübingen in
1979. The work had originally been intended to comprise two
volumes, but only the first, *The Problem of Induction*, remained
complete; of the second, *The Problem of Demarcation*, no more
than a few fragments have survived. We know that Popper drastically reorganized this early labour, and it appeared mercilessly cut
in 1934 under the title *Logik der Forschung*. The English translation of 1959, *The Logic of Scientific Discovery*, was considerably
expanded with both text and appendices. In the meantime the
philosopher had worked on further additions, remarks and clarifi-
cations in the expectation that they would be published twenty
years after the first German edition – hence their title, *Postscript
to the Logic of Scientific Discovery: After Twenty Years*. But many
more years were to pass before this work was eventually made
available to the public, both for reasons of health and because
Popper's philosophical interests were carrying him into territory
that was no longer exclusively or even mainly epistemological.

Die beiden Grundprobleme der Erkenntnistheorie (1979) and the
three volumes of the *Postscript* (1982) eventually came out within
a few years of each other, though belonging to periods far apart.
In Popper's first work there is a strong, though critically directed,
influence of logical positivism. As the author of the 1933 *Exposé*
himself put it:

15

This book is close to the modern ('logistically' oriented) positivism shared by Bertrand Russell, Moritz Schlick, Philipp Frank, Rudolf Carnap, Hans Reichenbach and Ludwig Wittgenstein. But this does not prevent it from engaging with this current in a radically critical manner, and from trying to lay bare the 'fundamental contradiction of positivism' upon which positivist philosophy *founders*.

(BG: xxxv)

In this work Popper draws a balance-sheet of all epistemological currents either influential in general or present within the tradition in which he himself was educated; his analysis focuses especially on empiricism and rationalism, but also examines the characteristic theses of intuitionism and conventionalism, and Vaihinger's view that scientific concepts are only useful 'heuristic fictions' that cannot be shown to correspond to reality. The book is thus quite useful for an understanding of the roots of Popper's philosophy: it makes explicit reference to his reading in this field, directly quotes from the authors under consideration, and sometimes comments on them in great detail. We learn, for example, that Popper is familiar not only with Wittgenstein and neo-positivists such as Schlick, Carnap and Feigl, but also with Hume, Kant, Mach, Duhem and Russell. Kant, in particular, stands out as his guide, as the one who offers him the means to criticize logical positivism: indeed, Popper feels it necessary 'indelibly to underline his debt to Kant' (BG: 320). At the same time, however, he does not actually subscribe to any of Kant's doctrines, and takes a clear distance from that 'apriorism' which seems to him irreconcilable with 'rational empiricism'. The critique of logical positivism, as of the other approaches just mentioned, proceeds through detailed analysis of and objections to the theories in question, followed by Popper's own wide-ranging and carefully constructed answers that provide his own solution to the 'two main problems of the theory of knowledge'. The first problem, induction, is solved through dissolution – as we shall see in a moment; while the second, the problem of demarcation, is here only touched upon, as much of the original material had been lost. In the introduction written in 1978 for publication the following year, the author critically evaluates his early work and does not hesitate to point out some errors or ambiguities of which he had been guilty in the first version (e.g., BG: xxii). But in effect he still endorses the main theses, at

16

most demonstrating the ways in which critics have misunderstood them over the years (BG: xxii–xxiv).

In the *Logik der Forschung* what remain, after the editor's drastic cuts, are the epistemological theses largely shorn of the meticulous critical history that Popper had provided as background in the first version. Although the indispensable historical references are in neither case omitted, of course, this preoccupation with theoretical aspects of the two problems of knowledge is also apparent in the fuller English edition of 1959, *The Logic of Scientific Discovery*, which displays greater expository and theoretical maturity, without anticipating the metaphysical conclusions that only become explicit from the mid-1960s on.

The themes of the *Logik* were taken up again in the first volume of the *Postscript: Realism and the Aim of Science*. Here Popper discusses and goes more deeply into a number of complex or disputed aspects of his theory, while also providing an overall framework for his epistemological thought as a kind of critical rationalism. As to the 'metaphysics', we find that orientation towards realism which, though not presented as such in the *Logic of Scientific Discovery*, was even there the hinterland of his epistemological thinking. *Realism and the Aim of Science*, like Popper's previous works, is an attack on inductivism, but at the same time it seeks to refute a subjectivist or sceptical view of rationality. The second volume of the *Postscript*, *The Open Universe: An Argument for Indeterminism*, is connected to the first by a 'mutual concern with the freedom, creativity and rationality of man' (P1: xiv) – problems which, in the author's view, can best be confronted within an indeterminist perspective. The third and final volume – *Quantum Theory and the Schism in Physics* – develops Popper's propensity theory of probability and relates it to the problems of interpreting quantum mechanics.

Last, we should recall the numerous articles written between 1952 and 1960 not only on the philosophy of science but especially on knowledge in general, the most important of which were collected in the volume *Conjectures and Refutations*. In a way, this compilation brings Popper's strictly epistemological production to an end; he applies his central thesis – that 'we can learn from our mistakes' (CR: vii) – to the most varied themes ranging from the history and philosophy of science to the history and philosophy of politics. A link is thus established between the two areas of reflection that had occupied Popper until that time. As we shall see, his horizon would now gradually broaden out into a veritable metaphysics – that is, into a conjecture about the composition and functioning of the world in all its principal aspects.

In view of the 'layered' character of Popper's epistemological works, it does not seem appropriate to examine them one by one. Such a procedure would involve inevitable repetitions and threaten to create chronological confusion, for Popper updated and revised his writings not only when they were first published many years after their original composition, but also when the world impact of his thought made new editions necessary over a period of time. It therefore seems preferable to give an account of the epistemological theory that Popper constantly upheld over a number of decades, whilst indicating the significant additions or revisions made to the theory. Mention will also be made – especially in the chapter below dealing with the metaphysical works – of any allusions to be found in his writings of the later period, when he reworked his epistemology in evolutionist terms.

The reader should finally be warned that towards the end of the present section, we shall touch upon an essay which, though conceived as a work of political philosophy, also constitutes a bridge between Popper's epistemology and his strictly political thinking. This, of course, is *The Poverty of Historicism*, which the author once described in a strong spirit of self-criticism as 'one of my stodgiest pieces of writing' (UQ: 114). The title alludes to Marx's *Poverty of Philosophy*, itself an ironical play on Proudhon's *Philosophy of Poverty*. Just as Marx intended his text as a critique of Proudhon, so does Popper aim to criticize Marx and his historicist philosophy. But on the same occasion, he elaborates a methodology of the historical and social sciences, with which he had not previously concerned himself in writing because his attention had been focused on the natural sciences.

THEORY OF KNOWLEDGE

To begin, let us consider what Popper meant by theory of knowledge during the 1930s: he argued that it constituted 'a general doctrine of the method of empirical science' or a 'general theory of method' (BG: 423); it was 'the theory of the knowledge and science of science' (BG: 424). As we shall see, Popper came to consider his theory to be less limited in scope, and eventually defined it not only as a methodology of science but as a theory valid for any form of knowledge and learning, although science always remained his main point of reference, the paradigm of rational knowledge. In a lecture prepared for delivery at Stanford in August 1960, the philosopher stated that his 'interest is not merely in the theory of scientific knowledge, but rather in the theory of knowledge in general' (CR: 216).

In Popper's view, 'epistemology, or the logic of scientific discovery, should be identified with the theory of scientific method' (LSD: 49). At the same time, however, 'scientific knowledge is merely a development of ordinary knowledge or common-sense knowledge' (LSD: 18), and if the former is preferred to the latter, this is only because it can be studied more easily with regard to evidence and because it amplifies problems typical of any form of knowledge. But methodology is not 'an empirical discipline, to be tested, perhaps, by the facts of the history of science. It is, rather, a philosophical – a metaphysical – discipline, perhaps partly even a normative proposal' (P1: xxv).

Popper's main aim in his early work was to formulate a theory of human knowledge as product of our intellectual activities, and not as the subjective product of an organism with psychological or physiological constraints. In other words, he wanted to probe the objective aspect of knowledge that is (at least potentially) inherited by every human being, rather than the individual elements that interfere in learning. For Popper, this approach offered at least three advantages: (1) it solved Hume's problem concerning induction; (2) it allowed theories to be objectively evaluated even before they were put to the test; and (3) it formulated a *critical* method for science which proceeded through trial and the correction of error. On the first point, it has to be said that there is a confusion with the much more important, Kantian problem of demarcation. According to Popper, it is only with Kant that the central problem of knowledge becomes one of finding a criterion that allows us to distinguish between what is and what is not entitled to be called science. Popper wants to reject the widely held principle that inductive logic provides an adequate criterion for the differentiation of the empirical sciences from metaphysics or other forms of non-scientific knowledge. His own view is well known: there is no induction, because there is no way of deducing universal theories from particular statements; all the numerous observations of white swans, for example, never logically justify the conclusion that all swans are white. Thus, if we consider the objective, public, and therefore testable, aspect of a theory (instead of viewing it as a private, subjective product of the person who puts it forward), then it becomes an object of discussion that can be (at least logically) criticized even before it is summoned for empirical testing. It is precisely from these features of objectivity and testability that Popper draws the inspiration for his alternative to inductivism – that is, the method of trial and error that we shall examine at length both in the context of his epistemological thought and in our concluding discussion of the main themes of his work.

THE CRITIQUE OF POSITIVISM

As Popper recalls in his autobiography (UQ: 80), he saw his first work as a 'critical discussion' of the doctrines of the Vienna Circle, with special regard to the solutions offered by Wittgenstein, Schlick and Carnap. These philosophers were, in fact, Popper's constant interlocutors, and they remained so even after he had had the opportunity to go more deeply into disputed areas of contemporary physics and to consider also the social and other less exact sciences.

Although Popper recognizes that logical positivism has 'the merit of being the only modern theory of knowledge to have fought for strict empiricism' (BG: 321), he cannot help opposing its 'thesis of the omnipotence of science' (BG: 315), which founders on inductivist prejudices and a specifically epistemological contradiction. For 'the *positivist interpretation* of scientific knowledge is in contradiction with the *actual procedures* of the empirical sciences, with the methods of scientific justification' (BG: 48). It is curious to note that the very same accusation would later be turned against Popper by Kuhn, Feyerabend and other advocates of the 'new philosophy of science'; in their view, his critical rationalism developed an ideal 'armchair' method, as it were, without taking into account the history of science and the actual practice of working scientists.

For the young Popper, on the other hand, not only did logical positivism fail to do justice to real scientific practice, it urged an unacceptable dogma to the effect that 'what we cannot know with certainty does not exist' (BG: 315). In other words, Popper thought it his task to refute the identification of thought (or rather, language) with being, on the grounds that being – and here we glimpse the realist commitment that would later be openly declared – always extends beyond thought. These were not initially the dominant aspects, however; what we find surviving in the *Logic* from the broad critical survey in the *Two Problems* are mainly the more technical elements, particularly the rejection of the verification principle as a criterion of meaning. According to this principle, as is well known, a non-analytic statement is meaningful if and only if it is empirically verifiable. Popper would not accept this as a criterion of meaning because, as he said in a lecture from 1953, he always regarded the problem of meaning as a pseudo-problem and never felt any interest in it. On the other hand, if the verification principle is taken as a criterion not of meaning but of demarcation between what is and what is not science, then the 'criterion is too narrow (*and* too wide): it excludes from science practically everything that is, in fact, characteristic of it (while failing in effect to exclude astrology)' (CR: 40). Two years later, in a contribution to a volume in honour of Rudolf Carnap, Popper noted with satisfaction that the philosopher of the Vienna Circle had long ago abandoned the 'naturalistic' theory of meaning taken over from Wittgenstein's *Tractatus* in his own *Aufbau* (CR: 259ff.), and that in *The Logical Syntax of Language* and *Testability and Meaning* he had accepted the criticism that hinged upon the impossibility of excluding metaphysics from the realm of meaningful discourse.

Furthermore, Popper insisted that the verifiability criterion deprived of meaning the most important scientific assertions – that is, scientific theories and especially the ones formulated as laws of nature. For in any theory we find universal statements which assert much more than what can be verified even in principle. 'Scientific method presupposes the *immutability of natural processes*, or the "principle of the uniformity of nature"' (LSD: 252), and this assumption already expresses a metaphysical belief in the regularity of the world that can never be empirically proven. Nevertheless, our attempts to acquire knowledge are nothing other than 'a quest for regularity: we cannot do otherwise than enunciate laws of nature, strictly general statements about reality, and subject them to testing' (BG: 79). Hence natural laws are not simply the record of a series of observations; they are something more than that, something different which involves a step beyond experience and is thus meta-empirical – that is, metaphysical and unverifiable within the parameters of a rigorous positivism.

21

In opposition to the verifiability criterion put forward by the Vienna Circle, Popper therefore advanced his own criterion of falsifiability – understood as a criterion of demarcation, *not* of meaning. The shift is more significant than it appears at first sight, or than it certainly appeared to Popper's first readers, and he continued for years to defend the concept right up to his major *Replies to My Critics*, published in 1974. According to the new criterion:

> statements, or systems of statements, convey information about the empirical world only if they are capable of clashing with experience; or, more precisely, only if they can be *systematically tested*, that is to say, if they can be subjected . . . to tests which *might* result in their refutation.
>
> (LSD: 313–314)

This implies that laws of nature, and in general all the assertions of a scientific theory, can only be *partly decided* – that is, are never verifiable but only falsifiable. So when, inevitably, a scientific theory draws conclusions that go beyond the observable data, it places itself on ground where experience cannot directly testify in its favour but can do so only indirectly, by showing that rigorous empirical tests have not refuted it. All experience can do directly is pronounce against a theory, by demonstrating that it conflicts with the sense data which it seeks to know and explain.

This new approach also permits us to tackle the thorny epistemological problem of induction, which, in Popper's account, has always been invoked to find a satisfactory answer to the problem of demarcation. Once this has been solved on the basis of a more adequate formulation, the problem of induction shows itself in all its inconsistency (BG: 327). For 'only if *the asymmetry between verification and falsification* is taken into account – that asymmetry which results from the logical relation between theories and basic statements – is it possible to avoid the pitfalls of the problem of induction' (LSD: 265).

Naturally Popper's conception had to face various comments and criticisms, which he meticulously answered in the *Postscript*. One objection was that the supposed asymmetry only concerned a purely verbal difference, as whenever we falsify a statement we automatically verify its negation. Popper replied to this by distinguishing between the logical aspect of asymmetry and the methodological or heuristic aspect. Logically, 'there can be no doubt that a (unilaterally falsifiable) universal statement is logically much stronger than the corresponding (unilaterally verifiable) existential statement' (P1: 184). The asymmetry, then, stems from the fact that whereas an existential statement is deducible from a universal statement – for example, 'the thing a has the property P' can be derived from 'all things have the property P' – the reverse does not hold. As to the methodological or heuristic aspect, Popper points out that for the verificationist 'ideally, science consists of all true statements', so that verified statements belong to it, whereas for the falsificationist, 'science consists of daring explanatory hypotheses' (P1: 184–185).

Another objection plays upon the fact that not even falsification can claim to be certain, inasmuch as it is not said that all the basic statements are actually true. Popper does not hesitate to admit this, but he denies that it refutes the asymmetry in question. For:

the asymmetry is that a finite set of basic statements, *if true*, may falsify a universal law; whereas, *under no condition* could it verify a universal law: there exists a condition wherein it could falsify a general law, but there exists no condition wherein it could verify a general law.

(P1: 185)

Not even falsification, then, leads to absolutely indubitable results, although the degree of uncertainty is quite different from the impossibility in principle (not merely de facto or by chance) of verification.

A final series of objections relates to the difficulty of falsifying a single hypothesis, given that the refutation of a conclusion does not say which of the premises used to infer it was responsible for the error. Popper agrees that it is possible to 'falsify only *systems of theories* and that any attribution of falsity to any particular statement within such a system is always highly uncertain' (P1: 187). Again, however, this does not invalidate the asymmetry in question; at most, its application is limited to systems of theories.

On this basis, Popper proceeds to deal with 'the two basic problems of the theory of knowledge'. Turning them inside out both theoretically and historically, he gradually offers a series of pointers towards a composite image of science that is very different from the ones presented by nineteenth-century positivism or twentieth-century logical positivism, and yet is still closely bound up with the epistemological tradition of the West.

THE PROBLEM OF DEMARCATION

This problem was most clearly and precisely identified by Immanuel Kant, who also made the first rigorous attempt to set the limits of scientific knowledge. To solve the 'Kantian problem', a theory of knowledge must offer a sufficient criterion to distinguish the propositions of the empirical sciences from non-scientific, and especially metaphysical, propositions (BG: 4). Popper maintains that the Kantian problem of demarcation is fundamental for empiricism and that it is expressed in the question: 'What procedure distinguishes natural science from metaphysics?' (BG: 287). For centuries the best-established response was the one that appealed to induction, but Popper claims to have a better criterion that allows us to avoid the aporias of inductivism. The first and most urgent problem to resolve is therefore the problem of demarcation. On this depends a solution to the complex associated question regarding generalization from experience, which was most trenchantly formulated by Hume. Let us now follow the order of priority laid down by Popper himself. The key reference-point, including in the nascent polemic concerning the demarcation problem, was always positivism in its two characteristic moments: nineteenth-century and Viennese. The early positivists admitted as scientific only concepts whose origin lay in experience, as these could always be reduced to sense data or impressions or memories of sensations. Their twentieth-century descendants, however, with whom Popper engaged directly, realized that science is not at all a set of concepts, but rather a system of propositions that can claim to be scientific only if they are reducible to 'protocol-sentences' – that is, to elementary statements describing a single experience, such as 'I, here and now, see a red spot'. 'It is clear that the implied criterion of demarcation is identical with the demand for an inductive logic' (LSD: 35). And so it is necessary to face all the difficulties of trying to justify or establish a procedure which, as Hume showed once and for all, has no logical foundation, nor even (as Popper added in criticism of Hume) a psychological foundation.

It was here that the logical positivists thought they had found the intrinsic difference between science and metaphysics, the latter being by its nature – at least according to the so-called principle of verification, or verifiability – no more than 'idle chatter'. In Popper's view, this was a false conclusion, drawn from a principle which, precisely at the level of meaning, was incapable of safeguarding the most important scientific propositions, the ones that express universal laws. He therefore sought to formulate a criterion that would be considered 'as a *proposal for an agreement or convention*' (LSD: 37), so that one could rationally defend it just by analysing its logical consequences and by demonstrating its fruitfulness. First of all, he wanted to deny that metaphysics is of no use to the empirical sciences; indeed, he openly stated that from a psychological point of view:

> scientific discovery is impossible without faith in ideas which are of a purely speculative kind, and sometimes even quite hazy; a faith which is completely unwarranted from the point of view of science, and which, to that extent, is 'metaphysical'.
>
> (LSD: 38)

Evidently this does not involve a methodological abandonment of experience; the theory of knowledge is understood precisely as a 'theory of empirical method' (LSD: 39) – but it is a theory which, in accounting for real scientific procedures and results, goes beyond the mere accumulation of experiential data.

In sum, Popper's problem is to find a distinction between science and pseudo-science that does not dismiss the latter as mere nonsense. Often theories start out as metaphysical or mythical and only subsequently acquire a scientific dimension; it hardly seems consistent to describe as simply unintelligible or meaningless, discourses which at a certain point show themselves to be endowed with meaning. Right from his early reflections, Popper was convinced that metaphysics is not nonsense and that it is impossible to rid science of every metaphysical element – although, of course, he thought it desirable to remove the metaphysical elements whenever that was possible (P1: 179).

However important this aspect may be, the demarcation problem is rather more complex than it appeared in the classical formulations of logical positivism, and it certainly cannot be reduced to the demand to distinguish between empirical or 'scientific' theories and 'metaphysical' theories. In fact, the question concerning demarcation is connected both logically and historically to what

Popper called 'the central problem of the philosophy of knowledge, at least since the Reformation' – namely, how we can 'adjudicate or evaluate the far-reaching claims of competing theories and beliefs' (P1: 19). This then leads to 'the problem of deciding whether it is possible or impossible to justify a theory rationally; and this, in turn, leads to the problem of distinguishing between, or of demarcating, rational theories and irrational beliefs' (P1: 161–162). In other words, the problem may be structured in three segments: (1) the problem of demarcation strictly so called, which is intended to distinguish between science and non-science (primitive magic, myth, metaphysics); (2) the problem concerning the rationality of scientific procedure; (3) the problem of the acceptance of theories for scientific or practical ends. As we shall see, Popper's investigations into these three problems led him not only to delineate a new concept of science, but also to make more precise the notion of rationality underlying the whole Western tradition in both philosophy and science.

Popper proposes, then, to 'admit a system as empirical or scientific only if it is capable of being *tested* by experience' (LSD: 40), where the testing should be understood not as verification but as possible refutation. In fact, theory does not undergo screening by experience in order to be verified – for the result would anyway be insignificant in any decision about the theory, given that not even a large number of detailed checks can exclude the future possibility of its being proved wrong. Rather, the purpose is to show that despite rigorous testing, the theory has not actually been proved wrong or does not actually conflict with the available experiential data.

Popper relates on several occasions [UQ, Chs. 8, 9; CR, Ch. 1] the route which brought him to prefer the quest for refutation to the acquisition of corroborating evidence. He soon became aware that in each case 'the world was full of *verifications* of the theory. Whatever happened always confirmed it' (CR: 35). He was referring here mainly to the theories of Marx, Freud and Adler, whom many of his friends admired and he himself had studied with enthusiasm until he saw the huge difference that separated them from Einstein's science. Whereas Marxism or psychoanalysis – or astrology for that matter – always found things to confirm it, Einstein made predictions and formulated hypotheses which ran the risk of being bawled out of court by experience. The continual confirmations that some took as so many proofs of their

26

theory seemed to the young Popper, from the winter of 1919–20, to be an obstacle to scientific practice. For 'irrefutability is not a virtue of a theory (as people often think) but a vice' (CR: 36); 'it is easy to obtain confirmations, or verifications, for nearly every theory – if we look for confirmations' [ibid.]. Popper is here stressing that the distinctively scientific approach requires us to look for drawbacks, weaknesses or inconsistency with empirical data, and not for just that number of proofs which any theory, even the horoscope, can claim because of a more or less fortuitous coincidence with reality. Basing himself on such considerations, and on a firm conviction that verifiability and falsifiability are asymmetrical, Popper went on to formulate his well-known but often misunderstood principle of falsifiability. This must be understood as a criterion not of meaning but of demarcation, and applied not so much to isolated theoretical statements as to entire theoretical systems. With these provisions, Popper argues that the principle is effective in defining science *vis-à-vis* other forms of knowledge, and that it opens the way for a characterization of scientific procedure that leaves induction out of the picture.

A further important clarification concerns the distinction between falsifiability and falsification. The first is a requirement that guarantees the empirical character of a system of statements, and as such it 'signifies nothing more than a logical relation between the theory in question and the class of basic statements, or the class of the events described by them: the potential falsifiers' (P1: xxi). Falsification, on the other hand, refers to a procedure that effectively refutes a theory and renders it unacceptable because false. There is falsification only when an empirical falsifying hypothesis is corroborated and the effect which it describes is enough to refute the theory. Popper himself offers an illuminating example: the statement 'all ravens are black' would be falsified if a family of white ravens were to be found; and so, if a family of white ravens actually exists in the New York zoo – something that can be intersubjectively tested – then the statement 'all ravens are black' will have undergone falsification. Naturally, it might be asked whether falsification can ever be so secure as to leave no hope for a theory that may in other respects be quite valuable. But Popper can reply without hesitation that ever since the first edition of the *Logik*, and even before in the original draft of *Die beiden Grundprobleme*, he always maintained 'that it is never possible to prove conclusively that an empirical scientific theory is false' (P1: xxii). However, this should not dishearten those who trust in science, because a number of important falsifications have a certain degree of definiteness, while leaving some possibility of error to remain (P1: xxiii). Thus, despite the practical difficulty of deciding whether a theory has truly and fully been falsified by observations, this does not in the least affect the essential argument *that potential falsifiability must always be assured*. For this reason, in the introduction that he wrote in 1978 for *Die beiden Grundpro-bleme* (BG: xxix), Popper tends to reject the term 'falsificationism' often used to describe his epistemology, on the grounds that it does precisely confuse the question of falsifiability and the distinct question of falsification. And yet, from the fact that no theory can be regarded as having been conclusively falsified, it does not follow that falsification does not play a role, and an important role at that, in the history of science. Popper himself demonstrates this through a series of historical examples, from Leucippus' refutation of Par-menides' theory that the world is full and motionless, to the most recent refutations (based on confirmed experiments) of Schröding-er's interpretation of de Broglie's theory (P1: xxvi–xxix). The requirement of falsifiability is so important for Popper that he considers it analogous to the principle of non-contradiction. It is obvious that contradiction is a sign of falsity and that a self-contradictory system must be rejected because it is false, and falsifiability has the same function on an empirical rather than logical level. It ensures that, in the event of a clash with the empirical basic statements, the theory will be excluded from the class of science (LSD: 88–89, 314).

Popper maintained his essential commitment to empiricism, but he limited the role of experience in scientific endeavour to one of indirect and unilateral testing, inasmuch as it can beget only falsification and never verification. Hence:

> the possibility of refuting theories by observations is the basis of all empirical tests. For the test of a theory is, like every rigorous examination, always an attempt to show that the candidate is mistaken – that is, that the theory entails a false assertion. From a logical point of view, all empirical tests are therefore *attempted refutations*.
>
> (CR: 192)

Observation, experiment, experience in general are here no longer the foundation upon which science is constructed or, as it were, the raw material of science itself; rather, they function as control instruments or as guarantees of scientificity, by signalling any violation of the frontiers of experience. It is easy enough to see the debt to Kant, and Popper himself more than once recognized it. For the Austrian philosopher, too, our hypotheses and our concepts have validity only within the limits of our sense experience, but this experience, unlike in the Kantian critique, does not necessarily have to be submitted to our a priori forms; it may even rudely and more or less definitively discredit them.

Popper is well aware that even in this variant of empiricism, it is impossible to ignore the problem of the 'empirical base' which concerns the relationship between perceptual experiences and the basic statements (that is, the propositions asserting a specific fact). Logical positivism tackled the problem from a standpoint that Popper considered to be still bound up with psychologism, with the doctrine that 'all we know about the world of facts must [. . .] be expressible in the form of statements *about our experiences*' (LSD: 60). Now, for logical positivists, the empirical base is constituted by sentences that represent experiences – what Carnap and Neurath call 'protocol sentences', intended to describe the contents of immediate experience. The progress here lies in Neurath's thesis that no sentence can be considered inviolable, and that even 'protocol sentences' are subject to possible modification or even cancellation if they disturb a well-constructed theoretical system. But Neurath does not supply rules to limit arbitrariness by keeping the function of experience within the ambit of scientific knowledge; he 'thus unwittingly throws empiricism overboard' (LSD: 60).

Popper, then, has in mind an empirical base made up of basic statements which, being capable of falsifying a theory, cannot be deducible from any universal statement, even if they may potentially contradict one another. It follows that '*basic statements have the form of singular existential statements*' (LSD: 102), precisely because they possess the two requirements given above. In other words, such statements assert that an observable event occurs at a certain point in time and space. If someone objects that it might be difficult even to agree on the basic statements, Popper's reply is that we would then have to declare language bankrupt as a means of universal communication and to bow before a kind of new Babel (LSD: 104). He therefore thinks he has defeated psychologism, because there can be no doubt that the decision to accept a basic statement is causally linked to, but cannot be justified by, our perceptual experiences. This means that basic statements are certainly derived from the totality of organized sensations to which we give the name of experience. But they do not constitute the incontrovertible foundation of that totality, because any basic statement may in turn be tested by others that are deducible with the aid of some theory (LSD: 104). It seems impossible, then, to arrive at a statement that expresses an experience in ultimate and neutral terms, 'since all terms are theoretical to some degree, though some are more theoretical than others' (CR: 119; cf. P1: 211). Adopting an evolutionist standpoint, Popper later said that 'sense organs incorporate the equivalent of primitive and uncritically accepted theories', and that 'there is no theory-free language to describe the data, because myths (that is, primitive theories) arise together with language' (OK: 146).

Let us now consider the first stage in Popper's thinking. After solving the problem of the empirical base – which, in Popper's scheme, is destined to be the touchstone of any scientific theory – he tackles another crucial question for his principle of demarcation. The falsifiability requirement for scientific propositions takes account of the fact that there are different degrees: some theories are more easily falsifiable than others. What counts for any scientific theory as a whole, however, is that it is possible to indicate the conditions under which it could be said to be falsified or refuted – that is, the class of its potential falsifiers – and that it is thus to some extent testable. Of course, the more precise a theory is, and the more detailed its predictions, the easier it will be to test.

> A theory which is more precise and more easily refutable than another will also be the more interesting one. Since it is the more daring one, it will be the one which is *less probable*. But it is better testable, for *we can make our tests more precise and more severe*.
>
> (CR: 256)

The passing of such tests will, as we know, not prove that the theory is true, or even probable, but only that it has been confirmed or corroborated. For Popper prefers to substitute the notion of corroboration for that of probability, as the latter seems to him gravely compromised with the inductivist view of science he is seeking to undermine.

Popper later came to feel that his solution to the demarcation problem was still rather too formal and non-realistic, since it is always possible to find a way of avoiding empirical refutation. At the same time, he was aware of the importance of not giving in too quickly to criticism, so that the theory would have enough room to develop its potential. But while he thus partly reinstated the dogmatic approach upon which he had previously passed final sentence, he felt it necessary, on the other hand, to extend the critical method to the empirical base itself – that is, to the observational propositions that serve as the means of testing. Criticisms made during the 1960s by various exponents of the 'new philosophy of science' were certainly not without a role in widening Popper's horizon in this way. As we shall see shortly, one result was that he could go on to develop a 'metaphysical' doctrine such as the one of the three worlds.

THE PROBLEM OF INDUCTION

Apart from solving what since Kant has been the central problem of the theory of knowledge – that is, the problem of distinguishing science from non-scientific knowledge – the new criterion of demarcation provides the starting-point for a reformulation and resolution of the problem of induction. Popper already came to this conclusion around 1927, having worked on it for some four years (OK: 1, 29), but he only made it public in 1933 in a letter to *Erkenntnis* entitled 'Ein Kriterium des empirischen Charakters theoretischer Systeme', later included as an appendix in *The Logic of Scientific Discovery* (LSD: 312–314).

The problem addressed in this text was the contrast between our wish empirically to ground the laws of nature expressed in universal propositions, and the impossibility of justifying non-singular statements on the basis of experience. Popper consistently maintained that:

> there is no induction, either in a logical sense or in the sense of the theory of knowledge. Natural-scientific theories are 'hypothetical-deductive' systems [...] Consequently, it will never be possible to *demonstrate the truth* of the laws of nature, which always remain only 'problematic regulative ideas' (Kant) or 'heuristic fictions' (Vaihinger).
>
> (BG: 326)

This thesis makes it possible to develop a new scientific method of trial and error, the *critical method*; for our reasoning winds its way not along the path of induction, from facts to theory, but through refutation and falsification.

In order fully to appreciate Popper's methodology, however, we need to bear in mind his criticisms of inductivist logic and of an empiricism exclusively geared to observation. To his own method he gave the name 'deductivism' (LSD: 30), precisely to distinguish it from inductivism. The two procedures have the same goal, to discover the regularities that make natural phenomena understandable; but for deductivism a long series of positive cases, even without any negative ones at all, is not sufficient to reach this goal. 'The fundamental weakness of inductivism lies in an extremely popular but thoroughly false theory of the human intellect, namely, the *tabula rasa* theory' (BG: xxxii), which states that our intellect is passive and merely registers the data supplied to it by the senses. The whole of traditional epistemology has been influenced by 'the Baconian myth that all science starts from observation and then slowly and cautiously proceeds to theories' (CR: 137). The Baconian myth held sway so long as it was a question of explaining why scientific theories are true. But once it is calmly admitted that we are only capable of establishing the falsity and not the truth of such systems of statements, there is no longer any reason for Bacon's supposition. We shall return to this aspect of Popper's thought. First, we must enter more deeply into the problem of induction, which must be solved before any alternative methodology can be developed.

According to Popper, 'in fact we *never* draw inductive inferences, or make use of what are now called "inductive procedures" ' (P1: 35). The radical character of this assertion is tempered a few lines later by the replacement of 'never' with 'hardly ever'. But the reason for Popper's strong aversion is to be found in his long and detailed analysis of the problem of induction, as it was formulated and solved by Hume. He was already criticizing Hume's doctrine in his earliest writings, and his approach remained fundamentally unchanged when he later considered the problem from an evolutionist standpoint in the light of his new theory of the three worlds (that is, in the essay forming Chapter 1 of *Objective Knowledge*). On the one hand, then, Popper finds convincing Hume's critique of inductive inference, on the grounds that nothing logically justifies the move from observed facts to laws; but on the other hand, he cannot accept Hume's psychological explanation of induction in terms of habit derived from repetition.

As regards the logical aspect, Hume correctly pointed out innumerable apparent regularities which everyone trusts in practice, and upon which scientists themselves base their theories. Such practice, however, conflicts with what Popper calls *the principle of the invalidity of induction*: namely, that 'there can be no valid reasoning from singular observation statements to universal laws of nature, and thus to scientific theories' (P1: 32). If we refer to repetitive induction or induction by enumeration, which is based upon the repetition of observations, then its invalidity is obvious enough: 'no amount of observation of white swans establishes that all swans are white (or that the probability of finding a non-white swan is small)' (MF: 104). Nor does 'eliminative induction' fare any better – that which aims at eliminating every false theory so as to establish the true one, as Bacon and Mill prescribed. For its proponents did not realize that the number of logically possible rival theories is always infinite.

The principle of the invalidity of induction also appears to clash with the *principle of empiricism*: namely, that 'we demand that our adoption and our rejection of scientific theories should depend upon the results of observation and experiment, and thus upon singular observation statements' (P1: 32).[1] Hume tried to solve the conflict by abandoning rationalism: if induction is not rationally justified and yet works, all we have to do is give up any appeal to reason and explain it in terms of habit. Popper, however, prefers to give up induction and to save rationalism by means of a further principle: 'We demand that our adoption and our rejection of scientific theories should depend upon our *critical reasoning* (combined with the results of observation and experiment)' [ibid.]. This *principle of critical rationalism* allows us to solve the Humean problem without relying exclusively upon the psychological explanations that Popper regards as unfounded.

Humean psychology, being a reformulation of diffuse popular beliefs, seems to Popper to be mistaken with regard to (a) the typical result of repetition, (b) the genesis of habits, and (c) the expectation of regularity characterizing both experiences and behaviour (CR: 43). First, it has to be said that repetition often results not in a conscious expectation of regularity, but rather in a loss of consciousness: for example, after repeating a passage many times on the piano, we can execute it without paying conscious attention, so that each movement of the hand becomes automatic. Second, habits do not derive from repetition; there are, to be sure, actions which 'deserve to be called "habits" or "customs" only after repetition has played its typical part; but we must not say that the practices in question originated as the result of many repetitions' [ibid.]. Only in special cases is the expectation of regularity sustained by frequent repetition; for a single important observation may be enough to create a conviction or an anticipation. In any case, from a strictly logical point of view, 'the central idea of Hume's theory is that of *repetition, based upon similarity* (or "resemblance")' (CR: 44). Here repetitions are no longer identical but may involve no more than resemblance; for there are various situations which we treat as equivalent and hence interpret from a point of view that must exist before any repetition and cannot itself be the fruit of repetition, on pain of infinite regress. Hume's theory, then, does not explain our expectation of regularity as the fruit of repetition. Rather, it is repetition-for-us (what appears to us as repetition but perhaps not to a spider) which results from our attempt to impose regularities upon the world.

> We try to discover similarities in it, and to interpret it in terms of laws invented by us. Without waiting for premises we jump to conclusions. These may have to be discarded later, should observation show that they are wrong.
>
> (CR: 46)

But whereas the inductivist lays the stress on positive instances, Popper places it on negative ones – on counter-examples, refutations and all kinds of criticism (OK: 20).

Taken as a whole, the above is Popper's most mature and comprehensive development of the critique of induction that he first formulated in *Die beiden Grundprobleme*. There, and in the drastically shortened *Logik*, he stated and solved the Humean problem in essentially the same terms, subjecting to detailed scrutiny the various inductivist positions – from positivism and apriorism to conventionalism and pragmatism. But given our own 'propaedeutic' goals, it would not be appropriate for us to follow all the nuances of Popper's rich and intricate analysis, which would be fraught with difficulties for a reader not familiar with the last two centuries of epistemological theory. Besides, the Popper of the 1930s used a language, style and references geared to other scholars of the same problem, whereas the mature Popper was already accustomed to the more heterogeneous audience that attended his classes and lectures.

The only way of solving the web of problems linked to induction is to provide a different criterion of demarcation between the empirical sciences and other forms of knowledge. Popper points out in this connection that 'inductive method, like the criterion of verifiability, implies a faulty demarcation' (CR: 53). To 'avoid the pitfalls of the problem of induction', it is necessary to take into account 'the asymmetry between verification and falsification [. . .] which results from the logical relation between theories and basic statements' (LSD: 265). It must also be borne in mind that particular propositions are *completely decidable* from an empirical point of view: that is, they can in principle be assigned a secure truth-value, whereas universal propositions are only *partly decidable* in that experience 'can decide only about *one* of the two values, about the truth *or* the falsity of the statement itself' (BG: 307). For the laws of nature are only falsifiable, but the negations of rigorously general statements about reality may only be verified, never definitively falsified. Thus the statement 'It is not true that all swans are white' can never be falsified, because experience will never be able to prove that all swans are white. The exclusion of induction from the characteristic procedures of science does not mean, however, that science can do without inductive direction – that is, the kind of reasoning which moves from theories with a low level of universality to ones with a high level of universality. Popper calls this tendency 'quasi-inductive', because although it is rigorously deductive, it leads to a more general statement. These points risk appearing otiose, if not actually contradictory, in the account given in *Die beiden Grundprobleme* (BG: 327–328). But they may become clearer when compared to similar pages in *The Logic of Scientific Discovery*, where the author says that:

> to obtain a picture or model of this quasi-inductive evolution of science, the various ideas and hypotheses might be visualized as particles suspended in a fluid. Testable science is the precipitation of these particles at the bottom of the vessel: they settle down in layers (of universality). The thickness of the deposit grows with the number of these layers, every new layer corresponding to a theory more universal than those beneath it. As the result of this process, ideas

previously floating in higher metaphysical regions may sometimes be reached by the growth of science, and thus make
contact with it, and settle.

(LSD: 277–278)

Examples of this process are atomism, the theory of terrestrial
motion, or the corpuscular theory of light.

For Popper, then, quasi-induction is a deductive movement
because it starts from a broader and more general conception than
the one at which it arrives. But since this theory is originally no
more than a metaphysical idea, or is at least impregnated with
metaphysical ideas, it acquires the status of a scientific theory only
when it succeeds in demonstrating its own testability and is thus
borne out by experimental controls. In short, the deductive procedure is supplemented by empirical testing that moves from the
bottom (particular observations or experiments) towards the top
(the theory subjected to testing) – and it is in this sense that it
follows an inductive direction.

INDUCTION AND PROBABILITY

'Probability comes in as the substitute, or surrogate, of certainty
– not quite the thing, but at least the next best thing, and at any
rate approaching it' (P1: 222). This question, though not logically
connected to the problem of induction, shares with it a not easily
removable prejudice: namely, that science must afford a high degree
of probability, even if it cannot deliver certainty. It is hardly
necessary to point out that for Popper, just as there are no inductive inferences, nor is there such a thing as probabilistic induction.
'Like inductive logic in general, the theory of the probability of
hypotheses seems to have arisen through a confusion of psychological with logical questions' (LSD: 255). Matters are indeed far
from simple, and Popper himself admitted that 'probability created
problems' for him – 'as well as much exciting and enjoyable work'
(UQ: 99). Ever since the first edition of the *Logik*, Popper had
been convinced that the term 'probability' was compromised with
doctrines very remote from his own convictions, and he was keen
to draw a distinction (including a terminological one) between
the various ways in which it had been understood. He therefore
embarked upon a lengthy discussion of the various theories of
probability that had been put forward and maintained. His main

concern, however, was to distinguish between interpretations of the probability calculus, according to whether they referred to the probability of events or to the probability of hypotheses, and to demonstrate that it was wrong to reduce the latter to the former.

Classical theory deals with numerical probability – that is, with the quotient obtained by dividing the number of favourable cases by the number of possible cases, as in games of chance where the probability that a dice will show the number 5 is 1 in 6. The theory is not univocal, however, and lends itself to a variety of interpretations both subjectivist and objectivist. In the first group, we find the psychologistic interpretation which measures the sensations of certainty or uncertainty that may be aroused by the expectation of particular occurrences. This acceptation of the term may satisfy us when we have to do with non-numerical statements, but it is of no use at all when mathematical values come into play.

Another variant is the logico-subjective theory, which Popper chiefly identifies with Keynes and his interesting work *A Treatise on Probability* (1921). Here too, probability is identified with the 'degree of rational belief', or 'the amount of trust it is proper to accord to a statement' – but the probability relation is treated as a kind of logical relationship between two statements, so that the degree of probability is highest (= 1) when one proposition is derivable from another, and lowest (= 0) when the two propositions contradict each other (LSD: 149). Popper rejects this conception as being of no use to science, for 'the logical probability of a statement is complementary to its degree of falsifiability: it increases with a decreasing degree of falsifiability. The logical probability 1 corresponds to the degree 0 of falsifiability, and vice versa' (LSD: 119). The aim of science, then, is not to achieve high probability: if it were, science would have to base itself upon a large number of trivialities with an equally high degree of probability. Rather, science is interested in theories with a high content, whose probability obviously decreases in proportion to the rise in content (LSD: 286–287). We shall return below to this point, which is particularly important because it involves a new concept of probability to which Popper gives the name 'corroboration', to distinguish it from others that refer in one way or another to the calculus of probability.

Before we explain Popper's own views, however, let us stay a little longer with his survey of 'subjective' and 'objective' interpretations of probability. Whereas 'the subjective theory of probability springs from the belief that we use probability only if we have insufficient knowledge' (P1: 281), objective theories 'take probabilities as properties of certain physical systems – experimental set-ups, for example' (P1: 295). The author of the *Logic* places in this group the theory of relative frequency, the only one he considers acceptable in the physical sciences. Only later does he introduce the propensity interpretation – the most important change in this area after 1934 – which Popper considers 'more adequate' from 1953 but properly develops only in the *Postscript* (P1: 282ff.; LSD: 147). The frequency theory, represented by Richard von Mises as well as by Dörge, Kamke, Reichenbach and Tornier, 'treats every numerical probability statement as a statement about the *relative frequency* with which an event of a certain kind occurs within a *sequence of occurrences*' (LSD: 149). This means that probability statements no longer concern a singular event, but rather a set of events, and that they indicate the frequency of a certain happening in relation to this set of events. Thus, to say that the probability of the next throw of a dice being 5 is 1 in 6, is to say that, within a class of throws, the relative frequency of the number 5 is 1 in 6. Numerical probability statements are thus admissible only if they can be explained in terms of frequency, and the interpretation does not apply at all to non-numerical statements because they do not involve whole sequences of events. This theory was criticized for its restrictiveness, but von Mises replied that it was necessary to distinguish between scientific use of the notion of probability and pre-scientific uses, which involve a greater number of aspects but are even less clear and rigorous. Popper's own objection seems more to the point. Von Mises' theory, he argued, operates with infinite sequences, because only they meet the requirements for the calculation of non-given probabilities on the basis of given probabilities; it is therefore important that the end-piece of a sequence should satisfy certain demands. 'But this means that any *empirical* sequence is simply irrelevant for judging any infinite sequence of which it is the initial segment' (UQ: 100). Popper had an opportunity to discuss this with von Mises, as well as with Hans Hahn. They both agreed with him, but von Mises insisted that it did not invalidate his theory because his concept of a 'collective' was an ideal mathematical concept, like that of a sphere, to which there could be only rough empirical approximations. Popper then proposed a different solution in the *Logic* (paragraphs 51ff.), but later became dissatisfied with it as he moved towards a propensity theory. This has some affinities with the classical interpretation that defined probability as the number of favourable cases divided by the number of possible cases. For 'the propensity interpretation is very closely related to the interpretation which takes probability as a measure of possibilities. All that it adds to this is a physical interpretation of the possibilities, which it takes to be not mere abstractions but physical tendencies or propensities to bring about the possible state of affairs' (P1: 286). In this hypothesis, relative frequencies are considered as 'the results, or the outward expressions, or the appearances, of a hidden and not directly observable physical disposition or tendency or propensity' [ibid.].

The point of introducing hidden propensities behind the frequencies becomes evident once we realize that it meets Popper's own objection that the frequency theory calculates the probability of a singular event only as an element in a sequence; 'the propensity interpretation attaches a probability to a singular event as a representative of a *virtual or conceivable sequence* of events' (P1: 287). According to the propensity interpretation, any singular event is the result of a propensity that may be subjected to statistical testing. In other words, whereas in the first case an infinite sequence is necessary for the calculation of probability, in the second it is sufficient to have, as it were, gathered the tendency or propensity from physical phenomena. Furthermore, this interpretation emphasizes the objective side of probability, which – contrary to the false view of subjective theories – is not at all dependent upon the imperfect state of our knowledge. The chief difference between frequency and propensity interpretations lies in the role attributed to singular statements. For if we consider that probabilities are dispositional properties that depend upon a set of generating conditions, then the probability of a singular event is 'a property of the singular event itself, to be measured by a conjectured *potential or virtual* statistical frequency rather than by an *actual* or by an observed frequency' (P1: 359). Popper has no doubt that propensities 'exhibit a certain similarity to Aristotelian potentialities' [ibid.]; where they differ is that they inhere not in individual things but in situations – for propensity is a relational concept, like force or, better still, field of force. Thus, the propensity to turn up heads or tails is not an intrinsic property of a coin, but varies with the conditions in which the coin is tossed – for example, on a hard surface rather than sandy or muddy ground.

One might say, then, that the propensity theory takes account of the relational saspect of phenomena, given that even in the simplest cases there are a number of variables in play. And so it is important – especially during experimental testing – to maintain at least those conditions which are relevant to any repetition of the event.

In the *Logic* Popper had further argued that it is wrong to identify the probability of hypotheses with the probability of events; it is a mistake which stems from the confusion (detectable even in Reichenbach) between the probability of a hypothesis and the probability of a statement, the latter being in turn nothing other than the expression of the probability of an event. In fact, Popper himself defines an event as 'what may be *typical or universal* about an occurrence' (LSD: 89); that is to say, events describe in universal terms what is in itself always particular and individually connoted, and so it is easy to identify events with the statements expressing them. The flaw in the argument, however, is to assume that a hypothesis is a sequence of statements, understood as descriptions of events. For the universal statements used in a hypothesis cannot be considered as sequences of basic statements, and the latter can never be derived from universal statements alone (LSD: 258–259).

If the probability of hypotheses cannot be reduced to the probability of events, it is still necessary to solve the problem of how theories are to be evaluated. Popper, when describing a theory's success in attempts to falsify it, prefers to use the term 'corroboration' – precisely to distinguish it from the probability that an event will happen. A hypothesis is then more probable – that is, more corroborated – than another hypothesis when it has been subjected to a greater number of empirical tests without being refuted. But to avoid confusions that might easily arise, Popper thinks that the term 'probability' should be used only in cases governed by the rules of the mathematical calculus of probability, and that 'corroboration' should be used instead in the comparative evaluation of hypotheses (P1: 223–227). At first Popper spoke interchangeably of 'corroboration' or 'confirmation', but he later came to regard the second of these as too much 'used and misused' (CR: 57). We shall therefore follow him in preferring the term 'corroboration' in this context.

A theory may be taken as corroborated to the extent that it stands up to testing. Of course, there are various degrees of corroboration that make a theory more or less desirable, more or less reliable, but contrary to what one might think, the number of corroborating instances does not count for very much. The key factor is rather:

> the severity of the various tests to which the hypothesis in question can be, and has been, subjected. But the severity of the tests, in its turn, depends upon the degree of testability, and thus upon the simplicity of the hypothesis: the hypothesis which is falsifiable in a higher degree, or the simpler hypothesis, is also the one which is corroborable in a higher degree.
>
> (LSD: 267)

Testability, then, is the opposite of logical probability; the most easily testable and falsifiable theory is the one that is least probable in a logical sense. Besides, 'if you value high probability, you must say very little – or better still, nothing at all: tautologies will always remain the highest probability' (LSD: 270). The probability of a theory is thus inversely proportional to its empirical content.[2]

In this optic it is possible to avoid any reference to truth values, which, unlike corroboration, do not depend upon temporal variables. For corroboration is always relative to a hitherto accepted system of basic statements which, insofar as it can undergo sudden change, may give rise to a different evaluation of the tested theory. 'Corroboration (or degree of corroboration),' Popper explains, is 'an evaluating report of past performance [. . .] it says nothing whatever about future performance, or about the "reliability" of a theory' (OK: 18). In speaking of 'degree of corroboration', Popper wanted to offer in one terse expression 'a report of the manner in which a theory has passed – or not passed – its tests, including an evaluation of the severity of the tests: only tests undertaken in a *critical* spirit – attempted refutations – should count' (UQ: 103). The practical problem of induction is thereby solved: it is transformed into the problem of testing a theory, not to be confused with the verificationist concept of 'support' for a hypothesis. For, 'while the verificationist view leads to the claim that every "instance" of h supports h', Popper holds 'that only the results of *genuine tests* can support h' (P1: 235).

THE CHARACTERISTICS OF SCIENCE

It should now be clear that for Popper the goal of science is not to acquire certainty or, failing that, the highest possible probability. Its task is, to be sure, 'the search for truth, that is, for true theories (even though as Xenophanes pointed out we may never get them, or know them as true if we get them)' (CR: 229). But science is not content with trivial truths; 'what we look for is *interesting* truth' which gives 'answers to our problems' (CR: 229–230). In other words, 'the aim of science is to find *satisfactory explanations* of whatever strikes us as being in need of explanation' (P1: 132). No explanation can be provided or even sought, however, if the idea of objective truth is left out of the picture; it alone gives meaning to the concept of error, and significance to the aim of rational critique. The very admission of fallibility entails that there is objective truth as opposed to error, despite the fact that we are never equal to it and that 'it is hard to come by' (P1: 260).

Nor should it be forgotten that truth is not only hard to come by but also hard to define. Popper was already aware of this as a young man when, although he accepted the traditional notion of truth as correspondence to the facts, he felt so uncomfortable with it that he avoided any real argument until his meeting with Tarski in 1935 gave him the key to a solution (UQ: 98–99, 141–142; cf. LSD: 274). The terms of the problem are well enough known: the notion of truth as correspondence to the facts is the commonsense idea, but it is not easy to explain philosophically the relationship between a fact and a statement – that is, between a linguistic entity and an extra-linguistic one. The young Popper was not happy with Wittgenstein's view in the *Tractatus* of language as a mere picturing or mirroring of reality, nor was he persuaded by Schlick's arguments in the *Erkenntnislehre*. Tarski, however, showed him convincingly that the much-disputed correspondence pertains between the *description of a statement* and the *description of a fact*, and that this correspondence is expressed by another statement, different from the first, which belongs not to first-level language (the language that speaks of objects, of reality) but to metalanguage (a higher-level language that speaks of language itself). After this encounter, Popper never had any second thoughts and declared in 1990 his '54-year-long adherence to the Aristotelian theory of truth, rehabilitated by Tarski and successfully applied by him and by Gödel to some mathematical problems' (WP: 6).

These considerations (which we have barely outlined here), together with his conviction that any rational critique must involve the possibility of showing that a theory is not true, led Popper to treat 'the classical idea of absolute or objective truth as a *regulative idea*; that is to say, as *a standard of which we may fall short*' (P1: 26). This is why, in two lectures delivered in part in the early 1960s and later published in full as Chapter 10 of *Conjectures and Refutations*, Popper introduced the concept of 'verisimilitude' or 'truthlikeness'. He defines it by means of a formula:

$$Vs(a) = Ct_T(a) - Ct_F(a),$$

where $Vs(a)$ indicates the verisimilitude of a theory a, $Ct_T(a)$ is a measure of the truth-content of a, and $Ct_F(a)$ is a measure of its falsity-content. It is evident that the truthlikeness of a theory is greater if there is an increase in $Ct_T(a)$ but not in $Ct_F(a)$, or if $Ct_F(a)$ decreases but not $Ct_T(a)$ (CR: 234). Thus, although we cannot expect to grasp the full truth, or to recognize it whenever we come across it, we can determine how close we are to it by comparing the verisimilitude of the theories with which we are working.

Popper is concerned to draw a clear distinction between the idea of approximation to the truth (that is, verisimilitude) and the idea of probability with which it has often been confused since the beginnings of Western philosophy. For the concept of 'like the truth' has been interpreted as equivalent to 'uncertain and at best of some fair degree of certainty', which is to say 'probable' (CR: 237). Popper here stresses again what he already explained in detail in the *Logic*: namely, that verisimilitude 'represents the idea of approaching comprehensive truth. It thus combines truth and content while probability combines truth with lack of content' (CR: 237). This combination of the concepts of truth and logical content, at least in the present sense, is attributed to Tarski, who figures as Popper's constant reference point. Indeed, although Popper is content to remain at a lower level of detail, his aim is to set forth a theory of verisimilitude with results like those obtained by Tarski's theory of truth: that is, to rehabilitate a commonsense concept which, though looked upon with suspicion by philosophy and science, is necessary if critical realism and the critical theory of science are to be maintained (OK: 60).

Another point that seems problematic in Popper's view of science is the question of its objectivity, for this does seem gravely

43

compromised as soon as we deny that scientific theories are fully justifiable or verifiable. Popper recalls that Kant used the term 'objective' for knowledge that was *'justifiable*, independently of anybody's whim' (LSD: 44), and he proposes in *The Logic of Scientific Discovery* to redefine it in terms of intersubjective testability. In a footnote added later, he talks of having generalized this formulation: 'for inter-subjective *testing* is merely a very important aspect of the more general idea of inter-subjective *criticism*, or in other words, of the idea of mutual rational control by critical discussion' (LSD: 44). Objectivity, then, is the result not of neutral and impartial observation but of critical effort (P1: 45–46). It is certainly true that our knowledge always derives from human actions that have the ineradicable mark of subjectivity, and yet objective knowledge (science) does exist, as a kind of 'social institution'. Like other institutions, science is the outcome of human intervention that is not always intentional, and whose consequences often cannot be foreseen. But as soon as the contributions imbued with subjectivity are put to the test, discussed and criticized, the jumble of impressions, prejudices and intuitions is transformed into objective knowledge, precisely because it has moved from the sphere of individual psychology into the realm of what can be tested by other conscious subjects (P1: 86–87). The view of knowledge as uncertain and relative (a view shared by Popper) has often led to the conclusion that it cannot be objective, and this is doubtless the case if we follow Kant in his demand for necessary and universal knowledge. But if we content ourselves with progressive and provisional levels of plausibility, then our knowledge can perfectly well be objective.

Popper contrasts his own conception of science to two traditional ones that he considers equally unacceptable: instrumentalism and essentialism. The first claims that scientific theories are nothing but instruments, more or less useful, but not true or false like descriptive statements; the second asserts that science should search for ultimate explanations in terms of essences, on the grounds that there is in each particular case an intrinsic principle which science is called upon to discover. According to well-known instrumentalists such as Reichenbach or Carnap (P1: 112ff.), scientific theories are no more than computation or inference rules that enable us to make predictions. Popper does not deny that they are *also* this, but he refuses to accept that they are *only* this – for a theory, unlike an instrument, can actually be refuted (CR:

111–114). Moreover, instrumentalism discounts as quite superficial a factor which, as we have seen, Popper regards as fundamental: the quest for truth. And conversely, our philosopher maintains that a theory is unquestionably either true or false, even if we are not able to establish which it is with certainty (OK: 80). In the end:

> the tendency of instrumentalism is anti-rationalist. It implies that human reason cannot discover any secret of our world. [. . .] There is no truth in science: there is only utility. Science is unable to enlighten our minds: it can only fill our bellies.
>
> (P1: 122–123)

For Popper, on the other hand, truth – understood as approximation to truth – is the ultimate criterion for the a posteriori evaluation of theories, based upon how they stand up to testing. Of course, within the epistemological framework of critical rationalism, any a posteriori evaluation largely depends upon the a priori value of a theory – that is to say, upon its content and its virtual explanatory power (OK: 143). For any a posteriori evaluation is meaningful when it applies to a theory that is not trivially true but interesting, innovative and barely probable.

Turning to essentialism, Popper takes as his prototype Aristotle's view that 'a definition is a statement of the inherent essence or nature of a thing' (CR: 20). With a similar perspective, Descartes claimed to have grounded physics on the notion that expressed the essence of the physical world – namely, extension. In short, the idea is to establish beyond all reasonable doubt the reality that lies hidden behind appearances. Popper is quite prepared to admit that 'much is hidden from us, and that much of what is hidden may be discovered' (CR: 105), but he thinks that to assume the existence of 'essences' is of no help to scientists, sometimes indeed a hindrance, because it may make them happy with a supposed description of the essential nature of the object and discourage them from further investigation. By way of example, Popper shows how an essentialist interpretation of Newtonian theory makes it impossible to probe the nature of the force of gravity or inertia, for as intrinsic properties of matter they are supposed to require no further explanation, except perhaps God's endowment of matter with such properties.

According to what Popper calls the 'third view', it is quite possible to accept the existence of something behind appearance without thereby falling into essentialism. We may, that is, work 'with the idea of hierarchical levels of explanatory hypotheses' (CR: 173). Such theories are not merely instruments for the prediction of what will happen in the world of appearances: science seeks to advance into the unknown and to *describe* reality by means of hypotheses; its aim is to develop *true* theories, even if – and here is the crucial difference from essentialism – we can never be completely and indubitably certain about them. It might be objected, on the basis of Tarski's semantic theory which Popper himself accepts, that a statement describes reality if and only if it is true, and that therefore the hypotheses of science, whose truth can never be established, cannot be descriptions of reality. Popper's answer focuses on three points: first of all, the hypothetical character of a theory does not invalidate its *claim* to pronounce upon what is and is not real; second, because it is possible to establish the falseness of a theory, its rejection will in such cases constitute a true description of reality; and lastly, the very fact that a theory is refuted by reality implies that it was a theory *about reality*, and not just an unsuccessful mathematical formula (CR: 116). In other words, 'although our theories are made by ourselves, although they are own inventions, they are none the less genuine assertions about the world; for they can *clash* with something we never made' (OK: 197). Thus, even if we can never succeed in describing the ultimate essence of reality, we are able to continue deepening our investigation of the structural and relational properties of the world, obtaining ever richer contents expressed in ever more coherent and organic forms.

Here we can already glimpse the kernel of Popper's 'metaphysics'. His open espousal of realism supports a whole epistemological edifice which, though its correctness can never be demonstrated, is designed to be 'internally, logically non-contradictory', as well as 'free of the difficulties that beset other points of view'. What is true of science in general thus also applies to Popper's epistemology: its falsity can be demonstrated but not its truth, and so it is necessary to be content with what proves free of contradiction, both internally and in relation to external reality.

We may now summarize the main theses of Popper's epistemology, which he developed also and above all in discussion with contemporary thinkers, and through reflection on the teachings of great philosophers of the past such as Hume and Kant. 'All scientific knowledge is hypothetical or conjectural' (MF: 93). The growth of knowledge takes place only through the correction of previous errors; for 'the advance of knowledge consists, mainly, in the modification of earlier knowledge' (CR: 28). The method of science consists precisely in learning from our mistakes, through critical examination of theories developed to address the problems that gradually present themselves to researchers. Experiments serve an irreplaceable function within the critical discussion of hypotheses, but they 'are constantly guided by theory, by theoretical hunches of which the experimenter is often not conscious' (MF: 93). Scientific objectivity consists solely in the critical method, which, if we are lucky, enables us to drive out any errors and prejudices that may creep into our theories. Of course, the individual scientist may defend his position, even in a dogmatic manner, because the critical approach is not necessarily present within individuals but must be present within the larger scientific community. Besides, if the criticism is not to be weak and superficial, 'it is extremely important that the theories criticized should be tenaciously defended' (MF: 94). A theory is scientific when it can tell us something about the empirical world – that is, when it may in principle clash with an observational statement. This means that a theory is scientific when it is refutable, and that the criterion of demarcation between science and non-science is falsifiability. Scientificity, we may say, is guaranteed by testability, which is itself a matter of degree: 'the testability of a theory increases and decreases with its *informative content* and therefore with its *improbability*' (OK: 17).

NATURAL SCIENCE AND SOCIAL SCIENCE

Popper rather sadly observes that although social and political reflection appeared soon after the investigation of nature, 'the social sciences do not as yet seem to have found their Galileo' (PH :1). The problem of method has not yet been solved, and scholars are divided between those who consider the method of physics to be applicable, and those who regard it as alien to the social sciences. The 'historicist' position is distinctive, however, in combining pro-naturalistic theses (favouring the application of physics) and anti-naturalistic ones (against its application). By historicism, Popper understands 'an approach to the social sciences which assumes that *historical prediction* is their principal aim, and which assumes that this aim is attainable by discovering the

"rhythms" or the "patterns", the "laws" or the "trends" that under-
lie the evolution of history' (PH: 3). Popper declares himself convinced that such a method is 'at bottom responsible for the
unsatisfactory state of the theoretical social sciences' [ibid.].

Historicism maintains that because of the historical character of
social laws, methods which are perfectly legitimate in physics can
seldom – or never, as in the case of generalization, for example –
be employed in sociology. For the regularities that present themselves in society are not eternal; they characterize a definite historical period, and depend upon the power of human beings to
intervene and change their own activity (PH :7–8). Nor is it possible to apply the experimental method to the study of social
phenomena, given that the artificial isolation of a number of individuals would rule out events and factors of the highest importance
(PH: 8). There is also the fact that the subject-matter of physics,
already less complex than that of the social sciences, is simplified
still further by experimental isolation and the possibility of leaving
certain elements out of consideration. Besides:

> social life is a natural phenomenon that presupposes the
> mental life of individuals, i.e. psychology, which in its turn
> presupposes biology, which again presupposes chemistry and
> physics. The fact that sociology comes last in this hierarchy
> of sciences plainly shows us the tremendous complexity of
> the factors involved in social life.
>
> (PH: 12)

Historicists further argue that the atomist approach in general,
which analyses individual parts, is not well suited to sociology
with its holistic focus on a living organism rather than inert matter
(PH: 17ff.); the method of the social sciences therefore needs to
be based upon a deep understanding of social phenomena and
geared to explanation in qualitative rather than quantitative terms.
In response, Popper admits that 'no doubt there are some differences here between physical and sociological methods', but insists
that 'the historicist contention rests upon a gross misunderstanding
of the experimental methods of physics' (PH: 93). At bottom,
historicism is *a poor method*, unable to yield the results it prom-
ises' (PH: 58). This is, above all, a poverty of imagination, for the
historicist never manages to explore the possibility of change in
the conditions of change, which he insists on regarding as immutable (PH: 130). To identify the most appropriate and productive

method, we need first to have a clear idea of the aims and competence of the social sciences. Their task 'is not, as the historicist believes, the prophecy of the future course of history. It is, rather, the discovery and explanation of the less obvious dependences within the social sphere' (OS II: 324). In Popper's view, indeed, it is not possible to make exact social predictions. For what he calls the *Oedipus effect* means that prediction can influence the predicted event and so thwart the prognosis; for example, the prediction of a fall in stock-exchange values over the next three days would probably lead to hurried selling and thus invalidate the prediction by precipitating a crash.

Far from making unreliable prophecies, sociological theory should 'trace the unintended social repercussions of intentional human actions' (CR: 342). Very often the consciously willed behaviour of individuals produces unintended and even unwanted effects: for example, someone who is looking to buy a house in a particular area would certainly not wish his action to help push up local property prices, but that is exactly what he does by appearing on the market as a prospective purchaser. This allows us to glimpse an important analogy between the social sciences and the experimental natural sciences: 'both lead us to the formulation of practical technological rules stating *what we cannot do*' (CR: 343); or, to put it in another way, both 'can never do more than *exclude certain possibilities*' (PH: 139).

It is necessary and possible to apply the same method, because, as in the natural sciences:

> most of the objects of social science, if not all of them, are abstract objects; they are *theoretical* constructions. (Even 'the war' or 'the army' are abstract concepts, strange as this may sound to some. What is concrete is the many who are killed; or the men and women in uniform, etc.).
>
> (PH: 135)

In this sense, Popper therefore agrees with historicists that sociology, like physics, has both a theoretical and an empirical character (PH: 35). What he contests is the frequent assumption that the social sciences deal with more complex objects. He puts this prejudice down to two sources. On the one hand, things are being compared which are not actually homogeneous, such as concrete social situations and artificial situations created in the laboratory. On the other hand, it is claimed that the account of a social situation should include the state of mind and even the physical conditions of the persons involved – a view which presupposes that social entities are not abstract models (as they in fact are) but concrete objects with individuals as their vital components. As to the supposed complexity of the social sciences, Popper notes that they are really less complex than the natural sciences, because in most social situations there is an element of rationality which makes it fairly easy to construct models to function as useful approximations (PH: 140–141).

This element of rationality in human action allows the social sciences to apply the 'zero method'. By this, Popper means:

> the method of constructing a model on the assumption of complete rationality (and perhaps also on the assumption of the possession of complete information) on the part of all the individuals concerned, and of estimating the deviation of the actual behaviour of people from the model behaviour, using the latter as a kind of zero co-ordinate.
>
> (PH: 141)

In the end Popper does recognize the difficulty of applying quantitative methods – especially methods of measurement – to the social sciences. But he points out that the difference is more one of degree than one of kind, and that such difficulties can and must be overcome [ibid.]. Indeed, he relates the insistence on the qualitative nature of sociological terms to the essentialist approach he has already criticized in the natural sciences, where essence is understood as the source of every potentiality in a thing that its various changes do no more than realize. The result, as we have seen, is that questions are no longer asked about how a thing behaves or how a phenomenon develops, but only about 'what is matter', 'what is justice', and so on (PH: 26–34).

To understand Popper's point of view better, we shall need to look in the next chapter at his theories concerning the philosophy of politics.

3

THE POLITICAL WORKS

HISTORICISM AS A PHILOSOPHY OF HISTORY

While Popper was working on *The Poverty of Historicism*, the problem of essentialism led him to make some points about Plato's *Republic* which struck his friends as rather obscure. He therefore set about developing this part into the nucleus of what would become an imposing two-volume work, *The Open Society and Its Enemies*. The author himself remarks that although it was complementary to the book on historicism, it was 'no doubt the more important one' (UQ: 91). For it showed with a wealth of argument and example that the critical method typical of science can be generalized into 'the critical or rational attitude', so that it can also be placed at the basis of the life of society [ibid.].

It may be worth recalling here that it was in March 1938, on the day when he heard the news of the Austrian *Anschluss*, that Popper took the final decision to work up into a book the material that had already been taking shape for some time (OS I: xi). The writing of it lasted until 1943, taking up years that were sufficiently grave and anxiety-ridden to justify Popper's harsh tone against totalitarianism and its 'false prophets'. Although no contemporary events are mentioned in the book, it was written to explain them and to discuss the questions that would probably emerge after the war – in particular, the relationship between Marxism and Western democracy.

Popper's general interest in social science and political thought was aroused precisely by his observation that neither the one nor the other had been able to explain the phenomenon of totalitarianism (OS I: xiv). His book was intended to fill this gap by showing that our civilization 'has not yet fully recovered from the shock

51

of its birth – the transition from the tribal or "closed society", with its submission to magical forces, to the "open society" which sets free the critical powers of man' (OS I: xiii). Of 'those philosophies which are responsible for the widespread prejudice against the possibilities of democratic reform', the most powerful is what Popper calls *historicism*. For it looks at institutions from a historical point of view, focusing on their origin and development, whereas Popper proposes a kind of social engineering or technology that asks simply whether a certain institution is functional and adequate to certain ends.

To grasp Popper's complex path in his political *magnum opus*, it may be useful to begin by explaining the concepts evoked in the title which lead straight to the heart of his political approach. As the philosopher himself points out, the expression 'open society' also carries an emotional charge: that is, it stems from the pleasant sensation he felt on arriving for the first time in England, a country with old liberal traditions, from a land threatened by national socialism; 'it was as if the windows had suddenly been opened' (RR: 22). In fact, the term was first introduced by Bergson, but Popper employs it with at least partly different meanings to refer to a society where 'individuals are confronted with personal decisions' (OS I: 173) – as opposed to 'closed society' with its characteristic belief in magical taboos and its basis in tribal and collective tradition, where 'the institutions leave no room for personal responsibility' (OS I: 172). The open society, then, involves a 'loss of [that] organic character' which made society feel like a real concrete group; the open society carries a risk of abstractness, for it is characterized not by its content but rather – as Franz Stark points out in a concluding note to *Revolution oder Reform?* – by the rules guiding social disputes (RR: 47–48). Open societies are thus not very stable (RR: 24), because, unlike dictatorships, they are exposed to critical debate and to constant review of the solutions adopted. For in keeping with Popper's well-known epistemological criteria, political solutions, like scientific ones, can never be more than provisional and are always open to improvement.

Among the most dangerous enemies of the open society are the champions of historicism, who reduce people to mere cogs in an uncontrollable machine. For the same reason, Popper argues against the basic prejudice of historicism: namely, the view that if the social sciences are to be useful, they must be capable of making prophecies (OS I: xv). The connection between these two points immediately becomes clear in the light of a further consideration. If the course of history cannot be changed by human action but is already marked down in one way or another, then human responsibility is considerably reduced, but at the same time, as a kind of compensation, it will be enough to discover the direction or basic laws of historical evolution to predict with certainty how it will unfold.

Historicism is present in different historical epochs and in conceptions otherwise quite distant from one another: those who see history as a manifestation of God's will are followed by those who replace the chosen people with the chosen race or class. In particular, Popper traces contemporary historicism (mainly represented by Marxism) back to Hegel and beyond him to Heraclitus, Plato and Aristotle. But before we run through these stages, it may be useful if we consider more closely Popper's framework for the discussion of this kind of philosophy of history.

Historicism lays great stress on the problem of change, which is especially important where social institutions are involved. For what changes must still have the same identity after the change has occurred, even though this is not always discernible in the case of the structures of social regulation that are modified in the course of history. For example, it certainly cannot be said that the government of Great Britain has remained unchanged for the last four centuries, and yet it could be argued that the essential identity of the institution has been preserved; the conclusion seems inescapable, therefore, that we cannot speak of change or development without assuming essences that do not change – that is, without involving ourselves in essentialism (PH: 32). Not only does historicism pay tribute to essentialism, however; it also makes its own the holistic way of regarding changes within society as if it were one physical body moving as a single whole along its course. The aim is to identify not just a tendency but something like the law of inertia formulated by Newtonian physics. For his part, Popper does not deny the existence of social trends or tendencies, but he emphatically asserts that 'trends are not laws' and that 'laws and trends are radically different things' (PH: 115–116). Trends are expressed by existential statements, whereas laws are universal statements which, instead of affirming that something exists, assert that something is impossible. It follows that it is possible to base scientific predictions upon laws, but not simply upon trends.

Popper claims to have located 'the central mistake of historicism' in the fact that:

> its 'laws of development' turn out to be absolute trends; trends which, like laws, do not depend on initial conditions, and which carry us irresistibly in a certain direction into the future. They are the basis of unconditional *prophecies*, as opposed to conditional scientific *predictions*.
>
> (PH: 128)

Along similar lines, there is a historicist conception of the task of politics as being 'to lessen the birthpangs of impending political developments' (CR: 338). This is why historicism does not necessarily entail fatalism or inactivity – as one might logically suppose it to do – but actually encourages every activity which furthers or facilitates imminent change. It would seem, then, that 'social midwifery is the only perfectly reasonable activity open to us, the only activity that can be based upon scientific foresight' (PH: 49) and that requires the help of human reason in telling us the direction of incipient change. No wonder that historicism attaches so much importance to the study and interpretation of history – with the aim of discovering the laws of its development (PH: 50–51). But this does not alter the fact that human action has rather little influence on history, given that the course of its evolution is essentially unalterable. As Popper summarizes the position, 'the historicist can only *interpret* social development and aid it in various ways; his point, however, is that *nobody can change it*' (PH: 52).

As the theorist of critical rationalism, Popper kept an optimistic belief in man's capacity to improve his own lot and to solve his own problems without intervention from on high. For this reason, he could not accept the 'deification of history' (CR: 346) through which historical determinism has replaced the naturalistic determinism which, further back still, once ousted theological determinism. Popper's objections are twofold: (a) historicists derive their prophecies from conditional scientific predictions; but (b) even conditional scientific predictions can lead to long-term prophecies 'only if they apply to systems which can be described as well-isolated, stationary and recurrent. These systems are very rare in nature; and modern society is surely not one of them' (CR: 339).

For instance, eclipse prophecies are possible only because the solar system is stationary, relatively free from outside influences, and of such a nature as to exhibit regularities and repetitions. Much the same can be said of natural phenomena based upon the alternation of the seasons. But the development of society does not display these characteristics, and at least in its most significant aspects it does not present a cyclical pattern – hence there can be no assurance that historical prophecies will be successful. The critique of historicism is thus closely bound up with the critique of determinism which Popper first made in an essay published in 1950, 'Indeterminism in Quantum Physics and in Classical Physics', and which he later refined in the second volume of the *Postscript*, some time after the period he devoted to his political works. This means that, as he recognized himself, the first edition of *The Poverty of Historicism* – published in three parts in 1944 and 1945 in the journal *Economica* – does not contain a real refutation of historicism. Yet one is already clearly outlined by 1957, in the edition of the essay that came out in book form after considerable further reflection.

To sum up, Popper's refutation of historicism is based on the idea that 'the course of human history is strongly influenced by the growth of human knowledge', and that since we cannot predict the future growth of our scientific knowledge, nor can we predict the future course of history (PH: vi–vii; OGOU: 16–17). We must therefore rule out any theoretical history corresponding to theoretical physics (that is, providing a scientific theory of historical development), so that the historicist aim of historical prophecy is without any foundation. Popper is not denying, of course, that we can foresee certain developments on the basis of certain conditions, but he does think we can dismiss any prophecy which does not take into account the unknown factor represented by the ceaseless growth of scientific knowledge. For 'if there is such a thing as growing human knowledge, then we cannot anticipate today what we shall know only tomorrow' (PH: vii).

Despite the radical nature of this critique, Popper accepts that as a reaction to the prevailing conception of history – for which human affairs turn upon the figure of the great man or leader, as if there were no other forces or factors in play – historicism may in some cases have a certain validity. Tolstoy is explicitly mentioned here as representing a form of historicist combination of individualism and collectivism; his *War and Peace* fresco demonstrates 'the small influence of the actions and decisions of Napoleon, Alexander, Kutuzov, and the other great leaders of 1812, in the face of what may be called the logic of events' (PH: 148). Popper sees no historical determinism in such events, but he can only admire Tolstoy's attempt to show the importance of the countless individuals who burned Moscow or invented the methods of partisan warfare.

With the strength of these convictions, Popper set out in *The Open Society and Its Enemies* to trace some moments in the history of historicism, so as to 'illustrate its persistent and pernicious influence upon the philosophy of society and of politics' (PH: viii). It is no accident that he originally intended to call the work *False Prophets: Plato, Hegel, Marx*, because he regarded these three philosophers as the peaks of historicist thought representing the main variations on the unrealizable claim to political prophecy.

PLATO THE TOTALITARIAN

As we have seen, historicism is a doctrine that addresses the problem of change, and as such it has its origins in the philosopher who first discovered and theorized becoming: Heraclitus. For him the world was no longer to be identified with the cosmos – that is, a kind of well-constructed edifice – but rather with a never-ending process in constant flux. This heightened emphasis on change, combined with a belief in the inexorable law of fate, gave rise to the first nucleus of historicism.[1] Popper suggests that Heraclitus' view of the world was inspired by the political disorders of his time (OS I: 12ff.), and that the same may be said of Plato, who 'summed up his social experience, exactly as his predecessor had done, by proffering a law of historical development' (OS I: 19). Plato held that all perceptible (including social) changes in the cosmos were a symptom of corruption, decay and degeneration, but that it was possible to interrupt this process by 'arresting all political change' (OS I: 20–21).

The dialogues in which Socrates' disciple examined social questions were the *Republic*, the rather later *Statesman*, and finally the *Laws*. In these works Plato describes the evolution of society in terms that would be taken up many centuries later, by Comte and Mill, as well as by Hegel and Marx, with the difference that whereas 'the aristocrat Plato condemned it, these modern authors applauded it, believing as they did in a law of historical progress'

(OS I: 40). In striving to understand and explain the political upheavals through which he had lived, Plato came to see the concrete and contingent forms of social organization as decadent copies of an ideal state. His historicist sociology thus located the cause of political change in the discord theorized by Heraclitus, which, in the political domain, was expressed through the class antagonism caused by divergent economic interests. Class struggle was thus the moving, and corrupting, force of history (OS I: 55).

Plato's account of the perfect state is usually seen as involving a programme which, though thoroughly utopian, is at the same time unquestionably progressive. Popper, however, regards it as no more than a nostalgic look back, towards a past forever lost. Let us now briefly recall Plato's main political theories, before considering the critical discussion of them contained in the first volume of *The Open Society*. The ideal state of the *Republic* is one where everybody helps to satisfy the needs of the collective, according to the characteristic personality of the part of the soul that prevails in them, so that society is divided into as many layers as there are parts of the soul. The working class, dominated by the concupiscible soul, is destined to satisfy the material needs of citizens; the warriors, in whom the irascible soul is uppermost, have the task of courageously defending the city from enemies; and men in whom the rational soul holds sway have the duty of guiding the state and providing for the citizens' education. In fact, in Popper's view, Plato's triple layers may be reduced to a canvas in which a class of armed and educated rulers or guardians stands opposed to the class of those who are ruled and who lack both arms and education (OS I: 46–47). For Plato is only really interested in the rulers' education: he may allow peasants and craftsmen to pass on their skills from father to son, but he prescribes exact laws of iron for the bringing up of the guardians of the state. For the warriors, the most appropriate education seems to be the traditional one revolving around gymnastic-musical *paedeia*, where music is supposed to mitigate bodily force and strength and to prevent these laudable qualities from turning into brutality. For the guardians, the question is rather more delicate: they must be philosophers, capable of rising above sensible things to the world of the Ideas. These layers – guardians and warriors – have no right to private property or to a family, as these would distract them from public life and pursuit of the common good. To this common good, Plato does not hesitate to sacrifice the feeblest individuals, such as the chronically ill or seriously deformed infants. Bearing in mind this broad outline of the project in the *Republic*, let us now consider Popper's view of Plato as a reactionary serving the cause of totalitarianism, with no more than a few humanitarian twitches (OS I: 87–88).

In the first place, Popper's reservations centre on the axial concept of the whole of the *Republic*, the concept of justice. In Plato's later works, too, this is presented in such a way as to overpower any egalitarian tendencies and to relaunch the claims of tribalism which lead directly to a totalitarian moral theory (OS I: 119). Plato, Popper is in no doubt, identifies justice with class privilege: he holds to be just that which serves the interests of the state, and so justice is a property affecting the state rather than relations among citizens. Whereas we are used to thinking of justice as the absence of privilege, Plato's concept actually legitimates and justifies the privileges that safeguard the stability and security of the state – including, for example, a rigid division into classes. Realizing that his theories would clash with the sensitivities of his fellow-citizens, Plato is said to have promoted a despotic state by showing that his totalitarian model, though disagreeable in appearance, was actually the most just (OS I: 90). Thus, in response to the challenge of the new egalitarianism and humanitarianism that was forging ahead in the society around him, Plato came forward with a set of diametrically opposite principles: in his discussion of the path to excellence, he asserted the principle of natural privilege against the egalitarian elimination of all privilege; for individualism he substituted holism or collectivism; and in opposition to the principle of protectionism, for which the state has the task of protecting the liberty of citizens, he argues that it should be the goal of the individual to maintain and strengthen the state (OS I: 94).

With regard to the first of these differences, Popper points out that the principle of egalitarianism – understood as the demand that citizens should be treated impartially – had found its most mature expression in the mouth of Pericles. Plato, considering the demand to be invalidated by the fact that all men are not equal [*Republic*, 433b], preferred to avoid a direct polemic against egalitarianism and to put the case instead for an anti-egalitarian alternative (OS I: 96). Secondly, he also made use of certain ambiguities in the concepts of 'individualism' and 'collectivism', identifying the former with egoism and the latter with altruism. In Popper's view, this is an invalid procedure because individualism and altruism are

not actually incompatible; indeed they are the two guiding ideas
of our Western society and the two components of the central
doctrine of Christianity, which exhorts the individual to love his
neighbour and not his tribe, as Popper ironically remarks.

> Because of his radical collectivism, Plato is not even
> interested in those problems which men usually call the prob-
> lems of justice, that is to say, in the impartial weighing of
> the contesting claims of individuals. [. . .] Justice, to him, is
> nothing but the health, unity and stability of the collective
> body.

(OS I: 106)

This brings us to the third and final opposition between egalitarianism and anti-egalitarianism: for Plato, the moral code should
conform to political utility, because the ultimate ethical criterion
is 'the interest of the state'; citizens count for nothing by comparison, and may even be sacrificed to the public good.

In the light of all that has been said so far, we can see why
Popper cannot even share Plato's conception of the leadership of
the wise; he thinks it was influenced by Socrates' moral intellectualism, which identified goodness with knowledge and asserted that
moral excellence could be taught (OS I: 128). Popper remarks
that Socrates himself was an individualist, that his intellectualism
had an anti-authoritarian bent, and that he identified knowledge
with the awareness of not-knowing. His teachings easily lent themselves to distortion, however, because of their insistence on the
need to be educated (OS I: 129). Plato, of course, exploited this
opening when he prescribed for the guardians an education that
deprived them of any originality or initiative, so that they would
defend the established order as zealously as possible. In return,
the guardians – who were all supposed to be philosophers – had the
right to lie and cheat, 'to deceive enemies or fellow-citizens in
the interests of the state' [*Republic*, 389b]. Popper considers this
blatantly to contradict the image of the philosopher as a man
dedicated to the love of truth; it is not a long way from making
usefulness to the state the very criterion of truth. But Plato did
not go so far, of course, because he still had enough of the Socratic
spirit. It was left to Hegel and his successors to take that step:
pragmatists such as the Marxists were content with a theoretical
move, but soon (and here Popper alludes to the fascist dictatorships

of inter-war Europe) racists were putting those principles into practice (OS I: 144).

Plato's philosophy is still a long way, however, from that modest seeker after truth and wisdom so lovingly depicted by Socrates. He looks more like a haughty proprietor of truth and wisdom, entitled to exercise the dual function of guardian and legislator without which society is doomed to collapse. Popper suspects that Plato's work, full as it is of references to its social context, is more than a theoretical treatise – rather, a 'topical political manifesto' in which a self-portrait lies hidden behind the picture of the ideal sovereign.

> The philosopher king is Plato himself, and the *Republic* is Plato's own claim for kingly power – to the power which he thought his due, uniting in himself, as he did, both the claims of the philosopher and of the descendant and legitimate heir of Codrus the martyr, the last of Athens' kings.
>
> (OS I: 153)

Popper was often attacked for his harsh treatment of Plato, and he was surprised and even incredulous at the virulence of some of the reactions. Against the charge that he had desecrated the most venerable philosopher of Antiquity, he calmly tried to show the correctness (including philological) of his analysis and to emphasize that Plato really was a reactionary for *his own* times, which were already saturated with the libertarian and humanitarian spirit that he resolutely opposed (OS I: 216ff.) Popper still believed Plato to have been the greatest philosopher of all time, but in his view this made it 'all the more important to fight his moral and political philosophy, and to warn those who may fall under his magic spell' (OS I: 226). Plato's seductiveness over the centuries is mainly due to a struggle that can be seen breaking out in his works – a struggle between the influence of Socratic individualism, and a need to oppose it rendered especially acute by his own class identity. This conflict means that some humanitarian elements remain in Plato's project and cause many people to interpret it in a wrong manner (OS I: 109). Another reason for this persistent legend of Plato's humanitarianism is the very sincerity or bona fides of his totalitarianism. For although he advocated a quite rigid form of government, 'his ideal was not the maximum exploitation of the working classes by the upper class; it was the stability of the whole' (OS I: 108).

Popper criticizes Plato's utopia not on the grounds that it was unrealizable – which is how it may appear today, though not perhaps in the future – but because it called for sweeping changes whose consequences could not be foreseen. Utopianism is characterized both by its radicalism (its declared intention of going to the roots of evil and tearing them up once and for all), and by its aestheticism (its goal of building a new world free of any imperfection). Such ambitions strike Popper as quite ingenuous, but also as perilously inclined to irrationalism: that is, they ultimately rely only upon inspiration, without taking into account that 'we can only learn by trial and error, by making mistakes and improvements' (OS I: 167). The utopian thinks we can successfully accomplish what we set out to achieve. But it is more reasonable to suppose that inexperience and the unpredictable effects of our own actions will necessitate ad hoc adjustments that cannot be built into the overall project from the start.

Popper's preferred system is one that does not go beyond a number of clearly defined problems, to be solved by institutions which can never be perfect because they are always subject to human limitations. 'Institutions are like fortresses. They must be well designed *and* manned' (OS I: 126). And so, where institutions are not working properly, we need to distinguish between institutional and personal factors in order to identify the reasons for the malfunction. Often those who are dissatisfied with democracy fail to make this distinction; they do not understand that democracy 'provides the institutional framework for the reform of political institutions. It makes possible the reform of institutions without using violence, and thereby the use of reason in the designing of new institutions and the adjusting of old ones' (OS I: 126). Democracy cannot, however, guarantee the necessary moral and intellectual standards among its citizens; that is a personal problem beyond the scope of institutions. 'It rests with us to improve matters. The democratic institutions cannot improve themselves. The problem of improving them is always a problem for *persons* rather than for institutions. But if we want improvements, we must make clear which *institutions* we want to improve' (OS I: 127).

Popper's critique of the historicism within Plato's sociology has thus shown us the contours of the state that the author of *The Open Society* himself considers desirable, not in some distant future but in the immediate present. For he is talking of an institutional form functioning here and now that should be applied in every circumstance. He offers a 'protectionist' conception of the state as 'a society for the prevention of crime, i.e. of aggression' (OS I: 111) – for freedom cannot be exercised unless it is guaranteed by the state. Only when this is firmly grasped is it possible to solve the so-called paradox of freedom, to tackle the argument that if there are no restrictions on freedom it may itself lead to serious curtailments and even allow the power-hungry to enslave those who are more docile by nature. To this may be added two further paradoxes that are regularly deployed in this context – the paradoxes of tolerance and democracy. If, it is argued, toleration is extended even to the intolerant, then the tolerant will themselves be destroyed; and democracy itself does not have the means to prevent the (at least theoretical) possibility that a majority will decide to hand over power to a tyrant. Popper maintains that the first two of these paradoxes can be solved if people demand a government which, in appealing to egalitarianism and protectionism, grants freedom and toleration to all who are prepared to offer the same; and that the third paradox is addressed if provision is made for public watchdogs of government and for the imparting of reliable information to the citizens. Such a regime would not be infallible, of course, nor would any prior measures of supervision and control. But there can never be infallibility in human affairs, and democracy remains the best constitutional form so far invented by human beings (OS I: 602n.).

Popper's radical critique of the Platonic edifice touches not only particular doctrines but the very matrix of his ideal state, the basic question that gives rise to all his unacceptable answers. Instead of asking with Plato 'Who should rule?', we ought to be asking 'How can we so organize political institutions that bad or incompetent rulers can be prevented from doing too much damage?' (OS I: 121). This merely underlines what we have already noted about Popper's limited, but in his view more credible and acceptable, objective: not, that is, to achieve perfection on earth, but to eliminate a little at a time the main causes of human suffering.

Anyone who believes in the legitimacy of the first question will answer with a 'theory of (unchecked) sovereignty', on the grounds that the holder of power cannot be controlled because political power is by its nature free of restraint (OS I: 121), and that it should therefore be in the hands of the person or group best able to create a good and reliable system of government. But things appear differently for those who believe that governments can also be evil and that those in charge of public affairs are liable to mistakes and shortcomings. If this is true, we will want to have forms of power and institutional control to offset the powers of the rulers, in accordance with the *theory of checks and balances* (OS I: 122). Essentially, there are only two types of government: those 'of which we can get rid without bloodshed – for example, by way of general elections'; and those 'which the ruled cannot get rid of except by way of a successful revolution – that is to say, in most cases, not at all' (OS I: 124). The only choice, then, is between democracy – which, for all its limitations and imperfections, guarantees the right to criticize and reform institutions – and tyranny or dictatorship, against which violence is the only means of struggle.

Popper's main political convictions, so far only outlined, will become clearer if we now turn to his critique of modern historicism, which in his view was responsible for the dangerous world situation into which humanity was plunged in the fourth and fifth decades of the twentieth century.

THE DOGMATIC CHARACTER OF THE HEGELIAN DIALECTIC

Exactly like Plato, neither Hegel nor Marx realized that the correct question was not 'Who shall be the rulers?' but 'How can we tame them?' (OS II: 363). It is obvious enough that, although some important ideas are common to Plato and Marx, there are also fundamental differences which have to do with the way in which history has developed. Popper does not even try to reconstruct the main stages of this process; he simply traces the fate of some of Plato's ideas in the system of Aristotle, who, despite his extraordinary culture and breadth of interests, cannot be considered an original thinker (OS I: 231). The only major correction he made to Platonism concerned the doctrine of change, which he no longer analysed pessimistically but saw as a possible progress if the final cause was itself good.

It is true that Aristotle espoused nothing that can be directly attributed to historicism, but it is also true that his essentialism provided some of the missing ingredients for the historicist philosophy to be rounded off.

Popper suggests, in a brief review, that the long period stretching from Antiquity to Hegel may be interpreted 'in terms of the conflict between the open and the closed society' (OS I: 252). During these centuries, the thought of Plato and Aristotle was used by a medieval authoritarianism that remained oblivious of the magnificent example of Pericles and the Great Generation, as well as of early Christianity with its revolt against Jewish tribalism and its rejection of God as a tribal divinity (OS II: 253–256).

Hegel is Popper's next target, described without hesitation as 'an indigestible writer [...] supreme only in his outstanding lack of originality. There is nothing in Hegel's writing that has not been said better before him' (OS II: 262). The reason for this extremely harsh judgement soon becomes apparent: Popper, the champion of the open society, regards Hegel as one of its main enemies, completely in the service of his employer, Frederick William of Prussia; and he sets out to show just how compromised Hegel was with the Prussian bureaucracy [ibid.]. Of course, Hegel exerted great influence on the philosophy of history, politics and education, and Popper himself recognizes that he is 'the source of all contemporary historicism' (OS II: 257). But however stimulating Hegel's view of history may be, the author of The Open Society considers it to have little to do with reality – except for the idea, only implicit in his work, that tradition is of inestimable value because it enables individuals to structure a 'world of thought' without having to start from scratch; for their ideas are largely the product of the culture in which they have developed (OS II: 289).

As to the more characteristic doctrines of the Prussian philosopher, it should be borne in mind that he believes history to display progress and enrichment, and not decline in the manner of Plato. Like Plato, however, Hegel sees in the state a special organism endowed with a conscious and thinking essence, 'Reason' or 'Spirit' (OS II: 267); and from Plato's doctrine that only Ideas are real, he adopts the equation '*Ideal = Real*' (OS II: 271). Finally, Hegel too places himself within a perspective that appears progressive and revolutionary, but he plays the game of reactionaries and comes up with clearly conservative results (OS II: 279). By the use he makes of dialectics, he passes himself off as a champion of progress, but in reality he is obsessed with immobility and the goal of a totalitarian regime.

Popper first criticizes the instrument (dialectics) and then refutes in several ways the result to which it leads – namely, an

ethical–juridical positivism which, having identified the good with
what prevails, concludes that might is right (OS II: 271). As far as
dialectics is concerned, Popper notes that its two constituent ideas
go right back to Heraclitus, who already emphasized the war of
opposites and their unity or identity. To this Hegel added the
insights of the Kantian dialectic, but only after he had made a
fateful revision. For whilst agreeing with Kant about the existence
of the antinomies, he did not see them as a problem and even
considered it to be the essence of reason to proceed by way of
antinomies and contradictions. Popper cannot help commenting
that 'if contradictions are unavoidable and desirable, there is no
need to eliminate them, and so all progress must come to an end'
(OS II: 269). However plausible it may appear, this attitude to the
Hegelian dialectic is somewhat tendentious: it serves the thesis that
Hegel, in his eagerness to dispense with critical argument and to
establish a 'reinforced dogmatism', made it impossible to overcome
contradiction; but this is to twist the significance of Hegel's doctrines in a way that seems hard to square with his thought in
general. Obviously we cannot enter here into the merits of Hegel's
work.

In this light, it is interesting to weigh Popper's most detailed
and exhaustive investigation, 'What is Dialectic?', which he wrote
in 1937, first published in 1940 in *Mind*, and finally included in
the *Conjectures and Refutations* volume. In this famous article,
dialectic is first compared and contrasted with the trial and error
method, which also involves a conflict between a thesis and an
antithesis, but which, instead of yielding a synthesis as in the
dialectical method, is able at most to eliminate either the thesis or
the antithesis according to which is judged less satisfactory (CR:
315–316).

Popper accepts that dialectic may sometimes be a useful key to
a problem and even complement the trial and error method: for
example, the corpuscular theory of light, having once been replaced
by the wave theory, is at least partly 'preserved' in the new theory
that has replaced them both. Nevertheless, dialectic involves too
many imprecisions which end up obscuring its role. For instance,
it is said that the thesis 'produces' its antithesis, whereas 'actually it
is only our critical attitude which produces the antithesis, and
where such an attitude is lacking – which often enough is the case
– no antithesis will be produced' (CR: 315). Similarly, a synthesis
is not simply a recomposition of the positive elements of the theses

from which it derives; it implies a new idea that cannot be reduced to earlier stages.

Beyond these methodological points, the heart of the matter seems to be the principle of non-contradiction itself. Science, and therefore knowledge, can grow only if it complies with this principle, for whoever admits two contradictory assertions can validly infer any proposition they like – and this would make any scientific activity both impracticable and lacking in significance. The dialectician has to make up his mind. 'Either he is interested in contradictions because of their fertility: then he must not accept them. Or he is prepared to accept them: then they will be barren, and rational criticism, discussion, and intellectual progress will be impossible' (CR: 317). Contrary to the view of dialecticians, the fertility of contradictions is not an intrinsic prerogative: it comes only from our refusal to resign ourselves in the face of contradiction.

Subsequently, with the appearance of Marxism, dialectic assumes an important role not only in philosophy but also in political reflection, thanks to an interpretation which stands opposed to Hegel's conservatism yet preserves its optimistic connotations (CR: 335).

Before we turn to Popper's critique of Marxism, we should briefly consider the other charges that he levels against Hegelian historicism: namely, that it laid the basis for the totalitarian nationalism which – as Popper clearly hints without ever being specific – reached its climax in the Nazi movement led by Hitler.

Modern totalitarianism, which 'is only an episode within the perennial revolt against freedom and reason' (OS II: 290), is seen by Popper as directly descended from Hegel, at least as far as its most important ideas are concerned. It has only added a little of that materialism inspired by the Darwinian theory of evolution which Haeckel championed in the late nineteenth century, drawing on Goethe's philosophy of nature, but which did not move far from monism and a rigid mechanicism. Modern totalitarianism owes to Hegel its historicist nationalism, its view of the state as the embodiment of the Spirit of the nation or race that created it (OS II: 291). Also Hegelian is the idea that the state, as the natural enemy of other states, will seek to affirm itself through war; hence 'the only possible standard of a judgement upon the state is the world-historical *success* of its actions' (OS II: 296). The state *is* the Law, and as such is exempt from any kind of moral obligation;

even mendacious propaganda and deliberate distortion of the facts are permitted if they serve the public interest. Whereas the state is amoral, war is not morally neutral: it is actually good, especially when it pits young nations against old (OS II: 293). It thereby becomes possible to assign new value to the Leader, a figure of cosmic significance who embodies the spirit of his people, and to provide a plausible basis for anti-egalitarianism (OS II: 303). Finally, it should be remembered that the conception of the Hero or Great Man is a typically tribalist ideal that enjoins people to live dangerously, in contrast to the dull mediocrity of the masses (OS II: 304). It thus clearly demonstrates the link between historicism (including its Hegelian version) and the nostalgia for a closed society that can be traced in modern totalitarianism (particularly in the climate in which German culture developed between the wars).

Popper argues that despite the ostensible optimism of Hegel's formula 'The real is rational', there is a wide margin for pessimism caused by the painful feeling that we are merely unwitting tools in the hands of an overpowering fate. This is also the atmosphere in the work of 'the two leading philosophers of contemporary Germany, the "existentialists" Heidegger and Jaspers' (OS II: 306). Both are openly given over to nihilism, which is 'a confession characteristic of an esoteric group of intellectuals who have surrendered their reason, and with it, their humanity' (OS II: 308).

Having pointed out this nexus between Hegelian historicism and the racist totalitarianism triumphant during his years of exile and political reflection in New Zealand, Popper moves on to explore what he sees as 'the purest, the most developed and the most dangerous form of historicism': that is, Marxism (OS II: 311).

MARX AS FALSE PROPHET

For all his humanitarian intentions, Marx is regarded by Popper as a false prophet – not so much because he made prophecies that did not come true, as because he encouraged the belief that 'historical prophecy is the scientific way of approaching social problems' (OS II: 312). Marx rightly saw that science can make predictions only if the future is in some way predetermined, and so he concluded that it was necessary to postulate a rigid determinism. We know that Popper did not share this determinist view in general; indeed he devoted a large part of the three-volume

67

Postscript to its refutation. And more particularly, he was opposed to a determinist conception of history, which – as he acknowledges – was widely accepted in Marx's time. (John Stuart Mill, to take just one example, developed a version of his own, tinged with psychologism.)

In Marx's teachings, instead of Mill's stress on the psychological, we find a new element to which he gave the name materialism. It is now economics which occupies the key position, so that 'the science of society must coincide with the history of the development of the economic conditions of society, usually called by Marx "the conditions of production" ' (OS II: 336). Popper admits that there is some validity in the idea that the economic organization of society is the basis of social institutions and of their evolution, but only if one accepts 'an interaction between economic conditions and ideas, and not simply a unilateral dependence of the latter on the former' (OS II: 337). Marx himself underestimated the power of thought, which became clear precisely in an event inspired by his teachings, the Russian Revolution, when Lenin's success in transforming an economic structure was partly due to the violent impact of a new idea.

Marx's materialism is, in Popper's view, at the root of a series of 'fatal mistakes'. Among these is the rejection of social engineering, on the grounds that it can never succeed where the organization of society is not determined by individuals but, on the contrary, individuals depend on the social system and, more precisely, on economic conditions defining their position within society (OS II: 344). Closely related to this is the notion that politics is impotent in the face of economic reality (OS II: 349). For Marx, the state is only one part of the machinery through which the ruling class struggles to maintain its power; it follows that 'in principle, all government, even democratic government, is a dictatorship of the ruling class over the ruled' (OS II: 350). Popper here repeats what he has argued before in the book: that 'state power must always remain a dangerous though necessary evil' (OS II: 360), and that it is best to limit it to the indispensable minimum, the defence of liberty. But he cannot accept Marx's case that it is in the end impossible to improve social institutions by legal means. He rejects the dogmatic view of economic power as the cause of all evil (OS II: 358) and calls for the role of class struggle in politics to be reconsidered – not because it is unimportant, but because its very significance bars us from concluding that *all* history is the history of class struggle (OS II: 346).

Popper insists that what is needed instead of holistic historicism is piecemeal social engineering. Careful study will show that Marx's aims and method are epitomized in the prophecy of a classless society arising from the conflict between the last two classes in play: the bourgeoisie, with its control of the means of production, and an ever more impoverished and alienated proletariat which will bring about a revolution when it has reached the limits of endurance. The classless society will then be established after an intermediate period of proletarian dictatorship.

The failure of Marx's prophecy was already evident during the Second World War, when Popper was writing his massive work on political philosophy. He saw the reason for this failure less in the inadequacy of the empirical base than in the poverty of the historicism on which the argument sustained itself (OS II: 423). Popper anticipated the objection that, even if the final prophecy has not come true, some of Marx's theories have corresponded to trends in the real world – for example, his trade cycle theory that predicted recurrent crises and the adoption of counter-measures tending to weaken the free market system. But Popper replied that a closer view of Marx's merits would show that 'it was nowhere his historicist method which led him to success, but always the methods of institutional analysis' (OS II: 427). In short, Marx brilliantly analysed the functioning of contemporary institutions, but he did not uncover anything about their true nature – that is, about the essence which, on a historicist view, is supposed to determine any future development.

As we have said before, Popper did not explicitly refer to events or figures of the time in which he was writing. Yet his discourse penetrated more and more deeply into the contemporary world, displaying between the lines all the bitterness and indignation of a sincere democrat who, banished to a kind of blessed isle, feared for the future of a Western civilization torn between the racist and nationalist totalitarianism of the Right and the ambiguities of the Left. For not only did the Left fail energetically to combat regressive tendencies when they first appeared; it even encouraged them in some cases, in the illusory belief that they would act as a catalyst for the final showdown (OS II: 393). In exploring the causes of the resulting disaster, Popper assigned the responsibility not only to the followers of loathsome German nationalism but also to those who, with their scant faith in democracy, played into the hands of the fascist groups seeking to destroy it.

Popper traces the inter-war options of the European Left back to Marx's view that capitalism cannot but be replaced by classless society. The stark choice between unbridled capitalism and communism seems to have been refuted in practice, for the facts give more support to the theory of a 'political remedy' – that is, to the creation of social institutions capable of intervening to protect weaker subjects from abuses of economic power (OS II: 370). Such a programme is rather more concrete than a good intention; everywhere the system so effectively described by Marx has given way to intervention in the economy, a form of social engineering that targets the relations of production (OS II: 710). As proof of changes effected in quite different ways from the revolution envisaged by Marx, Popper recalls that much of the programme contained in the *Communist Manifesto* has actually been implemented by the Western democracies. They have introduced a progressive tax on income, sweeping taxes that almost do away with the right of inheritance, the ending of child labour, and free public education (OS II: 371).

All this evidently implies a conception of the relationship between political and economic power which is diametrically opposed to the one held by Marx. For him, the economic base underpinning the whole society cannot be affected by the political apparatus; whereas for Popper, there is an implicit possibility that political power will act as a check on economic power (OS II: 356), and there is no historical mechanism which cannot be corrected and modified through appropriate piecemeal engineering.

> Thus Marx was quite right when he insisted that 'history' cannot be planned on paper. But *institutions* can be planned; and they are being planned. Only by planning, step by step, for institutions to safeguard freedom, especially freedom from exploitation, can we hope to achieve a better world.
>
> (OS II: 373)

In considering the pages of *The Open Society* devoted to Marxism, one becomes aware that the real core of the disagreement between Popper and Marx is not their economic or political doctrines but their anthropological conceptions. Marxism treats man as the product of the economic structure, as essentially reducible to his social being; Popper sees the individual as possessing an autonomy that gives him some protection from the necessity of social and economic mechanisms. On the one hand, therefore, Popper can accept that 'in a certain sense' man is a product of society; but on the other hand, he has no doubt 'that we can examine thoughts, that we can criticize them, improve them, and further that we can change and improve our physical environment according to our changed, improved thoughts. And the same is true of our social environment' (OS II: 439). In other words, contrary to what Marx thought, ideas can change the world.

THE OPEN SOCIETY

These theoretical reflections, combined with observation of what had happened in Europe after the First World War, led Popper to argue that a desire to control change through centralized large-scale planning had gained the ascendancy during that period. This had involved a holistic view halfway between Plato's theory, which aimed to hold back change as far as possible, and Marx's theory with its awareness of the inevitability of change. But Popper regards such an attitude as only apparently rational; in reality, 'it is well in keeping with the irrationalist and mystical tendencies of our time' (OS II: 443) – especially with Marx's doctrine that all our opinions are determined by the social-historical situation in which we live, and, above all, by class interests.

This position has developed into a real current of thought known as 'sociology of knowledge' or 'sociologism', of which Max Scheler and Karl Mannheim are the best-known exponents. In this approach, scientific and political thought is powerfully conditioned by the social atmosphere, which often exerts a quite unconscious influence because it is part of the habitat in which the individual is born and bred. The resulting prejudices are not merely personal but are characteristic of a particular time and social class; thinkers are not aware that they have them, but their existence and scope become clear as soon as the positions of two thinkers belonging to different epochs or milieux are confronted with each other. They are then seen to be inserted into two distinct ideological systems between which no communication or compromise is possible.

This leads to the conclusion that it is necessary to change society as a whole if certain negative phenomena are ever to be eliminated. But in opposing the idea of a centralized power that seeks to restructure society according to a comprehensive utopian project, Popper contrasts it with the 'piecemeal' activity of a social engineer whose task is to design, restructure and set to work all the social institutions – broadly defined to include a commercial business as well as a school, a church or a law court. The piecemeal technician is well aware that only a minority of these institutions are 'consciously designed', and that all the rest are 'the undesigned results of human actions' (OS II; PH: 65). Nor has he any illusion about how they function: he knows that, to a greater or lesser extent, this always depends upon the human factor – that is, on personal initiative and the involvement of suitable personnel. Unlike holistic or utopian social mechanics, the 'piecemeal' approach does not propose to mould the whole of society according to a plan established in advance, precisely because it recognizes the unpredictability of the 'human factor'. Institutions and traditions 'may emerge as unintended consequences' of conscious and intentional actions. By obscuring this element of uncertainty, the utopian 'violates the principles of scientific method' (PH: 69), but at the same time he must try to control the personal variables by institutional means and 'to extend his programme so as to embrace not only the transformation of society, according to plan, but also the transformation of man' (PH: 70). This being so, it may be worth considering for a moment the reasons why utopianism does not follow the dictates of scientific method. The fact that the ultimate aim of utopianism is to mould citizens to the new social structure, means that it cannot test by empirical experiment the success or failure of the new structure and, if necessary, correct it where it is defective. This shows the unscientific character of the procedure, because 'without the possibility of tests, any claim that a "scientific" method is being employed evaporates. The holistic approach is incompatible with a truly scientific attitude' (PH: 70). It is clear, then, that from a position like Popper's – which considers all knowledge to be hypothetical and provisional – it is not acceptable to embark upon a definitive political project that cannot be tested and (potentially) falsified.

Utopianism often manages to ally itself to historicism, for the two share a common holistic approach. Historicism describes the development of society as a totality, just as utopianism depicts a comprehensive model of society in which nothing escapes the planner. Both believe that social experiments, if feasible at all, have value only if they take in the whole society – a clearly mistaken view, because 'piecemeal' experiments are basic to any knowledge (including pre-scientific knowledge) that is social in character. No one will deny that there is a difference between a businessman who has experience and one who does not, and the same is naturally true of a politician or an organizer (PH: 85).

Popper therefore maintains that there are limits or criteria for both political action and social programming, above all when their aim is to create a better world. The only path towards that ideal is the one now being jointly taken by the West – the path of democracy, which is certainly not a panacea, but only one of the conditions for us to know the social consequences of our actions (PH: 88). The basis for the democratic regimes is provided by the set of principles which together constitute liberalism. Popper expressed his deep admiration of them in a lecture he gave in Venice in 1954, which first appeared in *Conjectures and Refutations* and later, slightly modified, in *In Search of a Better World*. To avoid misunderstanding, he immediately explains that he does not mean liberalism to refer to any political party, but only to a set of principles. The first one of these, upon which all the others rest, is that 'the state is a necessary evil: its powers are not to be multiplied beyond what is necessary' (CR: 350, and ISBW: 155). By analogy with Ockham's Razor, Popper calls this the 'liberal razor'; it underpins the protectionist view that the fundamental task of the state is simply to prevent crime, 'to protect the weak from being bullied by the strong' (OS I: 115). The second principle concerns the difference between tyranny and democracy, which is that the latter makes it possible to get rid of a government without bloodshed (CR: 350; ISBW: 156, and OS I: 123). Popper's third thesis defines democracy as 'a framework within which the citizens may act', but which 'cannot ... and should not be expected ... to confer any benefits upon the citizen' (CR: 350; ISBW: 156); its function is essentially negative – to ensure that no one harms others. The fourth point stresses that while democracy is certainly not infallible, its 'traditions are the least evil ones of which we know' (CR: 351; ISBW: 156). Hence – the fifth principle – traditions are important as a mediation between institutions, on the one hand, and the intentions and valuations expressed by the individual, on the other [ibid.]. The sixth thesis, then, is that no liberal utopia can design a state from scratch; tradition is always required to move from abstract principles to the solution of concrete cases. It should be noted that Popper is here thinking, above all, of the well-known predominance in English law of largely unwritten custom – that is, of precedents enshrined by a tradition that has established itself through everyday practice [ibid.].

This leads on to the seventh principle: that 'liberalism is an evolutionary rather than a revolutionary creed (unless it is confronted by a tyrannical regime)' (CR: 351; ISBW: 157). Lastly, Popper calls attention to the fundamental tradition involved in 'the "moral framework" (corresponding to the institutional legal framework). This incorporates the society's traditional sense of justice or fairness, or the degree of moral sensitivity it has reached' [ibid.]. To destroy this supporting framework would be extremely dangerous, because it would also dismantle the legislative apparatus and the rule of law. This does not mean that the moral tradition remains unchanged through the vicissitudes of history. But its slow adaptation to new conditions must remain a stable and reliable point of reference – for if it is marked down for destruction, as in the case of Nazism, the result can only be the dissolution of all human values. 'If democracy is destroyed, all rights are destroyed' (OS II: 391).

THE MEANING OF HISTORY

Another attraction of historicism is its posing of the question of the meaning of history, which Popper addresses in the concluding section of *The Open Society*. The various forms of historicism point to trends or directions supposedly marking the course of human history: for some, the full realization of the Spirit; for others, the establishment of a classless society, and so on. For his part, Popper is convinced that history has no meaning, and in justifying this view he makes some interesting remarks on the historical sciences.

Just to begin with, *'"history" in the sense in which most people speak of it does not exist*; and this is at least one reason why I say that it has no meaning' (OS II: 499). There is not and never can be a history of mankind, because it would have to include the history of every single man and woman. What is passed off as the 'history of mankind' and taught in schools is really the history of political power, the central framework into which all other possible histories are inserted. For political power affects all of us, and all aspects of human life (OS II: 500). History, moreover – unlike sciences such as physics or sociology, which are concerned with the formulation of universal hypotheses – seeks to explain particular events. It therefore bases itself on the existing sources, which include only those facts that have been considered worthy of being handed down in the light of certain criteria. And as no other facts are available to us, we cannot put to the test our 'general interpretations', which simply represent one of many possible points of view. We should not conclude from this, however, that all interpretations are of equal value; some fail to account for the existing testimony, while others may resort to ad hoc hypotheses with greater or lesser plausibility, and others still are successful in incorporating facts explained by other theories (OS II: 494–496).

> To sum up, there can be no history of 'the past as it actually did happen'; there can only be historical interpretations, and none of them can be final; and every generation has a right to frame its own. [...] It also has a kind of obligation to do so; for there is indeed a pressing need to be answered.

For example, 'we want to know how our troubles are related to the past' (OS II: 498). Someone might then object that historicist interpretation is also legitimate because it offers a point of view. But Popper insists that not all interpretations are acceptable. In particular, historicism has the defect of being so taken up with the hidden (and actually non-existent) meaning of history that it throws very little light on what is going on around us.

In this context, Popper takes issue with the Christian conception that God reveals himself in history, and that history is therefore oriented towards the end willed by God. The author of *The Open Society* remarks that no trace of this idea can be found in the New Testament, and that to conceive of history in terms of divine revelation and judgement is to believe that worldly success is the final judgement and the goal of human action. History is made up of sufferings, outrages and abuses of power which are not always punished, and these intersect with actions inspired by values other than power which often lose out because they are not able to prevail on the stage of the world. 'And in this not even man-made, but man-faked "history", some Christians dare to see the hand of God!' (OS II: 502). In support of his argument that historicism and Christianity are mutually incompatible, Popper quotes Kierkegaard's criticisms of Hegel (OS II: 505) and concludes that 'historicism ... is not only rationally untenable, it is also in conflict with any religion that teaches the importance of conscience. [. . .] The historicist element in religion is an element of idolatry, of superstition' (OS II: 509). A religion that wishes to make history understandable should not present it as a direct emanation of God's will, but rather as a product of struggle between the forces of good and the forces of evil, exactly as Augustine did in *The City of God*.

In opposition to such doctrines, Popper puts forward a set of three theses. The first of these is negative, in that it denies that we can discover the meaning of history. But the second is very positive: it states that we can do something much more significant than discover the meaning of history; we ourselves can confer meaning upon it, by deciding what are our goals and trying to impose them on history, instead of trying to fall in with the supposed force of destiny. Finally, the third thesis maintains that 'the attempt to give to our history an ethical meaning or aim need not always be futile' (ISBW: 147).

Now, the first thesis openly contradicts not only the nineteenth-century theories of progress associated with Comte, Hegel or Marx, but also Spengler's theory of decline or the cyclical theories of Plato, Vico and others. Popper does not mince his words: 'I regard all these theories as wrong-headed, and even, in a way, pointless' (ISBW: 140). For when people speak of progress or retrogression, they imply a scale of values that may be scientific, artistic or moral, and it is clear that while major advances are being made in one scale, stagnation or even retrogression may quite well be registered in the others. History is made up of a number of aspects, and as these do not move at the same pace or in the same way, they cannot all be reduced to a single general tendency. Unfortunately, Hegel's works and a fortiori Spengler's *Decline of the West* have led the public to expect philosophers of history to come up with predictions of the future. The demand fuelled the supply, and Popper now regrets the surfeit of arbitrary predictions that have only served the purposes of propaganda (ISBW: 143).

Popper's second thesis starts from Lessing's definition of history as 'the giving of meaning to the meaningless' (ISBW: 144) – which he uses to underline his point that history does not only consist of constant advances, but is also the result of human errors. Popper further endorses the view of H.A.L. Fisher that historians must recognize 'the play of the contingent and the unforeseen' – or that, in one way or another, history depends at least in part on ourselves (ISBW: 145).

The third and final thesis answers the objection that moral ideals have often ended up legitimating, or even provoking, savage crimes and acts of violence. Popper would not deny that such things have happened, but he is also concerned to avoid the opposite position – that no ethical objective can ever be attained. For criticism guided by moral principles has many times carried the day against a particular social order, or successfully confronted the worst evils of public life. This is possible, however, only if certain conditions are met; in the past, success came:

> only where people had learnt to respect opinions that differ from their own, and to be sober and realistic in their political aims: where they had learnt that the attempt to create the Kingdom of Heaven on earth may easily succeed in turning our earth into a hell for our fellow men.
>
> (ISBW: 147)

In a lecture that he gave in Zurich in 1958, Popper recalled that even the suppression of freedom and the violence which have stained the history of Communism have stemmed from faith in a theory that promised freedom to all human beings. Thus even 'the worst evil of our time was born out of the desire to help others and to make sacrifices for others' (ISBW: 222). Popper is not saying here, à la Leibniz, that ours is the best of all possible worlds, but 'only that our own social world is the best that has ever been – the best, at least, of which we have any historical knowledge' (CR: 369). The optimism of Popper derives from a positive evaluation of the present and the immediate past which is in turn based upon what appears, in the West, to be unassailable: for example, the now morally self-evident principle that no one must go hungry, or that an effective struggle must be waged against poverty (ISBW: 216). It is also now recognized that everyone should have the same equality of opportunity – for example, as a right to study for all who have the necessary abilities. And lastly, 'our time has stimulated in the masses new needs and the ambition for possession' [ibid.] – which also has a negative side, but was necessary if the poor were to take part in overcoming their own condition. The price for this self-advancement of the masses is the danger – let us not forget that Popper was writing in 1958 – that the Greek and Christian ideal of freedom as freedom from material

desires will ultimately be replaced by more frustration than satisfaction (ISBW: 218).

As we shall see, all these themes are rooted in Popper's unshake-
able belief in rationalism as the basis of political and social life.
By contrast, the pessimism embraced even by great philosophers
he judges to be only 'a dangerous fashion' (ISBW: 213). It should
never be forgotten, however, that 'no society is rational, but there
is always one more rational than that which exists, and we have a
duty to strive towards it' (RR: 29). In other words, beyond the
distinction between governments that can be brought down without recourse to violence and those that cannot, different societies
can display different degrees of openness. Thus, precisely insofar
as the open society is a reality, it also remains an ideal towards
which we indefinitely aspire (RR: 28).

4

THE 'METAPHYSICAL' WORKS

REALISM AS A METAPHYSICAL OPTION

The title of this chapter is not strictly correct, as it is more a question of metaphysical doctrines recurring within works that are also – perhaps mainly – devoted to gnoseological arguments. Someone might then object that Popper never concerned himself with metaphysics, and this would be true if metaphysics is understood as classical ontology rather than as what Popper meant by the term.

A number of points would therefore seem to require clarification, starting with the character of the principal works to be considered here. For, apart from the *Postscript*, we shall be looking at writings from the 1960s and later which tackle the question of knowledge from a new standpoint and draw out implications that Popper had previously left in the background. His chief interest is always the same: he remains with gnoseology and steers clear of 'what is sometimes called an "ontology"' (SB: 4). And whether referring to the *Postscript* or a fortiori to the *Logic of Scientific Discovery*, he stresses that he has not written books of metaphysics. The gnoseological origin of Popper's thinking also seems to be confirmed by the fact that he begins to speak of realism and determinism in the *Postscript* – a definitely epistemological work meant as a commentary on the *Logic* – which primarily addresses the problems of a special (however important and paradigmatic) form of knowledge. In the third volume of the *Postscript*, entitled *Quantum Theory and the Schism in Physics*, Popper openly states that 'realism is the message of this book', and that it 'is linked with rationalism, with the reality of the human mind, of human creativity, and of human suffering' (P3: xviii). This is all the more significant in that the context of Popper's strenuous defence of realism is here the purely scientific debate on quantum theory.

If we turn next to *Objective Knowledge*, a collection of essays written between 1961 and 1971, we can see that the very title betrays its gnoseological origins – even if some of its theses, such as that of the three worlds, go well beyond the traditional boundaries of epistemology or gnoseology. The same may be said of the weighty tome that he wrote together with the Nobel Prize-winning brain scientist John Eccles: *The Self and Its Brain*. Popper's essential aim is to identify and describe the origins of knowledge, yet this leads him into arguments that encompass anthropology and even in a sense cosmology, and into areas such as the conflict between realism and idealism, or the whole question of determinism, which – whatever his intention – recall some aspects of classical metaphysics.

It may be possible, therefore, to regard these works either as gnoseological (even predominantly epistemological in the case of *Quantum Theory and the Schism in Physics*) or as metaphysical, but it is this latter aspect which distinguishes them from Popper's earlier output. As we have seen, any doctrine, whether ontological or not, is defined by Popper as 'metaphysical' if it cannot in principle be falsified or refuted. On the other hand, many cosmological speculations, especially as initially formulated, are not open to empirical testing – and yet they may become honest-to-goodness scientific theories if and when, as research programmes, they somehow pertain to science and assist its development (P3: 31–32).

Popper certainly did not hold back from espousing what, on his own definition, were openly metaphysical theories – witness his unfailing advocacy of realism (RC: 963). '[I]n almost every phase of the development of science we are under the sway of metaphysical – that is, untestable – ideas' (P3: 161); scientists engage in metaphysical research programmes which, though mostly unconscious, are implicit in their judgements and attitudes. For Popper these are metaphysical 'because they result from general views of the structure of the world and, at the same time, from general views of the problem situation in physical cosmology' [ibid.]. And they are research programmes, rather than theories:

> because they incorporate, together with a view of what the most pressing problems are, a general view of what a satisfactory solution of these problems would look like. They may

be described as *speculative physics*, or perhaps as speculative anticipations of testable physical theories.

(P3: 161–162)

Already in the *Logic of Scientific Discovery*, Popper expressed his 'metaphysical faith in the existence of regularities in our world' (LSD: 252). And he even argued that:

scientific discovery is impossible without faith in ideas which are of a purely speculative kind, and sometimes even quite hazy; a faith which is completely unwarranted from the point of view of science, and which, to that extent, is 'metaphysical'.

(LSD: 38)

In the *Postscript*, Popper quotes these lines as evidence of his faith in metaphysical realism – a faith which, though not used in support of the core theses in the *Logic*, was still 'very much there' (P1: 81). But what does Popper actually mean by 'realism'? In his preface to *Die Zukunft ist offen*, Franz Kreuzer sums up critical realism in the formula:

this is not a world of the confirmation of truth, but a world of the refutation of errors. But there is the world, and there is also truth – only there can be no certainty about the world and about the truth.

(ZO: 9)

Popper himself had earlier said as much in a discussion-interview with Kreuzer (OGOU: 44), where he also defined the fundamental assumption of realism as being that 'the universe is independent of ourselves' (OGOU: 99). In short, to be a realist is simply to hold that the world exists and develops independently of human beings (OGOU: 100); to retain from common sense every individual's understanding that the end of his own existence does not mean the end of the world (OK: 35).

Popper does not seek to demonstrate the validity of realism, which is a conjecture (OK: 100), irrefutable (OK: 38) and therefore metaphysical. But he does try to show that the alternative theory – that is, idealism – is an equally metaphysical conjecture, with the difference that the weight of argument is clearly on the side of realism (OK: 39). Already on the next page, however, it turns out that most of the plausible, if not conclusive, arguments in favour of realism are actually arguments *against idealism*. All that is left for us is to follow the philosopher's trajectory in the *Postscript*, which certainly contains his most systematic treatment of the question but also has no shortage of incursions into gnoseology, once realism has shown all its desirability in that domain.

First of all, Popper appeals to the natural tendency of common sense to distinguish between reality and appearance, between surface reality and underlying reality, between different kinds of real things (OK: 42). From this he postulates the difference between scientific knowledge – which includes all knowledge, even the most elementary, capable of colliding with sense experience – and all forms of knowledge which do not have the 'real' world as their object. By 'real world', Popper understands the totality of things which 'can causally act upon, or interact with, ordinary real material things' (SB: 10; P2: 116). He accepts, of course, that real things display varying degrees of concreteness; fields of force, for example, are more abstract than material objects such as tables or chairs. But they are all 'real', even the theoretical objects of physics distinct from matter, because they have the capacity to interact with material objects. It is as well to stress this point and the examples given by Popper, because they make it easier to understand his theory of World 3, whose apparent idealism can be rather troubling in a context drawn in strongly realistic colours.

Second – a point of the highest importance – Popper appeals to science by noting that all or nearly all physical theories entail realism (OK: 40, 304). In 'The Aim of Science', an article written in 1957 and reprinted in *Objective Knowledge*, Popper affirms his commitment to realism, on the grounds that it would otherwise be impossible to understand the scientist's task of finding satisfactory explanations. By 'satisfactory explanation', he means one that can offer 'independent evidence' in its support – which would have no meaning if there were no object to be discovered with partial autonomy of the subject (OK: 203). He then adds, shortly afterwards, that it is not necessary for the method to presuppose metaphysical realism; it is enough to recommend the most severe tests, leaving to others the metaphysical speculation accompanying certain assumptions.

Some years later, however, in 1966 to be precise, Popper distinguished scientific theory from imaginative fancies by the different traditions in which they are embedded. The scientific tradition has been 'characterized by what may be called scientific realism. That is to say, it was inspired by the ideal of finding *true solutions* to its problems: solutions which corresponded to the facts' (OK: 290). It would seem reasonable to suppose, then, that in the years between 1957 and 1966 realism had figured more and more in Popper's thinking on epistemology, so that it eventually became the foundation without which the scientific edifice, and the world whose phenomena we try to explain through science, would collapse.

Despite the errors and misconceptions of idealism, we would be wrong to deny that it has a *raison d'être* in a real problem – in its discovery of the impossibility of justifying realism (P1: 85). This applies, in Popper's view, to *all* the other forms of the disorder, including positivism and the neutral monism of Mach or Russell (OK: 86). But although the theory of the world's independence of the knowing subject cannot be demonstrated, it should be stoutly defended because of its importance within the system inspired by critical rationalism; it is in this spirit that Popper takes his first steps away from the critique of idealism towards explicit arguments in favour of realism.

Popper's synthetic account of idealism takes its typical instances and considers them – rather imprecisely, it is true – in their simplest form, such as the thesis that 'the world (which includes my present audience) is just my dream' (OK: 38). But while combating idealism, Popper does not deny that the security of one's own existence is very strong; what he cannot accept is that 'it can bear the weight of anything resembling the Cartesian edifice; as a starting-platform it is much too narrow' (OK: 35). Yet it was precisely on the basis of Descartes' postulate that the first alternatives to realism developed – and made their official appearance on the philosophical stage with Berkeley, Hume and Kant. With regard to the first two, especially Hume, it should be noted that they initially appealed to common sense (which is profoundly realist), before being diverted towards 'an absurd idealism' (OK: 87). This idealism arose out of the belief that knowledge is no more than a special state of mind acquired thanks to the security of subjective experiences, which are in turn identified with experiences of an observational character (OK: 36).

Despite the justifications that idealism may enlist in its behalf, and despite the multiplicity of forms that it has assumed in Western thought, Popper rejects it as deriving from a more general subjectivist theory of knowledge – one which has largely prevailed since

Descartes, Hobbes, Locke and Hume, and which shares the false prejudices that have marked the commonsense theory of knowledge alongside its instinctive adherence to realism (OK: 3). According to this theory, all we have to do to know the world is open our eyes and look around us; our senses are thus our main source of knowledge, and our minds function merely as receptacles in which the material of sensations piles up (OK: 60–61). For Popper, things are not at all as simple as this 'bucket' theory suggests. For in reality, all our experience is 'decoded' by rearranging, organizing, ordering the chaotic messages we receive from sense perception (OK: 63). The theory so strongly criticized by Popper does not take into account this working up of the supposed sense-data; it does not realize that the results are by no means immediate and direct, but are the fruit of a perhaps incalculable series of trials and errors.

The theory is thus misguided for two reasons: on the one hand, it does not accept the existence of knowledge that is not subjective; but on the other hand, it takes as the paradigm of (subjectively) certain knowledge that which can be objectively demonstrated. This approach is contradictory, and it also fails to grasp that nothing can ever be demonstrated beyond the proven falsity of a hypothesis. Knowledge, as we shall see, is a Darwinian-type evolutionary procedure which gropes its way forward through trial and error, correction of errors and further trials; hence the structurally hypothetical character of any human pronouncement, including the ones made by scientists.

The subjectivist approach only became explicit with Descartes, but there was already a counterpart to it in Antiquity. It can be effectively challenged only through an objectivist theory that presents knowledge in an essentially conjectural manner. For, in Popper's view, it is not the subjective side of knowledge – the bodily dispositions whereby the knowing subject believes in a certain theory with greater or lesser force – which should be of interest to the philosopher. Rather, it is the objective side – the logical content of ideas, conjectures or suppositions, of theories made public and discussed, which should be assessed not in terms of the certainty they arouse but by virtue of their resistance to attempted refutation (OK: 73). In the latter case, it is possible to speak of 'knowledge without a knowing subject' (OK: 109), because abstraction is made from the mental and psychological dispositions of the knowing subject; a theory or idea is evaluated independently of the personal inclinations of its proposer and of the trust they may inspire.

The subjectivist approach can be criticized as a sign of psychological expressionism, which takes a person's work as an expression of an inner state. There is truth in this if it means that the world of knowledge is created by man, but not if it assumes it to be totally dependent on man (OK: 147). In fact, Popper thinks it a quite conclusive argument against subjectivism that 'scientific knowledge is certainly not *my* knowledge' (P1: 92); so many things are known to science without being known to me. Even the few fragments of knowledge that each one of us possesses:

> do not conform to the preconceived scheme of the subjectivist theory of knowledge: few of them are entirely the results of *my own* experience. Rather, they are largely the results of my having absorbed certain traditions (for example by reading certain books), partly consciously, partly unconsciously.
>
> [ibid.]

And 'absorbing a tradition is a process fundamentally different from that envisaged by the subjectivist theory, which wants me to start from *my* knowledge and, moreover, from my observational experience' (P1: 93).

Once it is agreed that personal experiences are not sufficient to explain the vast and complex phenomenon of knowledge, subjectivism loses all persuasive force. Nor is it of any avail to object that 'knowledge' is really only that which can be known, so that the concept of a knowing subject is contained within the definition itself. For one can quote examples of knowledge that is not 'known' by anyone but is nevertheless fully available; thus some people may know how to use a logarithmic table, and others also how to calculate and compile one, but no one will know all the information that it can potentially deliver. The same is true of any scientific theory: no one, not even its originator, knows all its potentialities.

The fact is that although objective knowledge derives from human actions, it often emerges without prior subjective knowledge. 'This is invariably the case in all calculations (so far as the man who makes them is concerned): here we wait for the result to emerge in some physical shape before we form the corresponding subjective conviction' (OK: 95–96). Hence we may regard the objective knowledge that culminates in science as a *social insti-tution*, or as a set of social institutions [ibid.].

These assertions closely recall the critique in Popper's political works of the psychologism and sociology of knowledge. They also suggest that when he stresses the objective side of knowledge, he is really thinking of its institutional aspect – the aspect which, hypostatized and isolated from the densely woven components with which it is usually entangled, makes up what Popper calls World 3. This emphasis is not so one-sided, however, as to make Popper forget that subjective knowledge plays an indispensable role in the growth of objective knowledge. Nevertheless, he considers it of scant interest for a philosopher, because it is located at a level that is neither logical nor epistemological, but rather psychological and biological (P1: 96).

Popper's aversion to subjectivism is quite understandable if we think of what is, in his view, its 'deepest motive': namely, the bitter realization that much of our ostensible knowledge is uncertain and is therefore not really knowledge, at least not in the Greek sense of *episteme* as opposed to *doxa*. And so it seems that we must fall back on the most certain basis we have, 'the experiences which are "given to me" ' (P1: 102). In this reconstruction, however, Popper overlooks the fact that Descartes himself – the supposed father of modern subjectivism, and indirectly also of idealism – denied any 'immediate' certainty of sense-data, and that this gave him the idea of searching for something evident beyond all doubt. Popper too denies any certainty or immediacy of so-called sense-data, but unlike Descartes he resigns himself to the uncertain, hypothetical and provisional nature of all human knowledge. Or at least, he sees no good reason why we should think it possible ever to meet with something evident beyond dispute. This is not the place to discuss such matters, which belong in an epistemological or gnoseological context, and so we shall just note that Popper essentially shares the view of modern rationalism that our senses deceive us and are not a source of reliable knowledge. The difference is that whereas classical rationalism found in reason sufficient strength to counter the distortions coming from sensory information, critical rationalism discovers in it a function which is more critical than constructive – not to speak of foundational.

86

THE THREE WORLDS AND THEIR INTERACTION

After the mid-1960s, Popper's insistence on the objective or institutional aspect of knowledge led him to develop his theory of
objective mind, or theory of World 3. In an address given in 1967
under the title 'Epistemology without a Knowing Subject', he
distinguished for the first time between an objective or 'third
world' approach and the 'second world' attitude of subjectivism:
the former bases itself upon the results of cognitive activity –
theories and arguments – whereas the latter approaches scientific
knowledge from the psychological and behavioural side (OK: 107).
This subjectivist viewpoint strikes Popper as incapable of grasping
the specificity of scientific work, because it does not take into
account that a theory may be discussed and evaluated only insofar
as it is *formulated* in an objective and communicable manner,
abstracting from subjective nuances and from the psychological
conditions in which it was conceived and developed (OK: 26).

It will be useful to remind ourselves here that between the late
1950s and the early 1960s, Popper's epistemology was systematically attacked by scientists and philosophers who advocated a new
philosophy of science that would, among other things, revalue the
role of 'personal knowledge'.[1] During the same period, he also had
to face the now famous challenge from Thomas Kuhn, whose
Structure of Scientific Revolutions (1962) shook the pillars of falsificationism by stressing the importance of non-rational, psychological factors in the adoption of scientific research 'paradigms'.

Popper responded to these criticisms by reaffirming that the
logic of discovery was more interesting and useful for science than
the psychology of research (NS: 58). His tone became more urgent,
however, when he warned of the need to distinguish clearly and
unambiguously between the two domains and thus laid the seeds
of the idea of a world divided into three related spheres:

> first, the world of physical objects or of physical states;
> secondly, the world of states of consciousness, or of mental
> states, or perhaps of behavioural dispositions to act; and
> thirdly, the world of objective contents of thought, especially
> of scientific and poetic thoughts and of works of art.
>
> (OK: 106)

Thus, World 1 is made up of the objects of physics, chemistry or
biology, including all the material objects that we normally

experience – whether chairs, tables, mountains, gases or animals. World 2 encompasses all our psychological experiences both conscious and unconscious, from states of mind to desires, from convictions to memories. And World 3 consists of all the products of the human mind: books, theories, scientific problems, works of art, ethical values, social institutions, and so forth (P2: 117–118). The distinction between the two human spheres is by no means insignificant, because it allows us to appreciate the difference between 'the world of thought-processes, and the world of the *products* of thought-processes. While the former may stand in causal relationships, the latter stand in logical relationships' (OK: 299).

As far as terminology is concerned, Popper chose 'World 1', 'World 2' and 'World 3' because they are neutral and colourless but not at all conventional. The numerical sequence corresponds to their respective age (ISBW: 9); for it seems well established that the physical world preceded the emergence of that set of perceptions, sensations and psychological reactions which comprise World 2, and that, on the basis of subjective human consciousness, World 2 in turn produced the evolution of strictly human language from which World 3 was forged (P2: 115–116).

Popper is well aware that philosophers have from time to time called one of these worlds into question: materialists have held only World 1 to be real; immaterialists – including some physicists – consider only World 2 to be real, agreeing with Berkeley that only our sensations exist. Then there are so-called dualists, who recognize that Worlds 1 and 2 are there for all to see, but would certainly have reservations about World 3, at least in the sense intended by Popper (ISBW: 9). In their view, books and works of art are certainly objects of sensory knowledge, but only qua objects in the physical world; they differ from materialists and immaterialists in not wishing to reduce World 1 to World 2, or vice versa.

Popper, undeterred by such objections, makes it clear that 'these three worlds do not belong to science, in the sense of natural science. They belong to a sphere that needs to be given a different name – let us say, metaphysics' (ZO: 74). Popper, then, does not claim here to be speaking scientifically – indeed, he knows that his thesis is disconcerting because it will 'strike many as extremely metaphysical and dubious' (OK: 116). Yet he considers it meaningful and important for science itself, both because it insists that a theory is not a purely psychological matter (OGOU: 76) but something which can be discussed, and because it allows the body–mind dualism to be overcome through an interactionist solution that rejects monism as well as dualism. In fact, Popper calls himself a 'trialist' (ZO: 32), following the example of other great thinkers from Plato to Frege and Bolzano. World 3, he explicitly accepts, has much in common with Plato's world of Ideas, the first discovery of a non-sensible yet intelligible reality. But of course, there are also differences: whereas Plato's third world was immutable, divine and inhabited by concepts, Popper's is changeable and man-made and consists of propositions, theories and assertions which not only contemplate truth but also turn out to be false; and Plato, unlike the contemporary epistemologist, maintained that such a world was capable of providing ultimate explanations in terms of essences (OK: 122–124, 300–301; OGOU: 90–91). Still, Plato should be credited with having revealed a world that was not the sum of the contents of consciousness, 'but rather an objective, autonomous third world of logical contents' (ISBW: 161–162).

World 3 also has some analogies with Hegel's objective spirit, with his changing and constantly evolving world of ideas. But Popper rejects the omnipotence that Hegel attributes to the world of ideas, which in the end abuses man and impedes his creative activity; nor does he accept that this autonomous world can be compared to a self, to a human consciousness. Finally, the Hegelian dialectic – which is supposed to be the law of evolution of the world, both ideal and non-ideal – assigns a positive role to contradictions, whereas the author of *Objective Knowledge* regards them merely as errors to be got rid of (OK: 125–126).

All things considered, Popper thinks that his third world is closer to Bolzano's world of statements-in-themselves and truths-in-themselves, but that it 'resembles most closely the universe of Frege's objective contents of thought' (OK: 106). Even here, though, Popper has his differences: he tries to clarify and define the relationship of Bolzano's statements-in-themselves to the rest of the world (OK: 126), and later, in *Die Zukunft ist offen*, he introduces a sudden epistemological break with Frege's 'Third Realm' when, without disregarding the contents of art, literature and ethics, he argues that 'the best contents of World 3' are scientific theories (ZO: 101).[2]

World 3, in sum, comprises all the products of every cultural activity (ISBW: 9); it embraces everything that is the work of the human spirit (OGOU: 77), considered in its intelligible aspect or its 'objective logical content'. Popper gives the Stoics their due for having extended the theory of World 3 from Plato's Ideas to theories and propositions (ISBW: 162), and distinguished between the objective logical content of what is said and the objects about which it is said (which may belong to any of the three worlds) (OK: 158).

It might be asked what are the signs from which Popper infers the certain existence of a world independent of man and distinct from the world of physical objects. His answer is clear: scientific theories (the main inhabitants of World 3) have an indubitable influence on the physical universe, and so they are themselves real by virtue of the definition we have already met of what is real – namely, everything that can causally act upon, or interact with, ordinary material things (SB: 10; P2: 116). Take, for example, the enormous influence of theories and ideologies – typical inhabitants of World 3 – upon our life and milieu. It is on the basis of theories that our habitat has changed to the point that we are able to fly or to communicate in real time with the whole world; while ideologies mark political and social life, shaping and directing even the personal, private choices of individuals. The influence of both is quite comparable to that of bacteria and the like (ZO: 101), as we can easily see if we think of the effects of atomic theory or of economic doctrines (OK: 159).

Popper offers two thought experiments in support of the existence of World 3. The first assumes that all our instruments and machines have been destroyed, as well as our subjective knowledge of them, but that libraries and our learning capacity have remained intact. In such a situation, the world might yet go forward and recover the lost patrimony. But let us then imagine a case where in addition the libraries have been destroyed; our capacity to learn from books would then be unusable, and humanity would be forced to begin again from scratch (OK: 107–108). It is therefore wrong to suggest that a book is just ink-spotted paper which acquires all its meaning from the reader; in fact, every book 'contains objective knowledge, true or false, useful or useless', and for it to be considered a part of World 3, it is enough that it could be understood and deciphered, even if this were never actually to happen (OK: 115–116).

World 3, then, is the world of products of the human mind that cannot be identified with any material object; a Mozart symphony, for example, does not exhaust its content either in the score, or in the listener's or composer's acoustic experience, or even in the sum of all actual acoustic experiences. 'In that sense the World 3 object is a real ideal object which exists, but exists nowhere, and whose existence is somehow the potentiality of its being reinterpreted by human minds' (SB: 450). The salient characteristic of World 3 is its particular relationship to man: on the one hand, it is exclusively the product of the human mind and of purposeful human activity; but on the other hand, it contains consequences not intended and sometimes not even imaginable by the human actor in question (SB: 547).

Popper himself clearly sets out a number of major ideas which refer to an objective mind originating in, but freeing itself from, the subjective mind. His main thesis overturns the traditional assumption that objective knowledge is derived from subjective experience; for 'almost all our subjective knowledge (World 2 knowledge) depends upon World 3, that is to say on (at least virtually) *linguistically formulated* theories' (OK: 74). As we have already seen, in fallibilistic gnoseology, knowledge begins not with the personal sensations dear to classical empiricists and positivists, but with the formulation of hypotheses that must then be put to the test. From this Popper concludes that insofar as traditional epistemology refers to subjective knowledge, it 'is irrelevant to the study of scientific knowledge' (OK: 111). Moreover, 'an objectivist epistemology which studies the third world can help to throw an immense amount of light upon the second world of subjective consciousness, especially upon the subjective thought processes of scientists; but *the converse is not true*' (OK: 112). The most widespread mistake in gnoseology, which even permeates common sense, is to deny the existence of that of which we are not conscious. In fact, problems exist even before anyone is aware of them, and so there is a sense in which World 3 is autonomous, because it can be the object of discoveries quite similar to the geographical ones we make in World 1 (OK: 74, 111).

Hence World 3 enjoys an autonomy of its own, and it is 'objective' in the sense that it does not entirely depend upon subjective mental states. Nevertheless, it is a product of human activity, of human beings, 'just as honey is the product of bees, or spiders' webs of spiders' (OK: 159, 111); it is 'the unplanned product of human actions' (OK: 159–160; ISBW: 164).

Whenever he has occasion to speak of it, Popper insists that World 3 is largely autonomous but is still a typically human product – so much so that it can exert a powerful feedback effect on its creator. For instance, we should not forget that when new problems are introduced in the realm of objective knowledge, World 3 has a crucial feedback effect upon World 2 by stimulating the mind to search for new solutions (OK: 122). In Popper's view, therefore, 'everything depends upon the give-and-take between ourselves and our work; upon the product which we contribute to the third world, and upon that constant feedback that can be amplified by conscious self-criticism' (OK: 147). Through such interaction between our actions and their results, we constantly transcend ourselves and our own talents, which gain strength as they contribute to the growth of objective knowledge.

Against this background, it is not difficult to argue that 'the Worlds 1, 2 and 3, though partly autonomous, belong to the same universe: they interact' (P2: 161). It is evident from what has been said so far that World 3 acts in many ways upon World 2 – for instance, whenever we learn something or take pleasure in a work of art. But nor can there be any doubt that World 2, the human mind, acts in turn upon the physical world, thereby demonstrating that it is a question of universes open to reciprocal influence (P2: 130).

The three worlds, then, are related to each other in such a way that they interact in pairs: World 2 interacts with both World 1 and World 3, while these last two cannot interact directly but only through the mediation of subjective and personal experiences (OK: 159). For technology manifests itself above all in the physical world, but it depends enormously on the theories inhabiting the objective mind (OK: 159; OGOU: 87).

Interaction between the three worlds is of the greatest import-ance, because it constitutes the 'shaping of reality' (ISBW: 26) that allows us to understand the spiral of reactions through which the world and we ourselves are transformed. For example, the dream of flying – which pertains to World 2 – gave rise to projects, endeavours and theories in World 3, which then had an impact on World 1 when the building of aeroplanes changed physical reality and the material conditions of human existence. But the spiritual conditions of humanity were thereby also affected, as aspirations, desires and intentions began to change, and the world of culture faced possibilities that had once been non-existent and unimagin-able. As we have already noted, such interaction is also especially significant for the solution of another problem that goes back to

Descartes: the relationship between body and mind. Not only does Popper recognize the existence of two distinct elements, with physical states being present alongside mental states not always reducible to them; he even accepts that sometimes, at least as far as the objects of World 3 are concerned, mental states may be separated from the physical phenomena of World 1. Popper is convinced that in order to grasp at a personal psychological level (and thus in World 2) an idea from World 3, it is not necessary to pass through World 1, which here consists only of brain mechanisms and their products. Indeed, he regards 'the thesis of the possibility of a direct grasp of World 3 objects by World 2 as generally valid' (SB: 549).

At this point, however, the reciprocal relations between the different worlds appear more confused than Popper is prepared to admit. For it is not clear how there can be a relationship between the subjective and the objective side of knowledge without the involvement of the brain and the sense organs (that is, of World 1). Nor is it easy to see what is the genuine middle in this group of three: the fact that 'all our actions in the first world are influenced by our second-world grasp of the third world' makes of the psychological world of subjective experiences a kind of unifying link between the first and the third world (OK: 148–149); but at the same time, the true middle between the two extremes seems to be World 3, which appears as the instrument favoured by inhabitants of World 2 to act upon World 1, to intervene in its mechanisms, and to explain its phenomena. For the grasping of an object in World 3 is an active process that involves a kind of re-creation of the object itself; and the mechanism is constantly being activated in every type of process of understanding, not least in that of persons and their actions – because in all understanding, 'the analysis of third-world situations is our paramount task' (OK: 167); 'or to put it in another way: the activity of understanding consists, essentially, in operating with third-world objects' (OK: 164). It would seem, then, that in striving to understand World 1, human beings (qua members of World 2) cannot avoid having recourse to the theories, models and schemas of World 3. But this means a *regressus ad infinitum*, since the understanding of a (World 3) theory required to explain an aspect of World 1 necessitates recourse to other (World 3) theories. Popper seems aware of this outcome when he says that the understanding of a theory is an infinite task which 'has, indeed, much in common with understanding a human personality' (OK: 299). But he does not appear to realize that this carries the risk of losing sight of the original reference object, which always belongs to World 1. Finally, we should note that in Popper's investigations accompanying the three-worlds theory, a certain confusion is created between two aspects of the physical world that cannot be treated in the same way, at least not in the perspective of World 2 where the personal experiences of human beings are to be found. For it does not seem correct to put on the same footing our relations with material objects and our relations with our own body and, in particular, with our own brain. Popper does not give any explicit reasons, however, why the body and its organs should be thought of as different from other material objects. There appears an ambiguity whereby the human body becomes hard to classify: it is certainly not part of either World 3 or World 2, but it also differs from the tables and chairs that make up World 1.

Turning now to Popper's theory of objective mind, we should first stress that it attributes a decisive role to language. For only insofar as a World 2 experience is linguistically formulated can it become communicable and therefore public, objective and criticizable. Until a thought is expressed on the outside, it does not become distinct from the person who formulates it: it is still only part of the conscious subject, like a feeling or an emotion. When it is articulated in language, however, it acquires an existence independent of the mind which thought it, and that mind too can then observe and criticize it as a separate object – in the etymological sense of *objectum*, thrown before the mind (SB: 451). But if language permits the exercise of criticism, it also makes it necessary; for human language, having developed the higher functions that govern description and argumentation, has introduced a possibility that does not exist for animals – namely, the capacity to speak falsehood. Whereas bees do not know how to lie when signalling the position of flowers to their companions (ZO: 36; OGOU: 85), the fact that humans can deliberately deceive makes it advisable for others to take a critical attitude.

At any event, although language is a man-made instrument like so many others, it is far and away the most important (ZO: 100), because 'our speech and writing create a third realm, made up of the products of our mind's activity' (ZO: 32). This enables us to make our thoughts objective and hence criticizable, to discover and correct the errors lurking in our theories. All this has been possible because man himself, beyond the expressive and communicative or signalling functions shared with animals, has developed two other functions: the descriptive one, which gives rise to the regulative idea of truth (since a description may or may not correspond to the thing); and the argumentative one, which makes it possible for us to test the adequacy of theories, their truth or verisimilitude (OK: 119–120; ISBW: 28–29; SB: 455–456).

EMERGENT CONSCIOUSNESS

The three-worlds theory has interesting repercussions on the way in which Popper views man and explains his peculiarities – indeed he ends up outlining a veritable anthropology. For we could say that man himself condenses the three worlds: this is obviously true of World 2, since although consciousness is not exclusively human – as Popper argues against Eccles (SB: 440, 446, 518–519) – it does certainly belong to man and even finds there its highest expression; but we can also say it of World 1, in which the body and its functions are located; and it is also true of World 3 which, despite its relative autonomy after being created, is nevertheless always created by man. Subsequently too, of course, man continues to participate in World 3, and his direct relationship with it makes mediation possible between World 3 and World 1. As we have seen, Popper accepts the view of man as divided into several heterogeneous components, and he thus openly espouses a theory of pluralism or, if it is preferred, 'trialism'. But he too has to face the main problem of the dualists: the relationship between body and mind. For Popper's pluralism is not like that of the atomists, for example, who invoked a plurality of heterogeneous elements to explain reality and its constant changes. It is more like a strengthened dualism, in that his three worlds are heterogeneous yet communicate with each other.

The starting point is Popper's conviction that human beings 'are selves; they are ends in themselves' (SB: 3), which he takes to be incompatible with materialism, his polemical target. As we have seen in another context, the theoretician of critical rationalism approaches questions mainly by examining and assessing the theses that seem to him unacceptable; an alternative hypothesis emerges only out of the opposition to these theories. Thus, to take a couple of significant examples, the principle of falsification developed out of a critique of the verification principle; and the defence of realism got going as a result of objections to idealism. In the present case too, Popper argues that to leave rival theories behind, it is enough to show that they do not explain what is readily intelligible in a well-constructed interactionism.

Whilst rejecting materialism, Popper recognizes that two of its opposed traditions gave considerable impetus to science: the Parmenidean theory of the *plenum*, which eventually led to the field theory of matter; and the atomism of Leucippus, from which modern atomic theory and quantum mechanics are derived. Modern physics, however, is no longer in tune with the classical materialist conception of the world as 'a clockwork mechanism of bodies which push each other like cogwheels' (SB: 6; ISBW: 10). Newton's theory of gravity, in which motion is explained in terms of attraction at a distance rather than contact pressure, already implicitly went beyond this older view; then Leibniz 'showed that atoms must be centres of repulsive force if they are to be impenetrable and capable of pushing' (ISBW: 10); and finally came Maxwell's theory of electromagnetism and, above all, the attempts of Einstein, de Broglie and Schrödinger to explain the nature of matter itself, as 'vibrations of an immaterial ether consisting of fields of forces' [ibid.]. Thus matter is no longer seen as substance, but rather as highly concentrated energy 'transformable into other forms of energy; and therefore something of the nature of a *process*, since it can be converted into other processes such as light and, of course, motion and heat' (SB: 7). Or again: 'the universe now appears to be not a collection of things, but an interacting set of events or processes' [ibid.]. Physics has thus gone beyond materialism, which can no longer be considered a possible solution to Descartes' problem.

What is needed is to find good arguments for the interaction between mental and physical states, bearing in mind that consciousness 'is produced by physical states; yet it controls them to a considerable extent' (OK: 251). The problem is anything but trivial, however, and more recently Popper himself, in an interview touching on *The Self and Its Brain*, stated that the book did not offer solutions to the body–mind problem and that he doubted whether any could be reached (ZO: 80) – although he also maintained that the problem had been modified through the introduction of World 3. In other words, Popper did not claim to have found *the* fully satisfactory solution to a difficulty which, as he was well aware, besets any dualist theory, but he did think he had contributed to a correct posing of the problem.

Let us now look at how Popper clarifies the interactionist position in his main work on the matter. We should begin by defining the terms of the debate. This may not be necessary in the case of the body, but the same cannot be said of the mind. Indeed, the authors of *The Self and Its Brain* feel the need to start by informing their readers that they have avoided any terms which might have a strongly religious connotation – such as the English word *soul* – or which might allude to particular philosophical doctrines. Their use of 'mind' is meant to be as in ordinary language, when we say, for example, 'I made up my mind' (SB: viii). As to the definition of the word, we have to be content with what is offered towards the end of this bulky two-authored work, when Popper says in his penultimate dialogue with Eccles that mind can be defined only negatively, as 'something utterly different from anything which, to our knowledge, has previously existed in the world' (SB: 553). This lack of further precision in definition may trouble many readers and even appear as a lack of conceptual clarity. But Popper reminds us here of his general aversion for 'What is . . .?' questions: he considers them unfruitful, both because they are compromised with the essentialism he so tenaciously rejects, and because they tend to degenerate into a verbalizing about the meaning of words and concepts that loses sight of the real problem (SB: 100).

Whilst respecting the philosopher's approach to these matters, we may perhaps try to identify a little less vaguely the reality indicated in the terms which he uses to describe human mental dynamics and the relations between the various functions involved in it. We may begin by saying that the various aspects of the human being can be considered in terms of two main components: one material (the body, including the brain) and one immaterial (including the mind, consciousness and self-consciousness). These unite and interact in the self, whose identity is given by the web of relations between physical and immaterial factors. The self, then, is not identical with consciousness – for there is also the large area of the unconscious, which is certainly no less important to a person's individuality (SB: 131). Indeed, as Eccles points out, a huge number of activities occur in the brain which never reach consciousness and about which the self-conscious mind itself performs a selection (SB: 476).

The self, then, does not coincide with consciousness or the self-conscious mind: it also combines all the unconscious activity of the brain, an organ belonging to the physical world which, in turn, does not exhaust either the functions of consciousness or the many-sidedness of the self. For the self includes moral character and will, which take shape in a social context and produce far from negligible effects in the brain. Clearly, the situation of human beings is rather complex, posing problems that range from gnoseology to ethics and from psychology to anthropology; these probably cannot be solved once and for all, but they require careful analysis, if only to ensure that they are posed correctly. Unfortunately, Popper does not tell us enough to know for sure what is the difference between the concepts of mind and consciousness. Sometimes he seems to use 'mind' as a short form for 'self-conscious mind'; sometimes it seems to indicate the domain in which brain activity and consciousness proper make contact – although in other respects this seems to be the end of a long evolution in which the emergence of mind was only the first step.

One therefore feels like asking how and why the absolute novelty that culminated in self-consciousness first made its appearance in the world. Popper himself asks this question, and his frank though hardly full answer is that it is like the question about the origins of life, for which we lack the necessary evidence. 'How did consciousness come to exist? I think that the main answer which we can give, and which has some evidence in its favour, though not very much, is the answer "by degrees" ' (SB: 438). However little can be established about the conditions of the emergence of consciousness – and Popper says that we do not have explanations even for the emergence of the human brain (SB: 563) – it constituted a novel and unpredictable fact (SB: 30), the point at which matter transcended itself 'by producing mind, purpose, and a world of the products of the human mind' (SB: 11).

Popper suggests, 'as a wild conjecture' (SB: 127), that consciousness emerges out of four biological functions: pain, pleasure, expectation and attention. But even that leaves to be explained the unity of our individual ego, which does not seem to be simply a matter of our biological situation. And the emergence of full consciousness, capable of self-reflection, is still shrouded in mystery (SB: 129) but is surely bound up with human brain activity and the descriptive function of language. In Popper's view, the brain (belonging to World 1) and the mind (belonging to World 2) evolved in interaction with the first product of the mind, language (belonging to World 3). For 'in choosing to speak, and to take interest in speech, man has chosen to evolve his brain and his mind; [and] language, once created, exerted the selection pressure under which emerged the human brain and the consciousness of self' (SB: 13). In this connection, it may be illuminating to hear Eccles – from his scientist's observation post – speak of self-conscious mind as an independent entity 'actively engaged in reading out from the multitude of active centres at the highest level of brain activity, namely the liaison areas of the dominant cerebral hemisphere' (SB: 362). The self-conscious mind carries out a selection on the basis of its particular interests and perspective. At each moment, it seeks to achieve the unity of conscious experience, which derives not from some final synthesis within the neural mechanism, but from the integrative action of the self-conscious mind in discerning which of the huge variety of mental activities is suited to this goal.

Unless I have misunderstood this difficult synthesis of philosophical considerations and neurophysiological data, Popper is here postulating a multitude of brain activities that would serve no definite function if there were not something like what Kant called 'transcendental apperception' – that is, self-conscious activity which unifies the various elaborations of the brain and inserts them into the framework of the individual's stock of knowledge. This is supposed to occur after selection of the data produced by the brain, on the basis of criteria provided by the mind which coincide with the individual's own interests, goals, values and expectations.

If we now put Eccles's scientific hypothesis together with Popper's philosophical statement, we could say that the central problem is to define the self in a way which best accounts both for the unity of experience and for the fact that the self operates through the brain (without being identical with it, as a materialist would argue).

All these considerations point towards the transcendence of the self *vis-à-vis* the brain. For, as Eccles sums up, the self-conscious mind does not only have a receptive function; its activity also tends to modify the brain, with which it is in a dynamic relationship that affords it a 'position of superiority' (SB: 552). If we were then to ask what this superiority consists in, we would receive Popper's precisely worded reply:

What characterizes the self (as opposed to the electrochemical processes of the brain on which the self largely depends – a dependence which seems far from one-sided) is that all our experiences are closely related and integrated; not only with past experiences but also with our changing programmes for action, our expectations, and our theories.

(SB: 146)

These philosophical points find a scientific counterpart in Eccles's assertion that 'the self-conscious mind is doing its usual job of trying to extract a meaning from the total cerebral performance that relates to its present interests' (SB: 521) Unless we have misunderstood both authors' views, this means that in conscious experience – which responds at least in part to conscious requirements – we find something over and above the results of brain mechanisms; that if the physiology of the brain and the nervous system do not ultimately explain consciousness in any shape or form, we cannot but postulate the transcendence of the self *vis-à-vis* its material organ, the brain.

It would be wrong to think, however, that this autonomous origin of the self with regard to the brain indicates an innate property which does not need to be acquired; 'we are not born as selves [. . .]; we have to learn that we are selves; in fact we have to learn to be selves' (SB: 109). To be a self, we have to learn many things – above all, to gain a sense of time that allows us to identify the self as stretching into the past (at least till yesterday) and into the future (at least till tomorrow). For this reason, Popper disagrees with the Kantian doctrine of a 'pure ego' implicitly prior to experience; on the contrary, 'being a self is partly the result of inborn dispositions and partly the result of experience, especially social experience' (SB: 111). One has only to think of what would happen to children if they lived in isolation (SB: 111, 448).

To conclude: for Popper, we do not know *how* mind and body interact, but we do know *that* they interact; nor should our ignorance appear so shocking, since in the end we do not even know how physical objects (or mental states) interact with one another (SB: 153). Certainly we do not know enough; but we should not therefore scorn the evidence that is available to us and helps us to formulate our working hypotheses. For example, we know that 'intense brain activity is the necessary condition for mental processes. Thus brain processes will go on contemporaneously with any mental processes, and being necessary conditions, may be said to "cause" them, or to "act" upon them' (SB: 99). On the other hand, according to recent research, 'it appears that the brain grows through activity, through having to solve problems actively' (SB: 112), and a number of experiments have confirmed that animals living in an environment rich in stimuli develop a heavier cerebral cortex. Eccles, for his part, backs up these ideas by stressing that the mind–brain interaction 'is a two-way process, the self-conscious mind receives and develops its experiences in all of its wide-ranging searching and selecting from the liaison brain. But also it acts back; and as it receives, so it gives' (SB: 473).

The human consciousness of self (that is, World 2) is thus 'highly complex', but it does not have the substantive character attributed to it within a certain philosophical tradition (P2: 153).³ Nor is that all: the complexity is heightened by the fact that the interaction is directed not only towards World 1 but also – indeed, above all – in the direction of World 3. For consciousness is intimately bound up with the development of language and the consequent elaboration of theories, which enables us to be a self and to visualize our self as something enduring (SB: 463). A kind of hierarchy is thus established in which World 3 transcends World 1 and World 3 transcends World 2 (SB: 563); for World 2 can develop and take shape only thanks to World 3. It might be said that culture forges individual consciousnesses and, in this sense, transcends them, but it needs to be added that culture results from the efforts of millions of individual consciousnesses to discover and understand the world around. 'As selves, as human beings, we are all products of World 3 which, in its turn, is a product of countless human minds' (SB: 144). The reciprocal influence of subjective consciousness and objective knowledge thus becomes central in Popper's philosophical anthropology. And World 1 is required to account for this interaction between World 2 and World 3 – which confirms that it is 'only in the brain that there can be interaction between World 1 and World 2, and in this we must really say that Descartes was our forerunner' (SB: 539). The fact that the brain is involved in many interactions between World 2 and World 3 should not make us forget that if something is going on in World 1, 'it depends partly on World 2. (This is the idea of interaction)' (SB: 537).

It is easy to understand why Popper, though no materialist, having argued a functionalist interpretation of the self, did not find sufficient motivation to affirm that the mind survives after death (SB: 556). For in his view the mind exists only as a *function* of the body. His agnosticism is not shaken by the urgings of his friend Eccles, who argues:

> Our coming-to-be is as mysterious as our ceasing-to-be at death. Can we therefore not derive hope because our ignorance about our origin matches our ignorance about our destiny? Cannot life be lived as a challenging and wonderful adventure that has meaning to be discovered?
>
> (SB: 557)

EVOLUTIONARY EPISTEMOLOGY

It should be clear from the last section that the background to Popper's theses is a biological view of consciousness as the product of a long evolutionary process, through which man has adjusted to his environment but also – thanks to the intervention of World 3 – tried to adjust the environment to his own requirements. Popper attaches so much importance to this aspect because the only original element in his three-worlds theory is its connection with Darwinism (ZO: 79). In particular, 'the theory of natural selection provides a strong argument for the doctrine of *mutual interaction* between mind and body or, perhaps better, between mental states and physical states' (NSEM: 351). Darwin's theory of evolution is incorporated into Popper's system with a few revisions that make it fruitful in an epistemological context and allow it to be something more than a 'logical truism'.

To clarify the function of Darwinism within falsificationist methodology, let us briefly recall the main stages through which the theory of the evolution of the species became established. One of the first significant figures was J.B. Lamarck, whose *Zoological Philosophy* (1809) maintained that the animal species developed one after the other in an order of increasing complexity, changing their own organs so as to adapt to their environment and then passing on favourable mutations by heredity. Some fifty years later, Darwin criticized Lamarck's positions on the grounds that they were based not upon experimental data but on various assumptions, such as the idea of a ceaseless perfecting of nature, which had no scientific credibility. By contrast, the English naturalist obtained his insights from a vast amount of observational material relating to flora and fauna in their natural setting. In his theory, evolution occurs through the struggle for survival, which leads both to the extinction of some species and to the appearance of new ones which have developed better-suited organs and thus been selected by the environment for their greater adaptability. Unlike Lamarck, Darwin held that the environmental influence on evolution was not rigidly determinist, and that some role was played by random variations which proved advantageous in the particular context facing an animal species.

Popper's objection to Darwin's theory of evolution is that it is really a kind of tautology: 'for the moment well adapted' is equivalent to 'has those qualities which made it survive so far' (OK: 69), so that the survival of the fittest basically means the survival of those who survive. Popper therefore argues for a restatement of the theory in which mutations are no longer interpreted as random or – the opposite – as resulting from deterministic action of the environment, but rather as the outcome of trial and error, of the efforts of living beings to solve problems that the environment has presented and continues to present (OK: 242). The basis for his reformulation is that 'all organisms are constantly, day and night, engaged in problem-solving', even if they are not aware of it [ibid.]. Problem-solving is always linked to the method of trial and error, whereby errors are overcome through the elimination of unsuccessful forms by 'natural selection' or through the correction or suppression of unsuccessful modes of behaviour.

Popper's second modification of Darwinism is to make action a two-way process or 'two-edged sword': 'it is not only the environment that selects and changes us – it is also we who select and change the environment' (OK: 149). The single organism is itself 'a tentative solution, probing into new environmental niches, choosing an environment and modifying it' (OK: 243).

Evolution, then, may be summed up as the passage from a problem (P_1) to a provisional or tentative solution (TS), and then to the elimination of errors (EE), which sets up new problems at once unforeseen and unintended (P_2). This process may be represented as follows:

$$P_1 \rightarrow TS \rightarrow EE \rightarrow P_2$$

Popper considers this schema an improvement and rationalization of the triadic movement of the Hegelian dialectic, with which it shares a conviction that 'critical error-elimination on the scientific level proceeds by way of a conscious search for contradictions'

(OK: 297). But the schema has the defect of not taking into account that there are normally a multiplicity of tentative solutions, so that it would be more accurate to draw it as in Figure 4.1 (OK: 243).

$$P_1 \rightarrow \begin{array}{c} \nearrow TS_1 \searrow \\ TS_2 \rightarrow EE \rightarrow P_2 \\ \searrow \qquad \nearrow \end{array}$$

$$\cdot$$
$$\cdot$$
$$\cdot$$
$$TS_n$$

Background Knowledge

Figure 4.1

As we can see, this tetradic model sums up the salient features of falsificationist methodology that were already taking shape in *The Logic of Scientific Discovery*. It is tempting to think that it is particularly well suited to describe the development of scientific theories or even of pre-scientific knowledge in general – not so much because theories obey Darwinian-type laws of evolution, as because the model was drawn from observation and reflection on the actual mechanisms of knowledge and only then, in a second stage, related to Darwinian standards. As a result, these standards had themselves to be modified in certain ways, for it to be possible to understand the particular type of evolution undergone by theories. The schema thus corresponds better to reality if it is given a more complex form that shows the large number of possibilities in any problematic situation (OK: 287).

$$P_1 \rightarrow \begin{array}{l} \nearrow TS_a \rightarrow EE_a \rightarrow P_{2a} \\ TS_b \rightarrow EE_b \rightarrow P_{2b} \\ \searrow TS_n \rightarrow EE_n \rightarrow P_{2n} \end{array}$$

Figure 4.2

The tetradic model may accordingly be used to describe the emergence of new problems, but also of new solutions, in an epistemological no less than a biological context – given that the evolution of knowledge is nothing other than a continuation of biological evolution.

Before we go more deeply into these ideas and try to grasp what is distinctive about evolutionary epistemology, it may be useful to draw out the main consequences of Popper's novelty in relation to Darwinism. In fact, evolutionism may give rise to two ideologies which, though resting upon the same assumptions, prove to be pessimistic in the one case and optimistic in the other. Let us follow Popper's own four-point summary (ISBW: 16).

1 In the pessimistic view, selective pressure wipes out what is unable to adapt, and so the environment is hostile to life; in the optimistic view, the pressure comes from within rather than without, and is highly favourable to life because it leads to a search for more advantageous environments.
2 In the former, organisms are passive, whereas in the latter they are active insofar as they are continually involved in problem-solving.
3 In the old ideology, mutations are a matter of pure chance; in the new perspective, nature and its organisms work inventively, through trial and error.
4 In the first case, the environment in which we live is hostile to us and results from the most ruthless selection; in the second, the first cell is still alive in any one of the living cells. 'We are all the primordial cell, in a very similar sense (genidentity) to that in which I am the same person as I was thirty years ago, even though perhaps not one atom of my present body existed in my body in those days' (ISBW: 15).

Now, Popper considers it possible to extend these features of natural evolution to the process whereby consciousness is produced – for 'new ideas have a striking similarity to genetic mutations' (SB: 440). Any one of them meets the requirement of finding a better mode of interaction with the environment or – if one prefers – of finding a satisfactory solution to a specific problem posed by life itself. The development of our knowledge, then, is similar to what Darwin called the process of natural selection, in that it grows through the selection of hypotheses which, by surviving and eliminating the less adapted, have shown that they are for the moment the best adapted (OK: 260–261). This is true also of animal knowledge and pre-scientific knowledge, but the struggle is harsher in the case of scientific knowledge where theories are deliberately exposed to criticism. What Popper is proposing is:

> a largely Darwinian theory of the growth of knowledge. From the amoeba to Einstein, the growth of knowledge is

always the same: we try to solve our problems, and to obtain, by a process of elimination, something approaching adequacy in our tentative solutions.

(OK: 261)

For Popper, then, there is an existential continuity between biological and epistemological evolution; theories, myths and all the other products of human culture are veritable organs evolving outside our bodies, which perform similar functions and correspond to similar (though not identical) needs as those performed and satisfied by the bodily organs. Knowledge is a human product, just as honey is a product of bees or a spider's web of spiders; their components are 'exsomatic tools' (OK: 286, 145; ISBW: 21). In keeping with his Darwinism, Popper points out that 'not only do we develop digits, eyes and ears, like other organisms; we also develop spectacles, we develop hearing aids, we develop every possible *instrument*' (ZO: 99); instead of strengthening our eyes or ears to perceive things better, we build microscopes, telescopes and telephones; instead of making our own legs faster and more robust, we build trains and motor cars; instead of expanding our brain and memory, we produce paper, pens, printing presses, libraries and computers. We thus carry to perfection the rudimentary exsomatic development found in animals when they set about building nests or (in the case of beavers) damming streams (OK: 238). Of all the tools invented by man, by far the most important is language. The development of its higher functions provides a new and effective means of solving problems, a bloodless way of testing proposed solutions that does not require the physical elimination of individuals (OK: 239–240).

Eccles, considering the matter from a scientist's viewpoint, stresses that 'these two, biological evolution and cultural evolution, act together in a way because the culture gives you the natural selection that selects for the better brain' (SB: 460). And Popper backs this up by arguing that the only difference between the two comes from our own initiative – since, without waiting for natural selection, we decide to eliminate our errors through conscious criticism (SB: 458). According to Dario Antiseri, we can even reverse the equation: not only is the growth of knowledge an evolutionary process; but 'biological evolution may be considered as a knowledge process'.[4] Popper seems to confirm this interpretation when he maintains that 'the adaptation of life to its environment is a form of knowledge. Without this minimal knowledge, life could not survive' (EE: 31). Obviously it is not a question here of conscious knowledge; and in speaking of primal forms of life we can use the term knowledge only by a kind of homology, exactly as we treat as homologous the arms of humans and the wings of birds. The basic feature of knowledge in this general sense is its capacity to anticipate the environment – as flowers, for example, open during the day and close at night, somehow 'knowing' in advance the alternation of the two (EE: 33). Besides, not even human knowledge is completely conscious; and most of our expectations remain unconscious, until the moment when they prove to have been unfounded (WP: 32). To borrow the title of a well-known book by the Nobel Prize-winning ethnologist Konrad Lorenz, we might add that 'living is learning' and that evolution works as does science, 'by means of tests and the elimination of error' (OGOU: 33; ISBW: 17), through which organism and environment progressively adapt to each other. Popper underlines that this is not an empirical method; it pertains rather to logic, albeit of a special type as in 'the logic of the situation' (OK: 70). By this he means a procedure which is not intended to be successful in every possible circumstance, but which – once a certain situation is given – becomes not just applicable but almost necessary from a logical point of view. Situational logic tells us only how things proceed in a certain context (where life is possible, for example); it does not pronounce on possibilities that might not become actual (UQ: 168).

These premisses make it possible to understand Popper's polemic with classical epistemology and its conception of sense 'data' leading to inductive theory-formation. For this involves a pre-Darwinian schema which 'fails to take account of the fact that the alleged data are in fact adaptive reactions, and therefore interpretations which incorporate theories and prejudices and which, like theories, are impregnated with conjectural expectations' (OK: 145). It follows that the process of knowledge cannot be cumulative or repetitive, because nothing is ever definitively acquired. At any moment the scientific patrimony is the fruit of ceaseless reciprocal adaptation between man and environment at three distinct levels: the genetic level, based on DNA structure; the behavioural level, based on the genetically inherited repertoire of possible behaviour complemented by rules handed down through tradition; and the scientific level, involving theories in which the tradition has placed its trust, as well as problems that are still open.

At every level of learning, therefore, two forces are in operation: the conservative power of *instruction*, and the evolutionary or revolutionary power of *selection* (SB: 133). The former has the task of safeguarding the goals reached by previous generations and passing them on to new individuals, so that they do not have to start from scratch each time, either at the genetic level or at the practical or theoretical level. The latter has the function of improving the biological and cultural legacy, by adapting it to new circumstances.

This being so, if the theory of trial and error is corroborated or at least made plausible by the evolutionist hypothesis, the theory of learning by conditioned reflex should be discarded even in the animal world. For Pavlov's explanation in terms of muscular stimulus and response reduces animal behaviour to a purely passive mechanism, whereas Popper attributes to it an active if unconscious interest in relation to its surroundings (SB: 133–134).

Finally, it should not be forgotten that Darwinism favours an interactionist solution to the body–mind problem, one in which mental states are produced by biological evolution and together generate World 3 as an 'exsomatic tool'. This does not, however, quite seem to explain the qualitative difference that Popper sees between World 2 and World 1; in fact, it would appear more consistent with evolutionary theory to speak not so much of three worlds as of different levels of development reached by life – which in the case of man has transcended the purely biological level of plants, as well as the rudimentary consciousness that might be attributed to animals. Nothing in Popper's system accounts for the qualitative leap represented by man's invention of language – indeed, the question tends to be simply ignored or passed over. But if it really is analogous in kind to biological evolution, then clearly we should say that men produce World 3 with their 'exsomatic tools' as bees produce honey and wax, and that World 3, exactly like honey and wax, should therefore be assimilated to World 1. In other words, if Popper wants to keep faith with his evolutionism, he should abandon the three-worlds theory; but if he wants to stand by the three-worlds theory, then he can no longer explain knowledge as a continuation of genetic and biological evolution.

Instead, Popper's enthusiasm for Darwin's theory of evolution, whatever its limits, led him to conclude that although it was 'metaphysical', 'its value for science as a metaphysical research programme is very great' (UQ: 172). Less than ten years after writing this, however, he changed his view and argued that the theory of evolution was a falsified and therefore scientific research programme (OGOU: 56). For in light of certain incongruities, especially in relation to sexual characteristics, he had to conclude that 'evolution by natural selection is not strictly universal, though it seems to hold for a vast number of important cases' (NSEM: 346).

On the other hand, Popper was already aware in the early 1960s of the difficulties inherent in Darwinism, when he discussed its weak points in detail in an article later republished in *Objective Knowledge* (OK: 269ff, 281ff.). This means that, despite all the changes of course of which we have spoken, Popper continued to be attracted both by evolutionism and by the three-worlds theory, the areas of friction between the two being left unmentioned.

In essence, Popper's criticisms of Darwinism only bear upon a rigid interpretation of natural selection in which animals are not allowed to be creative in a Bergsonian sense. His own inclination, at the very end of his dialogues with Eccles, is to stress that 'man has created himself, by the creation of descriptive language and, with it, of World 3' (SB: 566).

DETERMINISM AND INDETERMINISM

The creativity that we find not only in man but in the whole of nature would be inexplicable on the assumption of a determinist universe. The situation here is the same as in the case of the problem of realism: that is, we face two opposite and equally metaphysical conceptions of the world. Before, the opposition was between realism and idealism; now it is between determinism and indeterminism. Both are unfalsifiable theories that claim to pronounce on the world in its totality. But they are not, for all that, equivalent – indeed, Popper thinks that persuasive arguments can be given in favour of the second, and important objections made against the first.

The determinism combated by Popper is Laplacean 'scientific' determinism. This holds that 'the state of the universe at any moment of time, future or past, is completely determined if its state, its situation, is given at some moment, for example, the present moment' (P2: xx); or again, that 'the structure of the world is such that any event can be rationally predicted, with any desired degree of precision, if we are given a sufficiently precise description of past events, together with all the laws of nature' (P2: 2).

Quite different in kind is philosophical determinism, which is based upon a proposition so generic as to be perfectly compatible with physical indeterminism. For philosophical determinism states that every effect has a cause, or that like events have like causes; while physical indeterminism merely asserts that events in the physical world 'cannot be predetermined with absolute precision, in all their infinitesimal details' (OK: 220). The physical indeterminist does not deny that effects are produced by causes, but he does exclude the possibility of predicting them with absolute precision; the philosophical determinist, on the other hand, does not say anything about precision (OK: 220–221).

Popper has no doubt that determinism, even in its scientific version, 'does not belong to science, and has no explanatory power' (P2: 28). His most comprehensive and considered defence of inde-terminism is to be found in the second volume of the *Postscript*, the one entitled *The Open Universe: An Argument for Indetermi-nism*. In the preface he wrote in 1982, Popper vigorously re-affirmed what was already clear forty years earlier in his political works, namely, that he was 'deeply interested in the philosophical defence of human freedom, of human creativity, and of what is traditionally called free will'; he therefore intended the book to be 'a kind of prolegomenon to the question of human freedom and creativity' (P2: xxi).

A necessary but not sufficient condition to leave scope for free will is physical indeterminism. Popper reaches this through the tried and tested method of criticizing the opposite theory, starting with commonsense justifications and then moving on to deal with the philosophical and scientific arguments in support of determin-ism. Popper considers the determinist position to be religious in origin, bound up with the idea of divine omnipotence and omniscience according to which there is a being who not only has the power to determine the future but who has always known it; this leads to the conviction that every event has been fixed in advance (P2: 5).

The scientific version does little more than replace the idea of God with that of nature, and divine law with natural law. Unlike the inscrutable will of God, however, which can be known only through Revelation, the laws of nature may be discovered by human reason with the aid – as Galileo would have said – of 'sensory experience'. Scientific determinism may also be seen as deriving from a quite sophisticated critique of commonsense knowledge and its characteristic division of all events into two types: those that can be predicted, such as change of the seasons or the functioning of a clock; and those that cannot be foreseen, such as the movement of clouds (P2: 6). Newton's extraordinary success did persuade many, including Kant, that in physical terms there is not really any difference between the two cases, the apparent unpredictability of the latter being simply due to the insufficiency of our knowledge. But Popper stressed that although Kant accepted determinism as a proven fact of science, he could not tolerate it at a moral level – which led to an antinomy never fully resolved (P2: 7). As we shall now try to show, this ethical demand to leave room for human freedom was the main stimulus impelling Popper to uphold the cause of indeterminism.

There is also a 'metaphysical' version of determinism according to which all events in the physical world are predetermined and unalterable, so that the future can no more be modified than the past. This is, of course, an untestable theory, for even if the world continually had surprises in store, the future could still be predetermined and even foreseen by someone capable of reading the book of destiny (P2: 8). Metaphysical indeterminism, for its part, is equally untestable, and all it can do is examine and criticize the arguments used in support of determinism.

> One of the simplest and most plausible arguments in favour of determinism is this: we can *always* ask, of *every* event, why it happened; and to every such why-question we can always obtain, in principle, a reply which enlightens us. Thus every event is 'caused'; and this seems to mean that it must be determined, in advance, by the events which constitute its cause.
>
> (P2: 9)

To this it might be objected that commonsense answers to why-questions do not speak for the validity of determinism; for it is typical of common sense to ask why John has a fever but not to wonder why his temperature has gone up to 38.5 degrees rather than 38.6. The intuitive notion of causality at the root of common sense simply does not call for the quantitative precision which is so crucial to the theory of determinism, and even the commonsense notion of 'event' is essentially qualitative. The latter does, according to Popper, have validity within certain limits, but the same cannot be said of scientific determinism. Nevertheless, distinguished philosophers have made the mistake of thinking that the argument that every event has a cause can be deployed in support of determinism (P2: 11).

At the basis of all these arguments is an a priori conviction that the physical world is determinist, although this is by no means evident and needs to be demonstrated. Common sense itself involves the idea that there are clocks and clouds, predictable and unpredictable events; it therefore postulates a margin of indeterminacy. Furthermore, we can observe that organisms are less predictable than simpler systems, and higher organisms less predetermined than lower ones. If determinism were true, a physiologist without any musical sense would have been capable of predicting, from a study of Mozart's brain, the material signs that Mozart drew on paper at the moment of composition; but such conclusions from the hypothesis strike Popper as 'intuitively absurd' (P2: 28).

The burden of proof weighs considerably lighter on the indeterminist position; for all it asserts is that 'there exists *at least one* event that is not predetermined, or predictable' [ibid.], although 'of course many possibilities are excluded by the laws of nature and of probability: there are many zero propensities' (WP: 25).

With regard to the history of classical or World 1 determinism, someone might argue that it goes back as far as Leucippus and Democritus. But it would be easy to show that there were important philosophers in ancient Greece who were not determinists. Aristotle, for example, accepted the 'natural', indeterminist view of the universe; his unmoved mover was the final cause, and therefore not determining in the modern mechanistic sense (SB: 32). In fact, mechanistic determinism was not rigorously formulated before Laplace, who in his *Philosophical Essay on Probabilities* (1819) ruled out the possibility of any chance events; physical theory, together with the initial conditions at any given moment, completely determined the state of the universe at any other moment (SB: 22). In accordance with the laws of Newtonian mechanics, the world was supposed to consist of interacting corpuscles, so that full and exact knowledge of the state of the world at any instant would be sufficient to deduce its state at any other instant. As such knowledge was clearly suprahuman, Laplace had recourse not to an omnipotent God but to the fiction of a demon or a kind of super-scientist. After this crucial change, determinist theory lost the appearance of a religious doctrine and assumed that of scientific truth (P2: 30).

Since Laplace, determinism has been the dominant conception in the field of science; only quantum mechanics, especially with the work of Heisenberg and Born, has put forward the idea of absolute chance and postulated a 'quantum leap' which, though subject to probabilistic laws, is an absolutely unpredictable event escaping the laws of causality (P2: 125). The interaction between atoms or molecules does not obey exact mechanical laws; it has a chance or random aspect – by which is meant not only what Aristotle opposed to finality, but also what is subject to objective probability theory (SB: 34).

For Popper, then, determinism lacks any foundation, because it is not sufficient to know enough to predict every single detail about everything in the world, even the composition of a symphony.

> The world, as we know it, is highly complex; and although it may possess structural aspects which are simple in some sense or other, the simplicity of some of our theories – which is of our own making – does not entail the intrinsic simplicity of the world.
>
> (P2: 43)

Of course, Popper is not here denying that certain events are predictable or that science is capable of making predictions (since that is precisely its task). But he does want to distinguish between causality and determinism: if we accept causality, we recognize the cause–effect relationship once it has been determined in respect, obviously, of the past; but determinism involves the further claim to know in advance the precise effects that will be produced if certain initial conditions are given. Now, whereas causality is compatible with the horizon of fallibilism, 'scientific' determinism is contradicted by the approximate character of all (including scientific) knowledge. A defence of indeterminism is thus perfectly consistent with Popper's epistemology which, as we know, does not provide for certain and incontrovertible knowledge but insists that knowledge is always hypothetical in its structure. 'We try to examine the world exhaustively by our nets; but its mesh will always let some small fish escape: there will always be enough play for indeterminism' (P2: 47). If this is so, we might also think that the approximative and provisional character of our knowledge derives from the finiteness of man and not from an intrinsic openness of the universe towards novelty. But in that case, there would no longer be that creative aspect which Popper finds not only in man but in the whole of evolution.

Among the arguments for indeterminism, the second in importance is based upon the undeniable asymmetry between past and future. The past cannot be changed or even affected by any human decision; but although the future may be largely the result of the past, we constantly try to influence it with our present actions, because we think of it as still open (P2: 55–56; P3: 204; WP: 18). Interestingly enough, Popper seems won over by the idea that our actions are not constrained by determining causes but stimulated by the goals we set ourselves. For:

> it is not the kicks from the back, from the past, that *impel* us but the attraction, the lure of the future and its competing possibilities, that *attract* us, that *entice* us. This is what keeps life – and, indeed, the world – unfolding.
>
> (WP: 20–21)

To strengthen this thesis, Popper invokes the special theory of relativity, which postulates for every observer an absolute past and an absolute future, in accordance with Minkowski's four-dimensional double cone (Figure 4.3) (P2: 57).

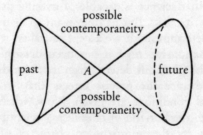

Figure 4.3

In this diagram A represents the present moment, the here-and-now to whose left lies the past and to whose right lies the future. The asymmetry consists in the possibility that a physical causal chain from the past may reach some point in the future, whereas an analogous effect cannot present itself between any point in the future and any point in the past (P2: 58). Hence:

> it may be said that, according to special relativity, the past is that region which can, in principle, be known; and the future is that region which, although influenced by the present, is always 'open': it is not only unknown, but in principle not fully knowable, since by becoming completely known, even to a demon, it would become part of the demon's past.
>
> (P2: 61)

A third argument for indeterminism is based on the fact that it is impossible to predict the results obtained through the growth of knowledge, since 'there cannot be a scientist able to predict [*from within*] all the results of his own predictions' (P2: 63). Evidently, if we predict today the ideas that will occur in the mind next month, then those ideas will present themselves to consciousness today and not in a month – therefore we could not have predicted correctly (P2: 65). In this sense, the Socratic ideal summarized in the injunction 'Know thyself!' proves to be unattainable. We cannot fully know ourselves or our limitations – at least those which define knowledge – because the solution of old problems inevitably raises fresh ones of which we cannot say if or when they will be solved (P2: 107).

A variant of this argument that is of some interest points to the impossibility of scientific self-prediction – that someone might deductively predict the results of his own calculations or forecasts. We may, of course, postulate non-scientific self-prediction, because this would not be based upon a universal theory but would also involve the mediation of the will in the process of reaching a decision (P2: 68). The impossibility of scientific self-prediction, however, is confirmed by the very successes of science in relation to systems barely influenced by the predictive process. None of this is sufficient to refute determinism, which Popper does not think possible to refute through pure logic. But it does serve to exclude 'scientific' determinism and to leave room for at least one non-predetermined event, and it does this precisely by appealing to the existence of rational knowledge, since 'there is a logical difficulty in considering rationality as predetermined, or as rationally predictable' (P2: 85).

To show that prediction is impossible from within the world does not automatically exclude the possibility that the world seen from outside – perhaps by the divinity – is predetermined. Such is the hypothesis put forward by metaphysical determinism, which cannot be refuted any more than can metaphysical indeterminism, because there is no way of demonstrating that there is not at least one undetermined event in the world, just as there is no way of excluding the existence of a spirit who enjoys full foreknowledge about the world (P2: 88). Popper remembers a conversation in which Einstein once spoke to him in favour of a determinism 'which amounted to the view that the world was a four-dimensional Parmenidean block universe in which change was a human illusion, or very nearly so' (UQ: 129). Popper opposes this on two grounds: he appeals to experience, which offers nothing to bear out a Parmenidean metaphysic; and he argues that the consequences of such a view would anyway be difficult to accept. For if it is inferred that the future is wholly contained in the past and hence quite redundant, we would have to conclude that the time we experience is an illusion, that 'time's arrow' is merely subjective, that there is not any particular direction in which time is flowing. Relating this argument to the work of Boltzmann and Zermelo (UQ: 156–162), Popper gave it a great deal of thought and published a number of contributions of his own in the 1950s and 1960s in *Nature* and the *British Journal for the Philosophy of Science*.

Popper's last point against the Parmenidean metaphysic stresses that even if the world were unchanging, there would be at least one changeable thing: namely, the conscious experience of human beings (P2: 91–92). Consequently, he declares himself in favour of an indeterminism even more radical than Heisenberg's, because it includes the thesis that classical physics is itself indeterminist (OK: 296). For physical indeterminism 'is merely the doctrine that *not all* events in the physical world are predetermined with absolute precision, in all their infinitesimal details' (OK: 220). And so convinced is Popper of the obstacles to exact predetermination or prediction of any event that he considers himself in agreement with Peirce, when he said that to some degree all clocks are clouds, and not vice versa (OK: 213; SB: 22; OGOU: 97).

To understand this seemingly hermetic assertion, we need to look at Popper's article 'Clouds and Clocks' (1965), reprinted in *Objective Knowledge*. First, let us remind ourselves that for common sense all events can be divided into two broad categories: those which are more or less clock-like in their predictability, and those which resemble the motion of clouds in the difficulty or rareness of their predictability. Clouds, then, 'represent physical systems which, like gases, are highly irregular, disorderly, and more or less unpredictable'; whereas clocks are the model of 'physical systems which are regular, orderly, and highly predictable in their behaviour' (OK: 207). In an ideal schema, clouds and clocks would be the two extremes towards which the various natural phenomena more or less approximate: for example, the seasons are more like clocks than clouds, but do not offer the same degree of predictability and precision; animals are closer to clouds, and plants to clocks; a cluster of gnats moving in an irregular way is very near indeed to clouds.

Now, Newtonian physics appeared to have firmly established that all clouds are clocks – that the world is physically determined and that the distinction between clouds and clocks does not reflect the nature of things but only our ignorance with regard to certain phenomena (OK: 211). Newton's physics did not, of course, draw quite those conclusions, but they were drawn by many followers of the great English scientist, so that in a world imagined as a 'huge and highly precise clockwork', there was no place for human decisions (WP: 7).

One of the rare dissidents in the period before 1927 was C.S. Peirce. He too believed that the world was a clock, but he denied that it was perfect down to the smallest detail; alongside Newtonian laws, the imperfection of any clock brings into play an element involving the laws of chance, disorder or statistical probability (OK: 212–213).

Others, such as Schlick, feared that the only alternative to determinism was pure chance; and to them Popper replied that 'what we need for understanding human behaviour – and indeed, animal behaviour – is something intermediate in character between perfect chance and perfect determinism – something intermediate between perfect clouds and perfect clocks' (OK: 228). Here the metaphysical question – in both the Popperian and the classical sense – turns into an ethical question. For Popper's question is really 'how such non-physical things as purposes, deliberations, plans, decisions, theories, intentions, and values, can play a part in bringing about physical changes in the physical world' (OK: 229). In other words, physical determinism is rejected on the grounds that it does away with the ideas of creativity and human freedom. But if it is true that some things happen which are not completely predetermined, then it is possible to find the necessary space for human intervention in the world (OGOU: 97). Indeterminism is necessary for this purpose, but it is not sufficient (OK: 230); as Popper entitles his afterword to volume two of the *Postscript*, 'indeterminism is not enough'. To leave space for human freedom and to make it understandable, we have to allow for causal actions that go from World 1 towards World 2, from World 2 to World 3, and vice versa (P2: 114, 127).

Our universe takes on a pluralist shape even in relations between events that actually happen: it is partly causal, partly probabilistic, and partly open; in short, 'it is emergent' (P2: 130). And there is no way of explaining life, with its incredible complexity and inexhaustible richness, unless we admit the creativity of the universe (P2: 171) and its highest expression in the products of human activity. Popper goes so far as to say that human freedom, while transcending nature, is part of nature itself (P2: 130). It is intrinsic to human beings in the same way as their capacity for speech, for example; but at the same time, just as language transcends its origin in nature and gives rise to the higher functions of culture, so is human freedom something which cannot be explained in purely biological terms. The exercise of freedom is intimately bound up with the creative capacity that makes it possible to develop not only new theories but also decisions or ways of thinking and behaving that have never existed before. The existence of creativity, at least at a human level, is demonstrated beyond doubt by the genius of a Mozart or Beethoven, an Einstein or Boltzmann. But on close observation, it can be seen in every human being, who is constantly finding original paths even in the simplest mental activities. Creativity manifests itself everywhere, even in what is thought of as induction; for simply by saying that all swans are white, reason goes far beyond what it has passively registered (OGOU: 62). These considerations are sufficient for Popper to conclude that the world is creative, because it 'has created a Mozart capable of creating the-works-of-Mozart' (OGOU: 63). And behind that, a proof of cosmic creativity is the fact that life once did not exist and then began to exist after a certain moment (OGOU: 64). We could also say, drawing on Prigogine's image of a bifurcation, that the same premises can lead through different tendencies to at least two different results (OGOU: 64–65); only thanks to the principle of creativity – which is also the principle of non-determinism – is it possible for new things to come into being. Popper is firmly convinced that science itself confirms the image of an inventive universe, 'in which new things emerge, on new levels' (NSEM: 342). For although science has attacked the view that reality is due to the miraculous intervention of a creator, it has 'left us with the marvel of the creativeness of the universe' (NSEM: 343).

To use a Kantian vocabulary, we might say that 'creativity is the a priori' (OGOU: 73); life itself is the context in which human affairs unravel and the emergence of the new becomes possible. The a priori should be understood, however, not in a rigidly Kantian sense but as a 'hypothesis to master the world' (OGOU: 71), so that the a posteriori is given from without while the a priori comes from within. For 'I see a posteriori that many swans are white. But the conclusion that *all* swans are white is an a priori reaction. We carry in our brain the law: thou shalt generalize' (OGOU: 72) – even though it is sometimes refuted by experience.

Popper's reasoning may thus be summed up as follows. If the world were a closed physical system, there would be no room for creativity and human freedom; but neither can one appeal to the indeterminacy of quantum theory, which leads to chance rather than freedom (OK: 254–255). We must therefore postulate that the world is a physical system open to the influence of World 2 and, indirectly, of World 3 (SB: 540). If the universe is open, there is a place for human freedom and creativity – but in that case the future will be open: it will not necessarily be like the past, but to some extent at least can be rationally decided.

Eccles, in full agreement with Popper, adds a further comment.

> If physical determinism is true, then that is the end of all discussion or argument; everything is finished. There is no philosophy. All human persons are caught up in this inexorable web of circumstances and cannot break out of it. Everything that we think we are doing is an illusion and that is that. Will anybody live up to this situation?
>
> (SB: 546)

We should note here that neither Popper nor Eccles really offers any proof in favour of human freedom; their arguments are based on a wish to avert a situation that seems to them undesirable. To conclude: it would appear that Popper is concerned to support indeterminism so as to leave space for human freedom, not because there is any evidence of it, but because without the possibility of self-determination, our situation as human beings – in which we behave as if we were free – would be no more than a tragic farce. Popper might object that the very use of reason speaks in favour of freedom of the will, since there would be no point in discussing with someone who was not free to make choices and decisions. But all this would prove is that rational argument is one of the factors determining human action. In the end, therefore, it would seem to be moral motives that carry the greatest weight in Popper's apology for human freedom. When the ageing philosopher declared that there are propensities and tendencies to realization which determinism is not prepared to admit, because it is stubbornly rooted to the idea that there is nothing new under the sun, he was essentially appealing to the human will, to a moral and not theoretical aspect of the individual. Unlike the determinist, he *wanted* to think of himself and his fellow-humans as being free; it is an aspiration that we have no difficulty in sharing, and would simply add – in line with Popper's own treatment – that it does not have any theoretical foundation.

Nevertheless, on the basis of this conviction Popper worked out a new cosmology. He only saw that one was possible towards the end of his life, but he had already for some time had the pivotal theoretical insight that 'the world is not a causal machine – it can now be seen as a world of propensities, as an unfolding process of realizing possibilities and of unfolding new possibilities' (WP: 18–19).

This conception is not compatible with determinism, because our own understanding of the world, and our choices that favour one possibility over another, modify the conditions of the world that is changing. Consequently, 'all properties of the physical world are dispositional, and the real state of a physical system, at any moment, may be conceived as the sum total of its dispositions – or its potentialities, or possibilities, or propensities' (P3: 159). Popper maintains that this doctrine – which could be expressed in the statement, 'Everything is a propensity' – synthesizes aspects dealt with in all the main metaphysical research programmes over the centuries, from Parmenides to the statistical interpretation of quantum physics (P3: 161–164, 205–208).

From the new propensity cosmology, Popper extracted ideas which went beyond physics and engaged with the problem of the organization of living matter in the individual. Sometimes this took in biological processes which, from the point of view of physics, often proved to be unexpected if not downright improbable, as if certain intrinsic propensities became actual by transcending the physical world and superimposing a hierarchy of ends. The elderly philosopher theorizing the universal radiation of propensity had travelled a long way since the composition of the *Logic of Scientific Discovery*. But in reality, his 'metaphysical epilogue' kept faith with the idea he had tenaciously upheld since his early opposition to Vienna Circle neo-positivism – namely, that science cannot do without metaphysics. Even if we admit – as Popper was the first to do – that his world-view was ultimately a picture or dream, rather than a testable theory, we should not forget that 'science needs these pictures' and that they 'largely determine its problem situations' (P3: 210).

Part III

5

THEMES AND MOTIFS

SCIENCE AS A SEARCHLIGHT

'I see in science one of the greatest creations of the human mind' (OK: 84), 'a magnificent adventure of the human spirit' (OK: 361). 'Science is not only, like art and literature, an adventure of the human spirit, but it is among the creative arts perhaps the most human' (P1: 259); on the other hand, science is nothing but 'enlightened common sense' (WP: 49) and 'suffers from our human fallibility, like every other human enterprise' (WP: 6).

By plucking such phrases from his various works, it is possible to synthesize Popper's conception of science, in which its results are never 'certain' because they do not spring magically from data, facts and observations that are free from any possibility of deformation [ibid.]. Science is, more modestly, the result of people's efforts to understand the world and themselves – hence its restructuring, as it loses much of its centuries-old authority; but hence also its greater flexibility, and a realization that it is part of the human creativity once reserved for the arts. This creative aspect strikes one immediately when one thinks that science invents theories on the basis of problems, and that the data would not yield anything if human beings were unable to connect and structure them in such a way that they provided an explanation of events and a plausible solution to the problem in question. This operation also involves the by no means neutral processing of what is given, the highlighting of certain aspects and the disregarding of others in accordance with the investigator's point of view. In this sense, 'science may be described as the art of systematic over-simplification – the art of discerning what we may with advantage omit' (P2: 44).

On the basis of these premises, it should not be difficult to understand the metaphor of science as a searchlight.

> What the searchlight makes visible will depend upon its position, upon our way of directing it, and upon its intensity, colour, etc.; although it will, of course, also depend very largely upon the things illuminated by it. Similarly, a scientific description will depend, largely, upon our point of view, our interests, which are as a rule connected with the theory or hypothesis we wish to test; although it will also depend upon the facts described.
>
> (OS II: 490)

Clearly, this image is in sharp contrast with the classical theory of science as an accumulation of observations; it emphasizes the theoretical element (even if this comes from myth or a metaphysical doctrine) as the guide and criterion of observation. The searchlight theory implies that science has a dual role: it not only solves existing problems but also creates new ones; not only uses observations, but prompts others and encourages different ways of interpreting observations already made (CR: 128).

Taking a further step in this direction, Popper also defines science as the totality of theories 'which appear to us at a certain moment of time to be better approximations to truth than other known theories' (CR: vii). For just as the searchlight image gives us a way of conceiving science in terms of brightness or intensity, so does it convey the sense of the explanatory range or extent of a theory in relation to the world and its various interconnections.

We may next ask ourselves what is the actual *task* of science. Here Popper's answer is clear and concise, but perhaps for that very reason it will profit from a few remarks. 'The task of science is partly theoretical – explanation – and partly practical – prediction and technical application' (OK: 349).

When it is a question of pure knowledge, the main theoretical requirement is to find an explanation. But what exactly is an explanation? One current definition takes it as a reduction of the unknown to the known, but Popper is far from happy with such an answer; indeed, he would prefer to say that a scientific explanation is the reduction of the known to the *unknown*. For in pure as opposed to applied science, the aim is to reach a higher level of universality, and this involves reducing theories and known facts to more general assumptions of which very little is known as yet, and which require to be accurately tested (CR: 63). In short, if theories are nothing but conjectures, then evidently they will always offer a hypothetical explanation; they will start from known and accepted facts, and move towards conjectures which still have to demonstrate all their effectiveness.

An explanation is always a logical deduction from certain premisses (*explicans*) to a conclusion (*explicandum*). As the premisses are usually of two different types – universal laws and initial conditions – we may draw up the following schema of explanation (OK: 351):

U (Universal Law)   Premisses
I (Specific Initial Conditions)   (constituting the *Explicans*)
E (*Explicandum*)   Conclusion

With regard to the practical task of science, however, the movement is in the opposite direction. For while the *explicandum* is theoretically known, it is necessary to find the *explicans* to derive predictions or to make a technical application – in other words, the point now is to discover the logical consequences of a known theory (OK: 353).

Having defined the province of science and illustrated its forward path, we may try to describe the picture that emerges from Popper's thinking. The most characteristic features of science are for him its provisional, conjectural and objective character, and a method that results from combining empiricism and rationalism but is not identical with either of the two.

Ever since the first draft of *Die beiden Grundprobleme der Erkenntnistheorie*, Popper has maintained that 'empirical-scientific theories (*general* statements about reality) can only ever be *provisional assumptions*, anticipations lacking a foundation' (BG: 8). For, as we know, induction is not logically admissible, and so we can only accept 'the impossibility of making definitive our knowledge of reality' (BG: 101). Not even the empirical base of science can be considered unchangeable, as the basic statements, in order to be objective, must undergo intersubjective testing and are thus falsifiable in principle if some of their consequences prove to be false (LSD: 47).

The empirical basis of objective science has thus nothing 'absolute' about it. Science does not rest upon solid bedrock. The bold structure of its theories rises, as it were, above a swamp. It is like a building erected on piles. The piles are driven down from above into the swamp, but not down to any natural or 'given' base; and if we stop driving the piles deeper, it is not because we have reached firm ground. We simply stop when we are satisfied that the piles are firm enough to carry the structure, at least for the time being.

(LSD: 111)

We see why Popper can say that 'our science is not knowledge (*episteme*)' 'we do not know; we can only guess' (LSD: 278). Later, when commenting in the *Postscript* on the human desire to find an unchallenged authority in science, he stresses that 'it is all guesswork, *doxa* rather than *episteme*' (P1: 259). Science is conjectural because it is unable to hold reality fast, but this does not nullify the effort to obtain knowledge and to go on seeking the truth. Despite its hypothetical character, then, science is not a mere instrument; it retains a value that goes beyond sheer biological survival. It might be objected that as science sometimes claims to say true things and not just refutable things, Popper ought to recognize that it has a theoretical aspect which is not simply a matter of conjecture. But instead, he stresses that 'the old scientific ideal of *episteme* – of absolutely certain, demonstrable knowledge – has proved to be an idol' (LSD: 280); and that scientific advance is due not to the accumulation of irrefutable facts but to the attempted interpretation of nature through bold ideas and unjustified (though significant) anticipations. These need to be criticized and discussed, however, 'for it is not his *possession* of knowledge, of irrefutable truth, that makes the man of science, but his persistent and recklessly critical *quest* for truth' (LSD: 281).

Let us now consider another major aspect of Popper's epistemology, before turning to the theme of truth that was so dear to him. Notwithstanding the hypothetical character of science that makes of it relative knowledge, scientific theories are and should be objective, in a sense that needs to be carefully defined. In the first draft of the work that made Popper's name as a critic of logical positivism, he identified the absolute with that which can be cultivated only subjectively; all objective (universally valid) knowledge, on the other hand, is relative. In fact, Popper held that the Kantian concept of objectivity has relativistic implications, but that these have nothing to do with the banal relativism of those who assert that everything is relative (BG: 94–95). This latter position he regards as 'one of the many crimes committed by intellectuals' (ISBW: 5; WP: 5), which stems from a confusion of the idea of truth with the quite distinct one of certainty.

Now, unless we have misunderstood the dense pages packed with quotations that the young Popper devoted to the question, we can say that something is 'objective' when it has an a priori basis that does not coincide with empirical perception (which is itself subjective). But the objectivity of which Kant spoke is guaranteed only on condition that knowledge is held within anthropomorphic limits; that which is valid a priori, and hence objective, really belongs not to the object but to the limits of human knowledge. For Popper, as we have seen, the a priori element is not a guarantee of validity, but only of refutability and therefore rationality. Objectivity is due entirely to the fact that a given theory lends itself to criticism and discussion; and because of the asymmetry between truth and falsehood, scientific theories are relative insofar as truth is unattainable and we have to be content with approximations of varying worth. For 'the objectivity of science is necessarily acquired at the price of its relativity (and whoever wants the absolute must go and look for it in subjectivity)' (BG: 136). In sum, science is conjectural and relative, it is 'built on piles'; and the much-heralded 'scientific objectivity' is not even an attitude pertaining to the individual scientist, as he may be a victim of prejudice like any other human being. Rather, 'objectivity is closely bound up with the *social aspect of scientific method*' (OS II: 447), which emerges not from any individual working alone but from the cooperative effort of the scientific community to test hypotheses and track down errors. Thus, 'objectivity can be described as the inter-subjectivity of scientific method' [ibid.].

It follows that the impartiality of the individual scientist is not a condition for, but a result of, the objectivity of science. For it is not true that we cannot modify our own presuppositions, as Kant thought, but it is true that we cannot modify them all at the same time – and so the critical contribution of our partners in dialogue can be useful in the highest degree.

Finally, we should recall that this conception of science:

connects a rigorously deductivist standpoint with a rigorously empiricist one. Like rationalism, this conception also
assumes that the most general propositions (axioms) of

natural science are (initially) put forward without any logical or empirical justification. But, unlike in the procedure of rationalism, they are not here accepted as *true* a priori (on the basis of being evident) but are simply posited as *problematic*, as ungrounded anticipations or tentative assumptions (conjectures).

(BG: 15–16)

A little further on, Popper accepts that his critical rationalism has been founded upon the modern notion of geometry, just as classical rationalism drew its inspiration from the older notion. Empiricism serves as a complement to rationalism; for we must try to falsify a theory by subjecting it to experimental checks, if we are to maintain it once it has passed those tests.

This famous thesis did, however, seem to be implicitly discarded in some of Popper's later writings. In his dialogues with Eccles, for example, he went so far as to argue that the data of perception, before becoming conscious experience, are interpreted hundreds or even thousands of times by the nervous system (SB: 431). And already in a note to the first English edition of *The Logic of Scientific Discovery*, he pointed out that observations 'are always *interpretations* of the facts observed'; 'they are *interpretations in the light of theories*' (LSD: 107). Well may we wonder whether, after such elaborate processing, sense-data can still be treated in the same way as the perceptions of empiricist gnoseology. In other words, some doubt arises as to how much Popper manages to save from empiricism – at least as this has been understood within the Western philosophical tradition. His friend Lorenz seemed to agree with this conclusion, when he said during one of their discussions that 'everything we experience is determined by what we have inherited: because we have a certain number of theories in our brain from which we cannot distance ourselves' (ZO: 30).

If this is the shape of science for Popper, it is hardly surprising that he does not regard scientific method as a special route to success (because there are no such royal roads), or even as a way of justifying scientific results (because a scientific result 'ought to be testable, and criticizable, but it will not be capable of being shown to be true' (OK: 264)). Popper is concerned to ensure that the philosophy of science, on the pretext of improving and even perfecting the mechanism that produces scientific knowledge, does not become a fashion or a specialism. For the only interest of that mechanism for science and philosophy is to enable us 'to learn something about the riddle of the world in which we live, and the riddle of man's knowledge of that world' (LSD: 23). When he wrote those lines in 1959, in the new preface to the *Logic*, this view was to some extent shared by the ordinary-language philosophers dominant in the Anglo-Saxon countries. But Popper was also at pains to differentiate himself from their approach to the problems of knowledge.

According to analytic philosophy, because scientific knowledge is merely an extension of ordinary knowledge, all we have to do is analyse the language in which it is expressed and the main gnoseological problems will come to light. Popper agrees with the first part of this statement, but he thinks that the most stimulating problems of epistemology – such as the growth of knowledge itself – escape those whose purview is essentially that of commonsense knowledge (LSD: 18). Rather, epistemology 'should be identified with the theory of scientific method' (LSD: 49).

This view does not, however, range Popper among those whose idea of studying 'the language of science' is to construct artificial models without significance either for science or for common sense (LSD: 21–22). He prefers to side with 'those who do not pledge themselves in advance to any philosophical method, and who make use, in epistemology, of the analysis of scientific problems, theories and procedures, and, most important, of scientific discussions'. In this group are numbered all the great Western philosophers, including Kant, Mill, Peirce, Duhem and Russell, who would fully agree that scientific knowledge is but a development of pre-scientific knowledge, but would also insist that it 'can be studied more easily than commonsense knowledge' (LSD: 22).

Popper, then, not only places science at the centre of his thinking; he accompanies his analyses of it with a series of remarks about the philosophy of science, and more generally the theory of knowledge, in an attempt to grasp the main mechanisms that make possible any form of human knowledge. The fundamental task of the theory of knowledge is thus to analyse the typical procedure of empirical science; it is 'a theory of what is usually called "experience"' (LSD: 39). But the empirical sciences are themselves nothing other than systems of theories, and so the logic of scientific knowledge may be said to develop a 'theory of theories' (LSD: 59) in which epistemological and psychological questions are kept clearly distinct. The former concern the foundation, legitimacy and validity of scientific theories – the *quid iuris?* – while the latter address the way in which knowledge is actually acquired, at the moment of discovery rather than justification – the *quid facti?* (BG: 4–5). In keeping with this premiss, Popper rebuts the charge made against him by Kuhn and Feyerabend in particular: namely, that the very history of science shows him to be wrong in arguing that methodology, rather than an empirical discipline, is 'a philosophical – a metaphysical – discipline, perhaps partly even a normative proposal' (P1: xxv).

Reflection about science therefore has a legitimacy of its own, quite apart from what actually *happens* in scientific tests and laboratories. And strange though it may seem, the basis for this statement is to be found in what Popper considers the *differentia specifica* of science – its concern for the truth, as the aim constantly before it. On the one hand, it is true that 'reason works by trial and error' (CR: 192), whether in creating myths or in developing scientific theories, which, like myths, are human inventions, 'nets designed by us to catch the world' (P2: 42). But it is also true that 'theories are seen to be the *free* creations of our own minds, the result of an almost poetic intuition, of an attempt to understand intuitively the laws of nature' (CR: 192). They differ from myths, and from the inventions of poets or technicians, in that their qualifying (if unattainable) goal is always the truth. It is true that theories are our inventions, but this has nothing to do with their scientific status, which depends upon such factors as simplicity, symmetry and explanatory power (P3: 41).

Before looking more closely at what characterizes a scientific theory, it may be useful to focus for a moment on a theme which Popper always thought of as closely linked to that of science, but which he never explicitly analysed: that is to say, the nature and value of metaphysics. We have seen that Popper consistently defended the meaningfulness of metaphysical discourse against the arrows of logical positivism; that he looked on it as a kind of embryo of science, and indeed thought some metaphysical ideas to be inevitable, if only in the form of a research programme; but that he also considered any metaphysical doctrine to be distinct from a scientific hypothesis. It would appear, however, that in the *Postscript* Popper changed his mind on this question. Now, he writes:

I look upon a metaphysical theory as similar to a scientific one. It is vaguer, no doubt, and inferior in many other respects; and its irrefutability, or lack of testability, is its greatest vice. But, *as long as a metaphysical theory can be rationally criticized*, I should be inclined to take seriously its implicit claim to be considered, tentatively, as true.

(P3: 199)

Popper goes on to explain that a theory may be considered rational if it attempts to solve certain problems and if it can be discussed in the context of the relevant problem situation. Whether it is metaphysical or scientific is not all that important: what counts is the way in which it solves the problems that gave rise to it, especially when it does this better than other theories with the same aim (P3: 199–200). There is thus a new criterion of demarcation within metaphysics, between systems devoid of rational value and systems worth discussing and thinking about. In the latter case:

the proper aspiration of a metaphysician [...] is to gather all the true aspects of the world (and not merely its scientific aspects) into a unifying picture which may enlighten him and others, and which one day may become part of a still more comprehensive picture, a better picture, a truer picture. The criterion, then, will be fundamentally the same as in the sciences.

(P3: 211)

Popper recognizes that what he has put forward is a 'metaphysical dream', based upon the non-scientific (because irrefutable) idea of indeterminism; but science has use for this dream and feeds on its pictures, which end up largely determining problem situations (P3: 198–199, 210–211). Nor does this dream claim the force of dogma; it is quite open to discussion and to comparison with rival conceptions that it intends to supplant. But 'the comparison should be in terms of simplicity, coherence with certain other theories, unifying power, intuitive appeal and, above all, fruitfulness' (P3: 201).

The difference between a scientific theory and an imaginary construct is entirely a matter of intent; the theory is 'inspired by the ideal of finding true solutions to its problems: solutions which correspond to the facts' (OK: 290; P3: 42). On the other hand, the notion of truth is implicit in the idea of objective knowledge, because a statement is objective – i.e. criticizable and refutable –

133

precisely insofar as a judgement can be made about its correspondence to, or at least its distance from, the truth. In this sense, truth – or rather, progressive approximation to the truth – is the 'general aim of rational discussion' (OK: 17), and not just of scientific knowledge. Popper may perhaps be accused of inconsistency in failing to draw all the consequences that follow from this principle. But he certainly cannot be accused of failing to see that the notion of truth is central to knowledge. For he clearly rejects the 'now so fashionable view that human knowledge can only be understood as an instrument in our struggle for survival' (OK: 264); and insists that science is a continual striving towards the truth, because 'truth is the fundamental value. What we cannot attain is certainty' (ZO: 51), or better, the certainty of having found the truth.

It might be said here that Popper still seems fixed on the thoroughly modern idea of an opposition between certainty and truth, which Descartes resolved by grounding truth not on certainty but on the overcoming of doubt. But Popper maintained that a pre-Socratic like Xenophanes already distinguished between objective truth (which is the coincidence of a statement with the factual data) and subjective certainty. Thus we can have convictions which, though wrong, are no less deeply rooted at a personal-psychological level, just as we can remain doubtful in the face of logically grounded truths; indeed, such is the normal psychological condition of the honest researcher, who can never be sure of having achieved some degree of truth (ISBW: 195). Contemporary thought mostly tackles the dilemma by denying truth in favour of certainty – or rather, by contenting itself with subjective certainties, until they are undermined by other, more convincing ones. Popper, for his part, is prepared to sacrifice certainty but not to give up truth; he defends this against scepticism by arguing that 'the concept of doubt already presupposes the concept of truth' (BG: 92), and by endorsing Wittgenstein's view that 'scepticism is *not* irrefutable, but palpably senseless, if it would doubt where a question cannot be asked'.[1]

At this point, it may be asked how it is possible to abandon all claim to certainty without also repudiating truth. Popper's answer is almost disarming in its simplicity: truth is elusive but is useful as a 'regulative principle' (CR: 226, 229f.). No theory, not even Tarski's much-admired account, is able to furnish a criterion of truth, because there is no such criterion. Yet it is clear that, whatever certain doctrines teach, truth cannot be confused with coherence or usefulness, since that is not the meaning which common sense attaches to the concept of truth – in a court of law, for example, where witnesses are asked to tell the whole truth and nothing but the truth. Closest to this commonsense usage is the correspondence notion of truth, most fully developed by Tarski (OK: 324), which manages to explain the fact that 'a theory may be true even though nobody believes it, and even though we have no reason to think that it is true; and another theory may be false even though we have comparatively good reasons for accepting it' (CR: 225).

The only point on which Popper diverges from common sense and the classical tradition (which both see truth as the end of all knowledge) is in relation to the possession of truth; for he sees man as tirelessly seeking after truth, but never as being in possession of it (OK: 47). There is no point in objecting that we can never test the acquisition of some indisputable truth, because what counts for Popper is certainly not self-evident truth that no one would ever dream of questioning, but 'interesting and enlightening truth' (OK: 55). Such truth is not manifest (PH: 157) and is 'hard to come by' (CR: 375), but we cannot do without it. For only if we stand by the idea that truth is beyond all human authority, can we appeal to 'objective standards of scientific inquiry' – otherwise any thirst for knowledge and any attempt to penetrate the unknown would be to no avail (ISBW: 51). Without this regulative ideal, it would be difficult to maintain the distinction between subjective and objective knowledge that was already so significant in Popper's epistemology before he formulated the theory of World 3. Thus, in *The Logic of Scientific Discovery*, he used the terms 'objective' and 'subjective' in a sense 'not unlike' Kant's, meaning by the former the characteristic whereby a statement is intersubjectively tested or criticizable, under 'mutual rational control by critical discussion' (LSD: 44). The distinction is also necessary, because scientific knowledge cannot be identified with the subjective knowledge of any scientist, however brilliant or erudite he might be (P1: 102).

KANT AND POPPER

Popper recognized that his conception of science underlined and integrated the acceptable elements of Kantianism (OS II: 736–737).

He declared himself a Kantian and, at least in his early days as a philosopher, thought that his critique of the Vienna Circle 'was simply the result of his having read Kant, and of having understood some of his main points' (UQ: 83). For in his view, one of the two fundamental problems of knowledge – that of the demarcation between science and metaphysics – had come to occupy its central position thanks to the author of the *Critique of Pure Reason* (LSD: 34). Popper could not conceal his opinion of Kant as 'one of the most admirable men we read about in history: completely honest, completely dedicated to knowledge' (ZO: 104), although he did not forget that the *chef d'oeuvre* of the Königsberg philosopher not only 'rested upon a misunderstanding' but also had led to the identification, at least in Germany, of the concepts 'hard to understand' and 'profound'.

Despite these qualifications, Kant's influence on Popper was enormous. It would appear to have especially involved two areas of great importance: the critical philosophy (which the Viennese philosopher intended thoroughly to revise), and the role of theory or of the a priori in knowledge. On the latter point, it is enough to recall that Popper, like Kant, was convinced of the existence of an a priori and of our imposition of order and structure on the world; but that, unlike Kant, he did not think these were necessarily valid a priori. Indeed, he reproached Kant for not being sufficiently Socratic, for not having understood well enough that we do not know anything (ZO: 68). Whereas Hume wrongly thought that we are unable to overcome our prejudices and beliefs through rational critique, Kant's error was in a sense the opposite: he thought that the theoretical apparatus we use to criticize our beliefs cannot itself be subjected to critical examination, but must be valid a priori (P1: 155; ISBW: 40). The *Critique of Pure Reason* sought to show that Newton's theory was true, whereas for Popper it is only a 'grand hypothesis' which we can never know to be true or false. He agrees with Kant's brilliant idea that it is not nature which dictates its laws but we ourselves who impose them on nature, but he does not think it necessary to conclude that our theories are valid a priori and incapable of being refuted (P1: 153). In other words, Kant 'was right to believe that knowledge was genetically or psychologically a priori, but quite wrong to suppose that any knowledge could be a priori valid' (UQ: 60; CR: 93–96; WP: 45). For Popper, the a priori is the indispensable and originating element in any form of knowledge, but not, as it was for Kant, the guarantee of its objectivity (OK: 24). Kant 'proved too much' (CR: 48) by building knowledge on a priori truth, instead of recognizing that it involved hypotheses which, as such, could be false (ZO: 31). In his early work, Popper makes the same point by arguing that Kant confused the psychological and the epistemological a priori (BG: 96); for although knowledge may be psychogenetically prior to experience, it is not apodeictic and its validity is ultimately dependent upon experience (BG: 106; CR: 47). Knowledge is a priori in respect of content, since we formulate our hypotheses without having recourse to induction; experience plays an important role in the phase not of formulating but of testing and eliminating conjectures, and our knowledge remains a priori if these should clash with reality (EE: 29–31). Popper therefore accepts the a priori, but he rejects the doctrine of apriorism according to which we can make scientific statements without subjecting them to empirical tests. Popper's a priori should not be thought of as a new version of innate ideas – a theory he dismisses as absurd. But he does accept that 'every organism has inborn reactions or responses' (CR: 47); each one of us, before reaching the conscious phase of life, has innate expectations which are not valid a priori and may prove false, however strong and specific they may be. For instance, Popper considers the instinctive expectation of the regularity of nature to be not only psychologically but also logically a priori – for, as we know, it guides any recognition of similarity and repetition – but it is not thereby *valid* a priori. In one of his last lectures, the theorist of critical rationalism clarified his use of the terms 'a priori' and 'a posteriori': the former referred to 'that kind of knowledge – of fallible or conjectural knowledge – which an organism has prior to sense experience'; and the latter to 'knowledge that is obtained with the help of the sensitivity of the organism to momentary changes in the state of its environment' (WP: 46).

What really counts in Kant's apriorism, however, is the assertion that not all knowledge comes a posteriori from observation and experience, that the knowing subject also makes a contribution by putting into knowledge what no sense perception could ever furnish – for example, the discovery of a connection between different phenomena, or of a general law supposedly holding for cases not yet observed. Popper is in no doubt: 'the creative is the a priori' (OGOU: 71, 73). For the presuppositions of thought are a priori insofar as they are our inventions; 'the a priori is a mutation through which we try to master the world' (OGOU: 71), and the world tells us a posteriori whether we chose the wrong path or whether there is some hope that we took the right one. For all these reasons, Popper argues that 'Kant anticipated the most important results of the evolutionary theory of knowledge' (WP: 46), but that it is necessary to go even further than Kant: for '99 per cent of the knowledge of all organisms is inborn and incorporated in our biochemical constitution' (WP: 46; EE: 36). This does not mean that the individual does not have an important function in the acquisition of knowledge: on the contrary, every new theory is a product of the knowing subject, an invention whose origin lies in the discovery of a new problem; and so the mind, far from possessing innate knowledge, is constantly straining to revise its cognitive inheritance (WP: 48–49). The really important point for Popper is that 'on every level, making comes before matching; that is, before selecting. The creation of an expectation, of an anticipation, of a perception (which is a hypothesis) *preceded* its being put to the test' (NSEM: 355).

One cannot help remarking that Popper's critical rationalism is somehow similar to Kant's critical philosophy: both attempted to rethink the situation of human knowledge on the basis of contemporary science, which in Kant's time was dominated by Newtonian physics and which is today a more intricate and altogether more problematic venture. In 1983, Popper stated once more that 'the real linchpin' of his ideas about human knowledge was fallibilism and the critical approach, which were what distinguished it from animal knowledge (P1: xxxv). Thanks to language, the possibility of expressing knowledge in statements allows us to be conscious of it and to make it 'objectively criticizable by arguments and by tests' [ibid.]. Criticism is, in a sense, the reverse side of truth. For although Popper demarcates science from myth by virtue of its regard for the truth, he adds in the *Postscript* that 'scientific theories are distinguished from myths merely in being criticizable, and in being open to modifications in the light of criticism' (P1: 7; CR: 127). Perhaps it would not be too imprecise to say that criticism is the instrument with which we try to draw closer to the truth and even to lay hold of it, although it remains impossible to rest upon a foundation of certainty. Criticism, then, is the supporting pillar of scientific method (P1: 7); the dogmatic attitude, by contrast, strives to verify and confirm suppositions (CR: 49).

If it is said that rational criticism too must base itself on some non-demonstrable assumptions, Popper replies that 'our criticism is, indeed, never conclusive' because we often work with baseless and unjustifiable presuppositions, but that this does not worry the critical rationalist, who is well aware that his own arguments are conjectural and open to criticism. Despite this lack of a certain foundation, there is no infinite regress because only the demand for demonstration or justification would actually lead to one; the critical rationalist feels no need to arrive at an endpoint of discussion (P1: 28–29; LSD: 104). In other words, Popper cannot be accused of not having grounded his own presuppositions, precisely because he makes no claim to have done so; his criticism is content to show that a given assumption may be not-false. Obviously, there is also what we might call 'logical' criticism, which employs methods other than empirical experiment and falsification, and which, to use Popper's categories, may be either immanent or transcendent. Immanent critique seeks to show that a theory does not adequately solve the problems it has set itself, or that it contains inconsistencies which make it unreliable (P1: 29–30). Transcendent critique, on the other hand, tries to show the superiority of a rival theory by lodging objections from its distinctive standpoint (P1: 30).

The thrust of these arguments is that Popper does not exclusively accept the 'principle of empiricism', according to which the adoption or rejection of scientific theories should depend upon the results of observation and experiment. He proposes instead the 'principle of rationalism', according to which the adoption or rejection of scientific theories should depend upon 'our critical reasoning (combined with the results of observation and experiment' (P1: 32). If this is a plausible procedure, then Popper's critical rationalism – together with the critical empiricism he also supports – is no more than 'the finishing touch to Kant's own critical philosophy' (CR: 27), underlining the sense of human fallibility which has always been a mark of great thinkers since the time of Socrates.

It was in C.S. Peirce that Popper found the first use of the term 'fallibilism', which he uses to denote this Socratic view of all human knowledge as uncertain. Indeed, fallibilism may be regarded as the *leitmotiv* of Popper's whole gnoseology: not only did he insist on it in everything he wrote; he directly linked it to the idea of an objective truth in relation to which we can recognize our errors. Thus it should not be seen as a pessimistic doctrine, for it theorizes the possibility of correcting our mistakes and implies the idea of objective, absolute truth. At the same time, fallibilism avoids lapsing into a position of arrogance, because it is acutely aware that the truth towers so far above us that we can never identify ourselves with it; what we can hope to do is gain some little scraps of truth.[2]

> This doctrine implies that we may seek for truth, for objective truth, though more often than not we may miss it by a wide margin. And it implies that if we respect truth, we must search for it by persistently searching for our errors: by indefatigable rational criticism, and self-criticism.
>
> (CR: 16)

Of course, the critical approach cannot be applied indiscriminately to all knowledge at the same moment: when we question one idea, we must at least provisionally accept a number of others that make up what Popper calls our 'background knowledge' – and which may in turn be critically examined at another moment.

> But almost all of the vast amount of background knowledge which we constantly use in any informal discussion will, for practical reasons, necessarily remain unquestioned; and the misguided attempt to question it all – that is to say, *to start from scratch* – can easily lead to the breakdown of critical debate.
>
> (CR: 238)

For Popper, then, the key gnoseological values are twofold: truth and the critical approach. And it is the latter which differentiates human from animal knowledge: between the amoeba and Einstein there is only one step, but it is a decisive step, because 'Einstein places himself in a *critical* relationship to his own solutions to problems' (ZO: 53). Although both apply the method of trial and error, 'the amoeba dislikes to err while Einstein is intrigued by it: he consciously searches for his errors in the hope of learning by their discovery and elimination' (OK: 70; WP: 51). Besides, the amoeba has to pay for its mistakes with physical elimination, whereas evolution has led man to master a language in which to express theories, so that human error is reflected in mistaken theory in a way that is not usually life-threatening (ISBW: 21).

Popper's two main theses in gnoseology may be summarized as:

(a) we are fallible but can learn from our mistakes; and (b) we cannot justify our theories, but we can rationally criticize and so improve them (OK: 265). It is a theory of knowledge which, on the one hand, grasps the finite nature of human thinking, and on the other hand, exalts the grandeur that we find in creativity, the growth of knowledge, and the active, not merely passive, role of our mental faculties in the learning process.

Popper is by no means unaware of the paradox implicit in his epistemology, but instead of trying to avoid it, he considers it fruitful for the advance of science and knowledge in general. He argues both that 'our knowledge is vast and impressive' and that 'our ignorance is boundless and overwhelming'.

> Both of these theses are true, and their clash characterizes our knowledge-situation. The tension between our knowledge and our ignorance is decisive for the growth of knowledge. It inspires the advance of knowledge, and it determines its ever-moving frontiers.
>
> (MF: 100)

The chief merit of Kant and his 'Copernican revolution' is to have finally shown that, although our location in the universe is irrelevant, there is a sense in which the world revolves around us; for 'we are discoverers: and discovery is a creative art' (ISBW: 132). Similarly, Kant was able to demonstrate that even ordinary experience, and' not just scientific experiment, goes beyond any observation, because 'everyday experience too must *interpret* observation; for without theoretical interpretation, observation remains blind – uninformative' (CR: 190).

THE ACTIVE MIND

It should now be clear that for Popper, the knowing subject plays a far from passive role in the acquiring of knowledge. He therefore openly polemicizes against adherents of the 'bucket theory of the mind', which 'views the mind as a bucket and the senses as funnels through which the bucket can be slowly filled by observations' (P1: 99). In this commonsense view, nothing happens to the mind unless it has first passed through the senses, and our expectations are merely the result of repeated observations made in the past (OK: 3).

The success of this theory is due to the extreme simplicity of its statement that we have only to open our eyes and look around us in order to know the world. Empiricist philosophers – of whom Hume is the prime example – have traditionally embraced this commonsense claim and shown a special liking for the metaphor of the *tabula rasa*, in which the mind is conceived as a kind of empty blackboard or unexposed photographic plate ready to be engraved with sense perceptions. A pedagogic variant of this theory reduces the learning process to the application of a funnel, so that the mind is still a container into which knowledge can more easily be poured. 'Our pedagogy consists in pouring answers into children without their having asked questions, and the questions they do ask are not listened to' (ZO: 52).

Popper does not deny that without our senses we would have no knowledge of the reality around us, but he does disagree with the view that all knowledge 'enters our intellect through our senses' (P1: 98) – even if this is amended so that the recipient, rather than being empty, is endowed from birth with something like a computer programme (OK: 61). In asserting that all knowledge is a modification of previous knowledge, Popper does not fear an infinite regress, because 'knowledge goes back, ultimately, to inborn knowledge, and to animal knowledge in the sense of expectations' (SB: 425). This should be enough to dispel any doubt that he wishes to rehabilitate the theory of innate ideas, and should also underline the need to revise the scope of sense experience in the flow of knowledge.

That the senses do not at all have the special role often attributed to them, is shown by the existence of someone like Helen Keller, who, though defective in what are for us the most important senses – sight and hearing – still achieved a correct and complete interpretation of reality (SB: 429). Only with this approach can we 'avoid being mere passive receivers of information' throughout our life (SB: 435). Popper refers here to an experiment mentioned by Eccles in the second part of *The Self and Its Brain*, which tends to show the importance of active participation by the knowing subject in all learning processes. Take two kittens from the same litter, leaving one free to explore its surroundings and suspending the other in a kind of gondola that is moved around by the first in the course of its explorations. Tests will then show that after a few weeks, the active kitten will have learnt to utilize its visual fields to obtain reliable pictures of the world, while the other will not have learnt anything (SB: 404–405). From the fact that we learn insofar as we are active, Popper concludes that even what Pavlov called the conditioned reflex is really hypothesis-making on the part of the dog (SB: 503). Such experiments exploit the plasticity of the canine dispositional system in the acquisition of food, given that hungry animals normally have to hunt and struggle, sometimes in adverse conditions, and must therefore be capable of adapting to circumstances. Pavlov's dog, then, reacting to a life-and-death situation in the artificial environment of the laboratory, adapted by simply producing a new hypothesis that linked food with the sound of a bell. 'Where the dispositions are less plastic to start with, or where the animal's vital interests are not involved, attempts to set up a conditioned reflex generally fail' (P1: 100).

The *tabula rasa* theory underpinning inductivism, which also constitutes its essential weakness (BG: xxxii), still reflects a pre-Darwinian view. According to modern biology, it is necessary to assume the existence of some form of knowledge – if only in the guise of dispositions or expectations – at every level of development of an organism. For 'there is no sense organ in which anticipatory theories are not genetically incorporated' (OK: 72). The 10 billion neurons and their synapses are material traces of largely unconscious knowledge incorporated into our genetic inheritance, without which we would be incapable of acquiring any new information (SB: 121). In this sense, we may say that every animal has some inborn knowledge – 'even though it may be quite unreliable' (MF: 96), given that the a priori is not synonymous with truth and validity.

Popper summarizes his views here by saying that the organism has its own inborn programme. But this makes it unclear how his theory differs from that of the 'modified receptacle' mentioned a moment ago. He might explain, of course, that for him the mind is *not* a receptacle with a programme enabling it to accumulate concepts and information; rather, it is an active organ proceeding not through accumulation but through trial and error, precisely thanks to the inbuilt programme. The fundamental difference with the *tabula rasa* theory, whether or not this involves the idea of a programme, is that for Popper 'we learn through activity' (ZO: 29) because the knowing subject, the observer, plays an important though very restricted role (OK: 73). The key point here seems to be choice of the term 'observation' instead of 'perception': as Kant taught us, there are no pure perceptions, because the sense material

143

is subject (within the container) to transformation processes similar to digestion or systematic classification (OK: 342).

Now, Popper only partly agrees with this thesis. Like Kant, he thinks that there are no pure perceptions; but he is convinced that the contribution of the knowing subject is not limited to automatic application of a mechanism. And whereas common sense blindly believes in the truth of the data of perception, Popper insists that we already learn as children to decode the complex messages reaching us through the senses, through a procedure based upon inborn dispositions which allows us to engage in trial-and-error-elimination (OK: 63).

It logically follows that knowledge starts neither from nothing nor from observation (CR: 33). Observation is by no means the origin, for perception becomes *observation* through a selective principle that is guided by a particular interest or a problem or an expectation. Hence the learning process leads not to the accumulation of mnemonic traces but to the modification over time of our dispositions to react.

> At every instant of our pre-scientific or scientific development we are living in the centre of what I usually call a *'horizon of expectations'*. By this I mean the sum total of our expectations, whether these are subconscious or conscious.
>
> (OK: 345)

When some of these expectations are disappointed by the observed facts, they become conscious and we are forced to correct them; we eliminate the false ones from our system in a process that we call learning. Unfortunately, the psychology of learning tends to ignore trial and error and to exaggerate the importance of repetition, which is actually useful not for learning but for forgetting, 'when we make something automatic so that it will not weigh too heavily upon us, in the sense of our not having to pay it any attention' (ZO: 24).

If, on the other hand, the most significant form of learning is that which leads us to discover new things, then we should conclude that it is the theoretical (as opposed to 'empirical', not to 'practical') element which plays the dominant role and steers not only knowledge – in the form of hypotheses, problem-formulation and reactive dispositions – but also experience understood as passive perception. This brings us back to the difference between the amoeba and Einstein, as a way of explaining the importance of the active component of knowledge. For both the amoeba and Einstein have innate expectations, but whereas the former cannot be critical of its own hypotheses, the latter is capable of correcting, integrating or replacing them, precisely because it does not just have to undergo them passively (OK: 24–25).

Against the receptacle theory, then, Popper opposes the searchlight theory of science and of the mind that produces it. The mind, that is, does not just bear the imprint of phenomena; it throws light onto that part of reality which at any moment appears problematic, or at any rate interesting. In this connection, we must not underestimate the role of unconscious knowledge in defining new problems and discovering new solutions. For what we call 'intuition' is often nothing other than a fragment of unconscious knowledge which becomes conscious (SB: 121). In the same way, we need to attach appropriate value to our creative imagination, which is what allows us to conceive of something never before expressed or to postulate hitherto unsuspected linkages (SB: 553). As Eccles also stresses, the imagination guides the active process of exploration, with its constant search for ways of improving our conceptual grasp and producing fruitful new syntheses (SB: 467–469).

LIFE AS PROBLEM-SOLVING

This interpretation is matched and confirmed by Popper's general vision of knowledge and of life in all its aspects. He is full of wonder for the miracle of life (P2: 122); its emergence was so unlikely that it now appears incomprehensible, given that 'an explanation in probabilistic terms is always an explanation in terms of a high probability: that under such and such conditions it is *very* probable that such and such happens' (SB: 561). Popper recalls that, according to our present knowledge of cosmology, space is largely a void; where there is matter, it consists of chaotic elements in which the probability of finding some form of life is virtually zero. This ought to convince us that although life is sometimes disdained and deprecated, it is really quite precious in its rarity (ISBW: 186).

Popper agrees with Lorenz that life is an adventure which, never satisfied with the conditions in which it finds itself, faces continual risks to create new ecological niches (ZO: 22, 20). It is hardly surprising, then, that from the very start life is 'sceptical' (in the etymological sense of reflecting or searching), because 'we are searchers' for a better world (ZO: 18).

Life cannot but present itself as a struggle against the obstacles to self-affirmation and to realization of the values of the individual – values which aim, more or less adequately, to improve the surrounding reality (SB: 558). By dint of facing up to such constant difficulties, life takes the form of problem-solving; problems qualify, as it were, the relationship between the living being and the world (OGOU: 74). We have already seen that Popper the epistemologist regards this relationship as the very origin of knowledge, which not only precedes experience but actually guides perception to come up with correct observations relevant to the problem it poses. As we know from studies of the behaviour of lower vertebrates, animals perceive what is relevant to their problem-situation and act accordingly. And if we transpose this model to human conduct, we find ourselves dealing with conscious personal goals and decisions (SB: 91).

Now, all problems – including the most complex theoretical ones – ultimately rest upon the practical problem of adaptation to the material environment, often by improving it, or upon the existential problem of the (more distinctively human) moral conditions of life. The problem-situation is so deeply rooted in life that any solution, however felicitous, 'opens up in its turn a whole new world of open problems' (P2: 162), which cannot be solved, at least not immediately, because knowledge cannot predict its own future conquests (P2: 109). Today's problem may be overcome tomorrow, but we cannot say today whether it will be solved, still less what consequences it will have. The knowing subject thus holds in itself an unknown world which will become clear as its relations develop with the surrounding reality.

An especially interesting treatment of problem-solving is contained in Popper's 'Epistemology Without a Knowing Subject' (1967), later incorporated into *Objective Knowledge*. In the last part of this article, where he draws out the existence of different levels of understanding, he shows how important it is for us to analyse the problem-situation, not only to devise a solution but even to understand the solution itself, by reconstructing the historical stages through which it was elaborated, criticized, modified and finally accepted (OK: 142–150).

Although Popper lays so much stress on the inexhaustibility of problems, he always exudes optimism in his writings and lectures, because he thinks that problems have been ever better tackled since humanity learned to kill off theories rather than those who advocate them – a procedure later theorized by critical rationalism. Reason, as the faculty of critical debate, plays an indispensable role in solving the problems raised by life, and 'rationalism is an attitude of readiness to listen to critical arguments and to learn from experience' (OS II: 455). However, Popper distinguishes between the true rationalism of Socrates – based on awareness of one's limits and intellectual modesty – and the pseudo-rationalism of Plato, whose intellectual intuitionism claimed to know with certainty and authority (OS II: 457). Popper's hostility both to uncritical rationalism and to irrationalism makes of him, in his own eyes, an Enlightenment rationalist.

THE LAST OF THE ENLIGHTENMENT THINKERS

In his long interview with Franz Kreuzer, Popper actually calls himself 'one of the last to join the Enlightenment' (OGOU: 22), whose basic imperatives are courage in seeking the truth and a call to tolerance. Contrary to first appearances, these two aspects are closely bound up with each other. Kant, the last great Enlightenment figure, was preoccupied in his life and thought with the struggle for intellectual freedom (CR: 177) – which speaks in favour of Popper's view that the commitment to reason is not so much intellectual as moral, for 'faith in reason, even in the reason of others, implies the idea of impartiality, tolerance, and rejection of any authoritarian claims' (RR: 39). We shall consider the ethical and political issues of tolerance in the next section. Here we shall focus on the theoretical side of Popper's Enlightenment thought, which inspires both his conception of science and his passion for philosophy.

At the price of attracting some caustic remarks, Popper maintained that the rational approach is nothing other than 'an irrational faith in reason' (OS II: 461; RR: 39; CR: 357). For, in the last analysis, it rests upon an irrational decision and cannot be justified by rational argument. Uncritical rationalism, for which 'any assumption which cannot be supported either by argument or by experience is to be discarded' (OS II: 460), falls into a paradox just like that of the liar, because it cannot itself be supported by argument or experience. But of course, this does not permit us to conclude that argument is of no help in making what is, as we have seen, mainly a moral choice. Popper's attack on irrationalism, ever since the troubled times in which he wrote *The Open Society and Its Enemies*, savours of a clear-cut moral challenge to those who make use of reason without feeling bound by its verdict (OS II: 473), on the pretext that only in this way is it possible to respect the deeper mysteries. Popper answers this kind of mystical irrationalism by quoting the words of Kafka, a great poet who certainly cannot be suspected of an excess of rationalism: mystics, he wrote, 'set out to say [...] that the incomprehensible is incomprehensible, and that we knew before' (OS II: 475). Popper also seems worried that the anti-rationalist mode pervading contemporary culture and threatening its survival has even contaminated science, with the result that the standards of scientific discussion have markedly declined (P3: 156). For all these reasons, the fallibilist epistemologist never hesitated to take the side of rationalism. Already in 1956 he wrote: 'I am a rationalist. By a rationalist I mean a man who wishes to understand the world, and to learn by arguing with others. (Note that I do not say a rationalist holds the mistaken theory that men are wholly or mainly rational)' (P1: 6). In fact, man is not so much a rational animal as an 'ideological animal' (MF: 82), ready to live and die for the ideas he believes to be true. This is evident not only from the various wars of religion, with their solely reprehensible motives, but also from other 'edifying aspects'; they all show the strength of ideas, albeit ideas transmuted into dogmas upheld with fanaticism and intolerance. For ideas are man's most precious treasure, and their lack is deplorable because 'criticism itself is constantly in need of new critical ideas' (ZO: 73).

At this point we must consider exactly what Popper means by the term 'rational'. Fortunately he made our task very much easier by stating that 'critical' was the best synonym of 'rational' (LSD: 16; OK: 66) and by underlining the critical – or, as he says elsewhere, 'negative' – function of reason (P1: 27). The critical attitude is not only the most important feature of science (CR: 256); above all, it distinguished the pre-Socratic dawn of philosophy, which began the tradition of discussion through arguments and objections, as well as dogmatic assertions (CR: 149). For the scientific mentality was born when the Greeks introduced a new approach to myths, so that what mattered was not the telling of some other tales but the replacement of dogmatic transmission with critical discussion of ideas (OK: 347–348). Today some philosophers of science – Popper explicitly mentions the book edited by Lakatos and Musgrave, *Criticism and the Growth of Knowledge* – do not attach sufficient value to the role of critical rethinking; whereas he himself believes that 'criticism is the prime *duty* of the scientist and of anyone who wants to advance knowledge' (P3: 33–34).

It is especially significant that, from Thales to Plato, ancient philosophy involves a succession of diverse cosmologies that never fail to surprise by their profundity and originality. This was possible because 'in this rationalist tradition bold changes of doctrine are not forbidden. On the contrary, innovation is encouraged, and is regarded as success, as improvement, if it is based on the result of a critical discussion of its predecessors' (CR: 151). Popper regrets that after two or three centuries, the spirit which moved the great philosophers of Antiquity grew so weak as almost to disappear, perhaps following Aristotle's reliance upon *episteme*, or certain, demonstrable knowledge, which fostered the idea that knowledge can and should be justified and not only criticized. Happily, the rationalist tradition was rediscovered in the Renaissance and rehabilitated thanks to Galileo and others. Since then, philosophy has swung backwards and forwards, in some cases going so far as to declare that there are no genuinely philosophical problems, or that philosophy is anyway powerless in the face of human vicissitudes. For his part, however, Popper stressed the importance of philosophy for both science and politics, because it does happen that philosophers produce ideas and 'ideas are dangerous and powerful things' (CR: 5); they can move mountains and retain all their force even when they are wrong (ISBW: 141–143). And so, we must definitely not undervalue the work of philosophers, who are engaged in what might be called 'the war of ideas'. As Popper points out:

> The war of ideas is a Greek invention. It is one of the most important inventions ever made. Indeed, the possibility of fighting with words instead of fighting with swords is the very basis of our civilization, and especially of all its legal and parliamentary institutions.
>
> (CR: 373)

As to the view that there are no genuinely philosophical questions, Popper tenaciously insisted that philosophy must return anew to the questions that fired the pre-Socratics – above all, cosmology and the theory of knowledge. For 'there is at least one philosophical problem in which all thinking men are interested: the problem of understanding the world in which we live; and thus ourselves (who are part of that world) and our knowledge of it' (CR: 136). It is probably true that a problem is never *purely* philosophical, that it always has some factual component and is linked to scientific problems; but it is also true that every problem presents aspects which 'need not be classified as belonging to science' (CR: 73).

Actually, Popper does not seem in the least perturbed by disputes about the existence of philosophy; he knows that they did not start yesterday but are 'almost as old as philosophy itself' (LSD: 51). His polemical thrust was mainly directed, in the 1930s, against logical positivism and its narrow view of human knowledge, and in the 1950s also against the ordinary-language philosophy inspired by the later Wittgenstein with which he had meanwhile had a chance to acquaint himself. Popper's main objection to the latter was that all philosophical problems cannot be reduced to questions concerning the use of language or the meaning of terms, for cosmology and all that goes with it raise genuine queries which cannot simply be conjured away as 'linguistic puzzles' (LSD: 15). Popper further argues that a philosopher must before all else tackle philosophical problems, as well as speaking of philosophy, for 'genuine philosophical problems are always rooted in urgent problems outside philosophy, and they die if these roots decay' (CR: 72). Any means to this end are valid: it is anyway sterile to try to define the correct method, because philosophy would then become application or technique rather than research.

Popper tries to be more precise by saying how he does *not* see philosophy (ISBW: 177–179): it is *not* the solving of linguistic puzzles, although this may be a necessary preliminary; it is therefore *never* the mere analysis of concepts or words; it is *not* a series of original and intelligent pictures of reality, because at least in Antiquity philosophers sought the truth more than aesthetic goals, unlike some more recent philosophers, such as Fichte or Hegel, who have shown more love for the brilliant system than for the truth. Thus philosophy is *not* 'a way of being clever', nor – as Wittgenstein suggested – an intellectual therapy; nor can its task be to study how to express things more precisely or exactly, because 'precision and exactness are not intellectual values in themselves'. Finally, Popper denies that philosophy is just an attempt to lay the conceptual basis for the solution of any future problem, as Locke considered it to be; and it is *not* an embodiment of the Hegelian *Zeitgeist*, because then it would be a slave of fashion and not a search for truth.

To those who reproach philosophy for its very existence, Popper replies that all men and women are philosophers, though some are more so than others (LSD: 15; ISBW: 174). Popper's essay devoted to an apology for philosophy, 'How I See Philosophy' (1978), reprinted in *In Search of a Better World*, helps us to understand this point better, as do the many references to it in his books.

All men and women are philosophers in that they more or less unconsciously adopt some stance towards life and death. Even their (often uncritical) expectations about what life should offer or what should be done to reach certain goals are philosophical attitudes (OGOU: 7). Perhaps not everyone is conscious of philosophical problems, but everyone does have philosophical prejudices – that is, theories they absorb from the environment in which they grew up, and then accept as self-evident (ISBW: 179). Such convictions would not be very important in themselves, if their influence on our actions and our life were not 'sometimes catastrophic'. To avoid disastrous errors due to naivety, we must critically discuss the assumptions underlying our choices and behaviour, and that is the same as the efforts of philosophical speculation to go to the root of what we do by instinct, education or conviction. This is the only possible way of justifying the desire and the commitment to keep philosophy alive, for like science it is nothing but 'enlightened common sense' (OK: 34). Thus:

> the task of the professional philosopher is critically to investigate the things that so many others accept as evident. In fact, quite a lot of such opinions are mere prejudices, uncritically accepted as evident but very often simply false. And to get away from them, perhaps something like a professional philosopher is required, who will take his time to reflect on them critically.
>
> (OGOU: 8–9)

Popper does not, however, share the view expressed by Fritz Waismann in the identically entitled article to which he replied in 'How I See Philosophy'.[3] The last of the Enlightenment thinkers does not agree that there should be an intellectual and philosophical elite which feels free to impress people by speaking in a pompous and incomprehensible language, in keeping with the far from praiseworthy tradition of intellectualism that flourished in Germany under Hegel and has been copiously imitated in the academic world (ZO: 103–105). Instead, in the awareness of their own privileged position, intellectuals should make a point of writing clearly and simply, avoiding obscure and overwrought terminology whose purpose is to convey a profundity and erudition that is not actually there. They should keep constantly in mind the example of Socrates, who expressed himself with the modesty appropriate to his self-proclaimed lack of any knowledge (ZO: 103; OGOU: 15). Intellectual humility follows directly from the commitment to reason, from 'the realization that we are not omniscient, and that we owe most of our knowledge to others' (CR: 356, 363). Taking issue here even with Goethe, who once said that only rogues are modest, Popper does not mince his words: 'Only intellectual rogues are immodest' (ISBW: 120).

As well as concentrating on minor questions that make it possible to pose as an expert, the philosopher should therefore critically reflect upon the great problems of the universe, man's position within it, the often dangerous power of knowledge, and the nature of good and evil (ISBW: 185–186). In this context, Popper makes a plea for a new professional ethics. Whereas the old professional ethics supported itself upon personal knowledge, upon certain knowledge implying a reference authority, the new one 'is based upon the idea of objective knowledge and of uncertain knowledge' (ISBW: 200). Before, the ideal was possession of the truth, and one of the injunctions was not to make mistakes – with consequences easy to imagine. According to the new ethics, there are no authorities and it is impossible to avoid mistakes, although naturally everyone has a duty to try to avoid them out of a love of truth, as well as to recognize their own mistakes. This is in keeping with the intellectual humility displayed by all the great scientists and scholars, which should also be recommended to technicians, professionals and intellectuals in general [ibid.].

As regards the specific themes of philosophy, Popper had no doubt in the early 1930s that they were problems of method (LSD: 55–56). For 'the problems of the theory of knowledge form the very heart of philosophy, both of uncritical or popular common-sense philosophy and of academic philosophy' (ISBW: 182). And in the *Postscript* too, he expresses himself in such a way as to suggest that philosophy is largely identical with the theory of knowledge (P1: 162). This is understandable enough if we think that, for Popper, philosophy 'never ought to be divorced from the sciences' (ISBW: 184). In science there is a horizon of accepted theories into which the individual scientist directly inserts his own contribution. But the philosopher is in a different position, he:

> does not face an organized structure, but rather something resembling a heap of ruins (though perhaps with treasure buried underneath). He cannot appeal to the fact that there is a generally accepted problem-situation; for that there is no such thing is perhaps the one fact which is generally accepted.
>
> (LSD: 13)

Still, Popper is not an Enlightenment thinker only because of his faith in reason, which implies both intellectual modesty and a certain confidence in philosophy. He is also convinced, like most representatives of the Enlightenment, that while reason is not an all-powerful instrument, it is adequate, if used well, to guarantee a life worth living at both an individual and a political level, which also allows progress towards a better world. Already those who have the good fortune to be born in the West live 'in a world which, relatively speaking, is the justest and the most caring of any in history' (ZO: 106; 42). For we inhabit a world where we can speak freely, and where the value of tolerance – the banner of the Enlightenment – has asserted itself, albeit with great difficulty.

THE ETHICS OF TOLERANCE

Following in the steps of Kant, Popper held that the principle of all morality coincides with the general prohibition on regarding one's own value as higher than anyone else's; this is the only acceptable maxim, given the notorious difficulty of being one's own judge. It also implies an attitude of being there for the other person, expressed in reasonableness and flowing into tolerance. A discussion must be two-way to be reasonable, and everyone must be prepared to learn from the other and to recognize, if necessary, that the other is right; otherwise, recourse to violence becomes inevitable. In fact, Popper confesses that his commitment to rationalism had a by no means rational motive in his abhorrence of violence (CR: 356), and therefore that rationalism is 'not self-contained, but rests on an irrational faith in the attitude of reasonableness' (CR: 357). He does not see how we can go beyond this to furnish positive motivations. But perhaps he could have asked whether his hatred of violence really is just an irrational passion, or whether it does not itself have a logical foundation. For the use of force is deplorable not only because most people do not like it, but above all because it tends to crush a person's psychological identity or even physical existence. And since no one using violence would wish this for themselves, it ends up in a contradiction or in an implicit denial that one's fellow-humans have the same rights as oneself.

On the other hand, it is to Popper's credit that he admits – through his distinctive apology for rationalism – that man is not entirely rational and that feelings have greater value for human life, although he does not feel the need to deny that an element of rationality is always present even in relations dominated by grand passions such as love (CR: 357). Popper also warns us to mistrust those who want to rule by love rather than reason: to love others means to want to make them happy, and there is a danger that happiness – even that of others – will be defined on the basis of one's own scale of values, which almost inevitably clashes with other scales of values and leads to hatred and intolerance (OS II: 465). Rationalism is thus preferable to irrationalism also as the basis for our life in society, because irrationalism necessarily tends towards dogmatism. Where there is no possibility of rational discussion, all we can do is choose between unconditional assent and total rejection; and conversely, rationalism is to be recommended because it demands 'recognition of the necessity of social institutions to protect freedom of criticism, freedom of thought, and thus the freedom of men. And it establishes something like a moral obligation towards the support of these institutions' (OS II: 468). Individual men and women, of course, in the richness of their singular experience, cannot by definition ever be completely rationalized, because the power of reason comes only from abstraction. But although it is precisely this uniqueness which makes life worth living, life itself gains from the existence of a 'field of abstract universals' (OS II: 475) as both the domain and the product of reason. For it is only thanks to reason and its products that individuality itself can survive, in both the literal and the metaphorical sense.

Consequently, Popper argues that reason must be the basis for political life; the only alternative is violence, and it would be 'criminal' to use this if it can be avoided (RR: 28). For reason enables us to criticize hypotheses that do not convince us, perhaps to prove them wrong and have them discarded, without at the same time physically or psychologically destroying those who advocate them (RR: 37). This attitude helps to create the tolerance which inevitably arises from a conviction that 'while differing widely in the various little bits we know, in our infinite ignorance we are all equal' (CR: 29). As Popper puts it, borrowing Voltaire's argument for 'toleration' in the *Philosophical Dictionary*, we are all continually making mistakes, so let us pardon each other's follies (ISBW: 190). This link between fallibility and toleration has been pointed out by all the great 'sceptics' of the past, all the honest searchers after truth, from Xenophanes to Socrates, Erasmus to Montaigne, Locke to Voltaire and Lessing. The ethical consequences of this commitment are far from negligible, because it requires us to be wary of our own sensations, however strong, but also to be unyielding with regard to those who lapse into intolerance, violence and cruelty (ISBW: 192).

In a lecture first delivered in 1981, 'Toleration and Intellectual Responsibility', Popper clearly poses the question that cannot be avoided in a democratic society. What should be done about minorities who accept the principle of intolerance? Should they be tolerated? 'If we do not tolerate them, we seem to deny our own principles: we seem to make concessions to intolerance, and so become hypocrites. If we do tolerate them, we may become responsible for ending democracy and toleration' (TIR: 19). In answering, we should heed the advice of the great champions of toleration – men like Mill and Voltaire who, although they did not envisage such a dilemma, clearly indicated that tolerance can exist only on a reciprocal basis and therefore finds its natural limit, so to speak, in intolerance itself. Popper goes further than this. Concerned about the practical difficulty of defining where rational debate ends and violence begins, he proposes that we should not tolerate even the threat of intolerance, especially if it becomes serious (TIR: 19).

Rightly or wrongly, the theorist of fallibilism was accused of fuelling relativism and its ultimate tendency to equate all values, including those relating to democracy and totalitarianism, and hence toleration and intolerance. But Popper insisted that fallibilism was quite innocent of these deplorable conclusions: to say we can make mistakes is to admit that the truth exists, that some actions are morally right and others are not; truth and good are not at arm's reach, as we know from how easy it is to fall into error, but they do exist and we can approach the ideals they represent. To guarantee mutual tolerance, then, it is sufficient that both sides accept this statement: 'I may be wrong and you may be right.' But to avoid relativism we must add something more: 'I may be wrong and you may be right; and by talking things over rationally we may be able to correct some of our mistakes and we may perhaps, both of us, get nearer to the truth, or to acting in the right way' (TIR: 26).

Popper attaches huge importance to this formula and analyses its three components in some detail. The first principle – 'I may be wrong and you may be right' – is a paraphrase of Voltaire and does no more than reaffirm Socrates's awareness of our boundless ignorance (TIR: 28–29). Contrary to first appearances, it cannot be simply taken up and used in favour of relativism. For relativism entails that both of us are right, whereas the principle of toleration implies that we may both be wrong and that on the question at issue there is certainly a right and a wrong point of view (TIR: 26).

The second statement – 'By talking things over rationally we may be able to correct some of our mistakes' – is the principle of critical reason, which seeks to discover not so much who is wrong and who is right, as what is true and what is false. This could be summed up in a simple slogan 'Words instead of swords!'. What matters is that thought, opinions, hypotheses should be publicly expressed in words, for theory that is merely thought is still part of its originator or supporter and cannot be discovered to be right or wrong, whereas theory that is communicated acquires objectivity or independence *vis-à-vis* the subject and can thus be critically assessed (TIR: 27–28). In this way, not only freedom of speech but also its limits are validated.

The third part of the formula – 'By talking things over rationally we may both get nearer to the truth' – establishes that we need not demand too much of rational discussion, that it will not necessarily bring everyone to agree. It will be fruitful, however, because those taking part will learn from their opponents' objections to explain more clearly the problem and their own views about it. It is hard to disagree with Popper when he says that 'we need others in order to put our thoughts to the test to find out which of our ideas are valid' (ISBW: 208). The history of science is rich in such episodes, one example in our own century being the discussion between Einstein and Bohr (TIR: 28). Their failure to resolve their differences was not a negative result, because:

> agreement is comparatively unimportant in the search for truth: we may easily both be mistaken. People did strongly agree, for a very long time, on many erroneous doctrines (such as the Ptolemaic system of the world); and agreement is often the result of the fear of intolerance, or even of violence.
>
> (TIR: 29)

Now, these principles which, in Popper's view, should be the basis of society find their most extensive application in the Western democracies, where most citizens consider liberty, non-violence, the protection of minorities and of the weak to be obvious values. This carries a danger in that it may lead people to lower their guard against the anti-democratic threat, in the belief that the long battle for democracy begun in ancient Athens has now been won. (Athenian democracy itself was rather imperfect, given that slaves existed alongside free citizens.) Naturally we cannot place our hopes in an ideal society; solutions are never simple and we should content ourselves with democracy, which – as Winston Churchill once said – 'is the worst form of government, except of course all those other forms of government that have been tried from time to time' (ISBW: 220). Thus, whilst being aware that no society is truly rational and that there is always another society more rational than the present one, we have a duty to become involved in improving our existing institutions and the way they work (RR: 29). In this sense Popper can say – perhaps a little mischievously – that:

> our western civilization is, in spite of all the faults that can quite justifiably be found with it, the most free, the most just, the most humanitarian and the best of all those we have ever known throughout the history of mankind. It is the best because it has the greatest capacity for improvement.
>
> (ISBW: 118)

According to Popper, the great merit of the West is what many see as its fundamental weakness: that is, the lack of a vigorous unifying idea. For:

we ought to be proud that we not have *one* idea but *many* ideas, good ones and bad ones; that we do not have a *single* belief, not *one* religion but many: good ones, and bad ones. It is a sign of the supreme strength of the West that we can afford that.

(ISBW: 210)

Alongside this belief in the West, Popper also expresses his optimism for the future; 'we live in a wonderful world, in a beautiful world' (TIR: 21), which has decided to combat poverty (ISBW: 217), to offer everyone the best possible opportunities. This optimism is due not so much to the actual solutions employed – which are not always effective – as to the driving intention of society as a whole to seek better living conditions for the greatest number of people.

To be sure, in a situation of this kind, the achievement of any value entails a conflict with other values, but what counts is that this conflict is not resolved through violence. Instead we have critical instruments at our disposal, so that the method which bears fruit in science – essentially, the identification and correction of errors – is also applicable in the case of democracy (OGOU: 20; ISBW: 119–120). Popper concludes:

If I dream of a democratic Utopia, it will be one in which a parliamentary candidate can hope to attract votes by the boast that he discovered during the last year thirty-one mistakes made by himself and has managed to correct thirteen of them; while his competitor discovered only twenty-seven, even though he admittedly also corrected thirteen of them. I need not say that this will be a Utopia of toleration.

(TIR: 34)

Popper's political perspective therefore makes it impossible for him to accept one of the most widespread commonsense theories: the notion of a social conspiracy. The evils afflicting humanity – poverty, war, unemployment and disease – are here blamed on the intentional acts or plans of certain powerful individuals or groups, who must be fought against if those evils are to be overcome. This was the path taken by Lenin, Mussolini and Hitler, among others, who tried to find scapegoats for the malaise of society and thereby caused unjust persecution and unspeakable suffering (ISBW: 180; CR: 342). Popper insists that although conspiracies do sometimes occur, they are rarely successful and the whole theory remains false and uncritical: the life of society cannot be reduced to a trial of strength between competing groups; it unfolds within a framework of traditions and institutions that mediate between groups and lead to unforeseeable reactions (OS II: 325). Were it not for tradition, there would not have developed propensities or dispositions towards such values as freedom or tolerance, or indeed their opposites (ISBW: 208). In the field of epistemology it would appear that tradition is the main source of human knowledge, for if individuals were unable to grow up with tradition as their base of support, they would not find it easy to set off in the direction of the truth, still less to make any headway (ISBW: 49; CR: 376). But then to be consistent, we ought to conclude that in the field of politics, institutions cannot produce the desired results unless they are able to draw upon tradition. For 'traditions are needed to form a kind of link between institutions and the intentions and valuations of individual men' (ISBW: 156; CR: 351).

In conclusion, Popper's view of the necessity of reason in science must also be applied in the field of politics, to oppose the use of violence and thus secure a world in which we merely eliminate unserviceable theories, instead of killing one another over them (OGOU: 19; ZO: 90). Peace, then, no longer appears to be against nature: it is even part of the evolutionary plan, which has provided us with the means to kill off theories in our stead (ZO: 90). We may legitimately hope that military conflicts will disappear from the face of the earth. In democratic countries, wars of aggression have already become all but impossible from an ethical point of view; the free world is prepared to take up arms, 'but it will do this only if it is faced with unambiguous aggression' (CR: 372).

When Popper voiced his favourable predictions in 1956, he may still have appeared too optimistic. Today, after the events that led to the collapse of Communism in Eastern Europe in 1989, and after the conflict in the Gulf in 1990 and 1991, there are still bloody tensions in the international arena. But at least the threat of nuclear war seems to have sharply declined, and as Popper foresaw, the dangers come not from the Western democracies but from securely illiberal and intolerant governments.

6

THE CRITICISM

Once Popper's theories first became known through the publication of the German edition of the *Logic* in 1934, they had a huge impact not only in logical-positivist philosophical circles, but also in England where he was invited to lecture the following year. He recalls that the *Logik der Forschung* had 'more reviews, in more languages, than there were twenty-five years later of *The Logic of Scientific Discovery*, and fuller reviews even in English' (UQ: 107). After that, Popper's fortunes never declined; indeed, as the years went by, his fame spread beyond geographical and academic limits into the literary pages of daily newspapers, establishing itself even among those who were not professional philosophers. Popper's success was undoubtedly favoured by his clear and intelligible style, but this did not spare him a whole series of misunderstandings. He replied to these in detail at the end of a collection of essays on his thought published in 1974, in a section entitled 'Replies to My Critics'.

In the vast bibliography of works about Popper, of which a considerable selection is offered at the end of this book, we can identify a number of recurring lines of interpretation as well as major differences of evaluation. For some, the wide variety of themes treated by Popper results in a harmonious 'unified vision' (Watkins, Giorello, Buzzoni), while for others, there is an underlying monotony because he was really the author *unius libri*, *The Logic of Scientific Discovery*, even if he later reached out to the human and social sciences (Antimo Negri). There are also those who deny the continuity and coherence of Popper's thought, arguing that it is marked by the turn he made when he linked his theory of knowledge to Darwin's view of evolution (Moravia).

As to the merits of Popper's contribution, Buzzoni (1982) draws what we might call a 'geographical' distinction between German-speaking scholars – whose assessment tends to be 'more keenly gnoseological' – and others in the English-speaking countries who pay more attention to his methodological proposals and his writings on the actual progress of science.

In a complementary classification, Lentini (1991) identifies three fundamental lines of interpretation. The first, which mainly refers to *The Logic of Scientific Discovery*, dominated the scene in the period between the first German edition of 1934 and the English edition of 1959, seeing Popper's theory of knowledge as essentially located within the tide of logical positivism; it was first advanced by Viktor Kraft, but it was taken up by other researchers and still has some supporters. In the second account, however, which began to gain currency in the 1960s, Popper is a radical anti-positivist whose epistemology provides an alternative to the Vienna Circle (Skolimowski). Others still have oscillated between these two interpretations: Francesco Barone, for example, a careful and renowned Italian scholar, did not oppose the view of Popper as a dissident in the first edition of his book on logical positivism (1953), but then in the second edition (1977) he partly changed his mind and argued that Popper was less an inheritor than a critic of logical positivism, though more influenced by it than he was prepared to admit. This combined assessment has tended to prevail in recent years, so that Popper is seen as having unsuccessfully attempted to achieve full harmony between elements of logical positivism and other, opposing elements.

How did the logical positivists themselves react to the *Logik der Forschung*? In a review that appeared in *Erkenntnis*, the official journal of the Vienna Circle, Carnap found substantial areas of agreement between Popper's conception and the conventionalist, positivist theses of Circle members. Neurath, on the other hand, reviewing the book in the same journal, referred to Popper as the official opposition to the Circle. Quite unconvinced by the objections to inductivism, he pointed out that Popper could show no reason why – in the case of a clash – we should not discard the falsifying rather than the falsified theory. Reichenbach agreed that there were difficulties in justifying the principle of induction, but he was not willing to conclude that scientific method could do without it; that would be to reduce scientific discovery to 'divination'. Carnap, while recognizing that the content of theory could not be reduced to the cases confirming it, emphasized the empirical necessity of some form of induction. Geymonat appeared equally critical in the review he wrote in 1936, and his assessment was no different in 1983 when he published a short book on Popper and Kuhn.

Neurath also remarked that when a theory was in danger, Popper tried to step up the attack; whereas it would be rather more interesting to examine the case for the defence. But of course, not everyone among the logical positivists shared Neurath's harsh judgement. Hempel was one notable exception, and Viktor Kraft – in a later volume on the Anglo-Austrian philosopher edited by Schilpp in 1974 – insisted that Popper's thought could only be understood on the basis of its close ties with the Vienna Circle. In the same collective volume, however, Skolimowski maintained that the author of the *Logik* had departed from logical positivism not just on some discrete points, but on the whole conception of science and human knowledge.

As we can see, views were far from unanimous about placing Popper in the context of 1930s epistemology. One thing is certain: when the reputation of Popper's epistemological works rose again in the 1960s with the publication of the English edition of the *Logic*, there was no shortage of criticisms and attacks that partly took over the objections made by Neurath before the break-up of the Vienna Circle. This was especially the case with his argument that Popper's methodological rules represented an ideal of research, quite remote from the actual practice of science. Similar reservations, at least as regards the goal, can be found in Salmon, a pupil of Reichenbach's, as well as in Agassi and Lakatos, who all held that Popper's combination of anti-inductivism with the concept of corroboration made his position ambiguous and ultimately threw it back onto the ground of induction.

Be this as it may, Neurath's objections were taken up and intensified by the more radical critics who went on to found the 'new philosophy of science'. Indeed, some authors (H.I. Brown, for instance) have seen Popper as merely a transitional figure between logical positivism and the conception of science most widespread today, with Thomas Kuhn as one of its most significant figures. In his *Structure of Scientific Revolutions* (1962), which won quite unexpected fame for his theses, Kuhn argued that Popper had characterized the whole of scientific activity in a way that was valid only for its revolutionary components. For criticism was not the distinguishing feature of science; and during periods of research, scientists gave it up and placed their trust in a commonly accepted 'paradigm', trying to solve problems on the ground defined by it. Only if a paradigm was no longer working and anomalies could not be integrated through patient research work, would a crisis develop and favour the revolutionary introduction of a new paradigm. If this then won through, it was not only for logical or experimental reasons but also because of psychological or sociological factors – a position that coflicted with the distinction drawn by Reichenbach in 1939, and accepted by Popper, between the psychological context of discovery and the strictly logical context of justification.

Aware of the weakness of some of the master's theses, a number of his disciples tried to amend the original theory of falsificationism. Agassi, one such 'revisionist', criticized the role that Popper attached to corroboration, on the grounds that it had no probative force (and hence no epistemological value) but carried only social and moral weight. For science too had an institutional and sociological side, which displayed all its importance when it became clear that demonstrations were not enough to win people away from their established convictions. According to Agassi, then, the degree of stability we find in science is not intrinsic to it, but derives from the social institutions that manage and apply the scientific inheritance – the inheritance of a *science in flux*, to quote the title of Agassi's well-known book. On the other hand, the new appraisal of empirical testability, which Agassi considers so necessary, leads him to stress the role of metaphysics in a rational understanding of the world.

Among the more orthodox Popperians, Alan Musgrave actively participated in the debate but did not distance himself in any significant way from fallibilist rationalism. The only point he conceded was that the methodological proposals of the philosophy of science had prescriptive force not for individual scientists (who were also free to work on research programmes apparently refuted by the facts) but for the scientific community as a whole, which could not allow itself to concentrate on theories with little corroboration in experience.

While it is true that Popper's followers did not question the fabric of critical rationalism, it is also undeniable that they discussed a number of related and far from marginal issues. The liveliest and most thorough debate concerned the function of metaphysics. Lakatos, the most heterodox Popperian in the group, regarded metaphysics as the 'nucleus' of the research programme, while Watkins saw it as having an external 'influence' on science; for Agassi, it might be thought of as the foundation of future science, often conflicting with current theories and thus acting as a stimulus for them to be superseded, or at least developed and improved. Many of the differences between Popper's disciples were probably, as Antiseri (1982) suggests, due to a careless ambiguity on his part when he originally relegated metaphysics in general to the sphere of non-science, without taking the trouble to distinguish this clearly from pseudo-science.

According to W.W. Bartley, however, the main issue at stake was rather the distinction between critical and non-critical or pseudo-critical theories, and the epistemological problem *par excellence* was the criterion for telling which was a good and which a bad idea. In Bartley's own view, no tool could work perfectly in this respect: good ideas could be distinguished only gradually from bad ones, following the three phases of Darwinian evolution: variation–selection–preservation.

Among Popper's disciples, Lakatos was certainly the one who came up with the most original variant, in that it went beyond the 'naive falsification' of which at least the early Popper had been guilty. For 'naive falsificationism', if rigorously applied, would not allow any new theoretical approach the time to survive and grow stronger by overcoming the many initial anomalies that can only be cleared up through further research. Lakatos therefore proposed the method of scientific research programmes, which recognizes that any scientific theory contains a hard core of metaphysical principles that inspire the theory itself and should be accepted by way of hypothesis; this core is surrounded by a protective girdle of variable and refutable elements that have to be continually tested by means of a negative heuristics, whose function is to show the paths to be avoided, and by a positive heuristics, which indicates the paths to be followed.

Lakatos, then, is convinced that strict falsificationism cannot be sustained: it claims infallibility for the empirical base and thus puts forward a new criterion which excludes falsifiability itself – that is, simply, 'a theory is scientific (or acceptable) if it has an "empirical base"'. Lakatos' crucial difference with Popper is that he rejects the hasty discarding of a theory in its early stages, and insists that, as an element in a research programme, it should not be taken in isolation from its own theoretical context. To criticize a whole project is thus a long process, and the programme should be given time to develop sufficiently to show its potential.

Lakatos' revision grew out of a concern to save the kernel of Popper's methodology, while taking account of the various criticisms to which it had been subjected. He hoped that Popperism would come out of this less exposed, but also that it would avoid the irrationalist and subjectivist tones present in Kuhn's approach. Meanwhile, a debate flared up and caused Popper himself to allow a certain legitimacy to dogmatism in scientific research; but, at the same time, he continued to affirm that:

> the important thing is not the explanation of the knowledge we all have, but rather the new, revolutionary knowledge that does not coincide with what we already know and almost forces us to revise or reject some of its elements.
>
> (EE: 40)

Nevertheless, whether the corrections to the theory came from its originator or were added with care by his followers, they can hardly be considered sufficient. As Paolo Parrini, an Italian scholar, has put it, 'neither in Popper, nor in Lakatos' method of scientific research programmes, can we find any indication of when dogmatism and criticism are legitimate and when they become excessive'.

In Popper's 'Replies to My Critics', as already in some remarks in articles from the 1960s, he regretted that his careless use of terms had often led him to be misunderstood, for he had never paid as much attention to linguistic precision as to matters of substance (OK: 58). But more than a slight role had also been played by the spreading of a 'Popper legend' that distorted the reality and intentions of his thought (RC: 964). According to this legend, Popper was a positivist who favoured the adoption of a criterion of meaning (failing to distinguish this from a criterion of demarcation), and who actually introduced falsifiability in order to arrive at a criterion of conclusive verifiability (RC: 965). This legend, though without foundation, had been fuelled by the warm reception given to his criticisms by certain members of the Vienna Circle (RC: 967).

At any event, the debate between Popper's detractors and defenders was central to epistemological thought in the 1970s and 1980s. Two particularly significant solutions began to emerge: the moderate one of Laudan, and the radical one of Feyerabend. In fact Feyerabend, having for some time been a disciple, turned into Popper's sharpest opponent – although he did admit that critical rationalism was the most liberal of the positivist methodologies. His own view was simply that science does not follow, and never has followed, a precise method or even rationally defined canons. In *Against Method* (1975), which rejected both Popper's original theory as well as Lakatos' corrections, he openly laid claim to irrationalism – at least with regard to science, which, like any other human venture, did not take a predetermined course.

To meet these anti-rationalist attacks that have shaken science in the last few decades, Larry Laudan has felt it necessary to 'tone down the concept of rationality', so that it is seen only as the preferred faculty for the formulation and selection of problem-solving theories. The problem – already the starting point in Popper's epistemology – forms the core of research, but it is inserted into a particular research tradition that has to face a number of competitors. The historical aspects of science thus acquire a weight that was not recognized either by Popper or by the logical positivists.

The current panorama includes in the ranks of critical rationalism not only such epistemologists as Agassi, Bartley, Watkins, Musgrave, Albert and Stegmüller, but also such well-known scientists as Bondi, Eccles, Medawar and the anthropologist Ian Jarvie, who have publicly sung the praises of Popper and his method. But there are also a number of critics (Miller, Tichy, Ackermann, Johannson) who, though having reservations about various points or theses, consider themselves essentially in agreement with much of Popper's doctrine and certainly do not share the relativism and irrationalism of a Feyerabend or Kuhn.

The debate between Popper and the new generation of epistemologists has aroused considerable interest, and some of them – especially those like Johannson for whom Popper's methodological rules do not fulfil their promise – have tried to draw a balance sheet of the dispute. The results are far from unanimous, of course, but the main doubts about the theorist of critical rationalism have been that he reduced (or tried to reduce) gnoseology to methodology without discussing the relationship between the two; that Popper's methodology may not be wholly compatible with the new evolutionary approach (Ackermann); that he failed to distinguish between what the various inductivist philosophies require of observational evidence (Grünbaum); and that his theory of rationality is too limited because it only takes in the critical approach and leaves out creativity. Still others have, as we shall see, judged Popper himself responsible for the irrationalist and subjectivist turn in recent epistemological thinking.

Finally, we should not forget the relationship between Popper and Wittgenstein, marked by divergences of both views and temperament that have been investigated by several complementary researchers. While Weinheimer broaches the question in a more general chapter on Popper's relations with the Vienna Circle, Munz stresses that both Popper's falsificationism and Wittgenstein's later philosophy were reactions against logical positivism. For Radnitzky, on the other hand, the differences between the two thinkers were far from negligible, and although they did not really come into the open during Wittgenstein's lifetime, they later surfaced in the criticisms of Popper made by Toulmin, Kuhn and Feyerabend, all greatly indebted to the later Wittgenstein.

Clearly Popper is one of those authors liable to upset everyone: the strict positivists who would like to see off not only metaphysics but philosophy *tout court*; the critics of logical positivism who want to save the 'transcendental conception of philosophy' but not metaphysics; and the orthodox metaphysicians for whom there is no rational foundation outside metaphysics itself. This is a fate shared by many of those who, not recognizing themselves in any of the most widespread solutions to a problem, seek to synthesize elements deriving from the various proposals and end up drawing the wrath of all. In our view, however, what makes Popper's quest so inviting is precisely this attempt to find a balance between divergent or even opposing theories, to draw out and combine that which is plausible in each.

For the study of Popper's epistemology, the monographs by Johannson, Ackermann, Döring and Weinheimer are all quite useful. Also of interest are the studies of Popper's relationship with philosophers who either directly inspired him or stimulated him through their criticism. Here we should mention first Focher's recent work, in which Hume, Bacon, Kant and Socrates are identified as 'Popper's four authors', but there are also useful indications to be found scattered in more general works. Other authors (Johannson and Ackermann, to name but two) have investigated his relationship with – and possible responsibility for – the 'new philosophy of science' current around Kuhn, Lakatos and Feyerabend, which started from shared premises but then developed in an anti-Popperian direction. Of course, the idea of rationality permeates the whole of a theory which its author himself called 'critical rationalism' – yet for Capecci, to take one example, Popper saw scientific rationality as the only one possible, elevating it to the 'court of reason'. This identification, more implicit than declared, was fraught with consequences, because it created the opportunity for a radical critique of rationality that used Popper's own analysis of the inherent precariousness of science.

It has been argued that a shrewd irrationalist actually lies disguised behind the rationalist defender and admirer of science. Thus for Stove, the intellectual origins of modern irrationalism are to be found in Humean scepticism; and Popper and his followers (some only seeming opponents) did no more than return to Hume's fallibilism and scepticism, which, when combined with deductivism, led them to deny the existence of rationally dependable knowledge. O'Hear, for his part, argues that Popper tried to reconcile the radical scepticism of his epistemological theses with his longing for objective truth, but that this proved an uphill task because of an aversion to justificationism which was only the reverse side of his scepticism. He therefore lacked the most suitable means to his declared goal of combating relativism – and this, according to Burke, became the central theme of his thought, both intellectually and morally.

Not everyone agrees with this interpretation, of course, and others such as Bartley prefer to emphasize the way in which Popper gave reason a new critical perspective in place of its function of justification. Hans Albert, for example, defends critical rationalism as nothing less than the methodological equivalent of the principle of non-contradiction.

Many are the scholars who have neglected the political side of things and concentrated almost entirely on Popper's epistemological theories: not so much to revise or criticize his overall approach, as to take up specific questions such as his concept of verisimilitude (Miller, Tichy), his treatment of induction (Grünbaum, Morpurgo-Tagliabue), or his theory of knowledge and evolution (Campbell, Moravia, Currie, Alt, Buzzoni). Moravia, while lauding Popper as the founder of a modern epistemology based upon natural selection, denies that knowledge can be considered solely in terms of a progressive adaptation to the environment, because it also has the function of devising new and different situations. On Popper's behalf, Munz complained in 1982 that many scholars had misunderstood his thought by ignoring its most significant aspect: the change that appeared with his evolutionary turn. The new ideas developed by Popper in the 1960s and 1970s did not mark an actual break in his thought, because the source of his earlier ideas had been and remained his solution to the problem of induction. Yet Munz insisted on the originality of Popper's evolutionary epistemology, which would not have been possible simply on the basis of falsificationism. What was new in Popper's later work was precisely the attention that he paid to biology and the auxiliary sciences, his refusal to limit himself, like most researchers, to the domain of physics.

Turning now to the political works, we should realize that these have generally commanded less attention, been more 'dabbled in' at length than really 'studied', as Fornero put it. This is partly due to the already mentioned 'legend' of Popper the logical positivist, which meant that his epistemological ideas long overshadowed ethical, anthropological and, above all, political themes. But as Cotroneo has argued, there is also the fact that he put forward his own political theories through a critique of great philosophers of the past, such as Plato, Hegel and Marx, with the result that he was largely seen in the context of the history of ideas; indeed, the objections made by such scholars as Levinson or Cornforth were more philological than philosophical in character, relating to the interpretation of certain passages or theses from Plato (much more than Marx) and only seldom directly addressing Popper's own views. Finally, in the years when the cultural hegemony of the Left could be felt not only in Italy but a little everywhere in Europe, Popper's unbending aversion to Marxism certainly did not help to make the anti-historicist theses of The Open Society any more popular.

Today, the political collapse of Communism has led to a reversal on the cultural plane, and this has even affected the ideas that Popper developed at a time when no one imagined the present outcome. It thus seems proper to consider Popper's arguments in defence of democracy, as has been argued by Bryan Magee, an admirer and disciple of Popper within the British Labour Party. For even if Popper was wrong on points of history, The Open Society and Its Enemies would still be a key book for its attempted combination of democracy and science with humanitarian principles. That ought to be enough for those like Levinson, de Vries or Bambrough who have accused him of misreading Plato.

It is particularly interesting that Popper's liberal defence of

Western society invokes arguments that are closely bound up with his epistemological conceptions (see Magee). According to Montaleone, the bonding between the two parts of Popper's philosophy can be seen in an article from 1940, 'What Is Dialectic?', where he uses his elaboration of the trial-and-error method to mount a series of objections to the Hegelian dialectic, without sparing Marx's variations on it.

Left-wing culture (Adorno, E.H. Carr) attacked Popper as a conservative interested in safeguarding the existing order. For others, however, his gradualism is the sign of a conviction which only rejects the dream of total regeneration, but which is not at all moderate in its refusal to set any limits to reform; indeed, he thinks that it should be as radical as possible, 'conserving' nothing but democracy and freedom (Antiseri, Cotroneo). In the similar interpretation proposed by Ruelland, the whole of Popper's philosophy revolves around the idea of freedom, in whose name he denounces the historicist conception and sets out the conditions for an 'open society'.

For Dahrendorf, Popper's work on both political and epistemological theory makes him the champion of a form of neo-Enlightenment anti-romanticism, with obvious roots in Kant and the eighteenth century. Similarly D.E. Williams, in his study of Popper's social and political thought, maintains that his ideals are essentially those of the Enlightenment and that the arguments he deploys against ostensible enemies are strongly inspired by Kantian philosophy. For Popper's determination to treat human beings as 'ends in themselves' underlies the whole of his thought, even in the field of epistemology; the choice of one among several competing theories is never just an intellectual question but always also a moral decision. Moreover, as Williams wishes to indicate by the very title of his book (*Truth, Hope and Power. The Thought of Karl Popper*), without a belief in the possibility of objective truth there can be no hope for the open society, as there would then be no non-violent, non-coercive means by which liberalism could combat illiberal power.

Even before the dispute with the Frankfurt School, we find Geymonat criticizing the theses of *The Open Society* from a clearly opposing standpoint. Although he recognizes that Popper, unlike Croce, did not even try to invent a metaphysics of liberty, he still sees him as the official philosopher of anti-communism and asserts against him the superiority of dialectical materialism. Non-

Marxists also put forward criticisms of Popper: according to Negri, for example, his hypercriticism 'did not help' either in constructing a liberal political theory, or in keeping the liberal ideal in a 'robust' condition; while for Alcaro, the grave defects of Popper's thought were its failure to provide a method for the criticism of governments, and its naive assumption that, in combating the unequal distribution of power, we ought to vote for the very system of political power that was historically produced by the causes we wish to eliminate.

When we come to the admirers and followers of Popper, some have praised the fact that he investigated the phenomenon of totalitarianism in the painful and distressing climate of the late 1930s; Bellino, for example, compares him in this respect to the other great political theorist, Hannah Arendt, whose *Origins of Totalitarianism* appeared not long after his own work.[1] For Cubeddu, who is more cautious but also essentially favourable in his judgement, the historicism targeted by Popper should be identified not with the conception of reality as history advocated by a Dilthey or a Weber, but with the nineteenth-century philosophies that sought to reveal the meaning and purpose of world history. In support of this reading, we might quote the view expressed by Pietro Rossi in one of the first articles on Popper to appear in Italy: namely, that the object of the Anglo-Austrian philosopher's attack was precisely the romantic variant that had already come under fire in contemporary German historicist thinking, from Dilthey to Weber. The latter, in particular, had pointed to the pretext-like character of the counterposition between natural and social sciences, and stressed the explanatory task and scientific claims of the social-historical disciplines – much as Popper would do later, without being aware of this 'solidarity' with Weber or even of the differences within the historicist conception.

The same issues lay behind the dispute at the congress organized in 1961 by the Tübingen Sociology Institute, where Popper and Adorno divided the participants over the method of the social sciences and the function of dialectics. While the debate spread out to the Frankfurt School, which took the side of its director, one of the most prominent supporters of critical rationalism, Hans Albert, accused Habermas and his Frankfurt colleagues of being ignorant of the law that value judgements cannot be derived from judgements of fact.

According to Todisco, the clash between Popper and the

Frankfurt School stemmed from differing assessments of the 'ideological conjuncture'. And indeed, whereas Adorno and his followers thought that the identification and solution of problems required insight into the present course of history, the author of *The Open Society* regarded as illusory, or even deleterious, any such claim to grasp a constant direction in human affairs. In Cipolla's account of the dispute, however, it was no more than a missed opportunity for sociology, because the contestants almost never hit the right target. Popper attacked Adorno by imputing Hegel's ideas to him, just as Habermas criticized Albert in lieu of the Vienna Circle or, at least, without appreciating the distance between critical rationalism and logical positivism.

To sum up this brief survey, we can say that the reactions to Popper's thought demonstrate, if nothing else, the fertility of his philosophical teachings. His follower, W.W. Bartley, has affectionately recalled the master's seriousness of purpose, his painstaking criticism of those studying under him, and his hostility towards contemporary English philosophy – all reasons why Sir Karl earned the reputation of being a 'difficult man'. But Bartley also thinks that it was precisely this 'culture clash' which allowed Popper to develop the clarity and trenchancy of argument that are universally attributed to him. This 'difficult man' never ceased urging his young disciples to seek out fresh problems and to work hard at them, instead of limiting themselves to a single theme. To them and to all his readers, he left numerous points for further thought and development in nearly every branch of philosophy.

NOTES

1 THE LIFE

1 See the interview given to *Corriere della Sera*, 8 October 1990.
2 *Corriere della Sera*, 16 July 1992.
3 *Corriere della Sera*, 28 August 1991.
4 *La lezione di questo secolo*, Venice, Marsilio, 1992. An English edition is forthcoming (Routledge 1996).
5 *Corriere della Sera*, 16 July 1992.

2 THE EPISTEMOLOGICAL WORKS

1 For a 'weak' formulation of the same principle, see *Objective Knowledge*, p. 12.
2 This idea of the empirical content of theory 'as a measure of the class of its signifiers' is regarded by Popper as 'perhaps the most important logical idea of *The Logic of Scientific Discovery*' (P1: 231).

3 THE POLITICAL WORKS

1 It also, of course, led to discussion of the well-known problems associated with becoming.

4 THE 'METAPHYSICAL' WORKS

1 See N.R. Hanson, *Patterns of Discovery*, Cambridge University Press, Cambridge, 1958; M. Polanyi, *Personal Knowledge*, Routledge & Kegan Paul, London, 1958, and *The Tacit Dimension*, Routledge & Kegan Paul, London, 1967; S. Toulmin, *Foresight and Understanding*, Hutchinson, London, 1961.
2 In 1918, in 'The Thought: a Logical Enquiry' (translated in *Mind* 65 (1956), pp. 289–311), Frege developed a theory of knowledge based upon three distinct realms: the mental, the physical, and a 'third realm' of objective thoughts quite independent of our knowledge and our capacity to express them in language. Popper's World 3, by contrast,

NOTES

is closely bound up with language, without which it could not be expressed.

3 What Popper means is that consciousness is not an entity alongside the brain but a *function* that develops on the basis of the brain, selecting, organizing and connecting the results of brain processes. The brain is in turn modified by the work of consciousness, so much so that its own capacities are improved. Someone might, of course, object that on this reading there is no room for any mind–brain dualism, and that it would have been more consistent if Popper had simply admitted that the brain serves a plurality of functions. This point is worthy of further discussion, but we shall here merely suggest that for Popper such a solution would have called into question the three-world structure as we have described it so far.

4 See the Italian edition of *Die Zukunft ist offen*: *Il futuro è aperto*, Rusconi, Milan, 1989, pp. 8–9.

5 THEMES AND MOTIFS

1 Ludwig Wittgenstein, *Tractatus Logico-Philosophicus* 6.51, Routledge & Kegan Paul, 1981, London, p. 187.

2 See Karl Popper, 'The Place of Mind in Nature', in R.Q. Elvee, (ed.), *Mind in Nature*, Harper & Row, San Francisco, 1982, pp. 38–39.

3 F. Waismann, 'How I See Philosophy', in H.D. Lewis, (ed.), *Contemporary British Philosophy*, third series, second edition, George Allen & Unwin, London, 1961, pp. 447–490.

6 THE CRITICISM

1 Hannah Arendt, *The Origins of Totalitarianism*, third edition, George Allen & Unwin, London, 1966

174

BIBLIOGRAPHY

Abbreviations used:
BJPS = *British Journal for the Philosophy of Science*
PAS = *Proceedings of the Aristotelian Society*

SELECT BIBLIOGRAPHY OF WORKS BY POPPER

This bibliography is reproduced from the one contained in Karl Popper, *Unended Quest: an Intellectual Autobiography*, revised edition, Routledge, London, 1992, pp. 245–259, together with further material published since 1992. The lettering system used in the original has been omitted here.

1925 'Über die Stellung des Lehrers zu Schule und Schüler. Gesellschaftliche oder individualistische Erziehung?', *Schulreform* (Vienna) 4, pp. 204–208.

1927 'Zur Philosophie des Heimatgedankens', *Die Quelle* (Vienna) 77, pp. 899–908.
' "Gewohnheit" und "Gesetzerlebnis" in der Erziehung' unpublished; a thesis presented (unfinished) to the Pedagogic Institute of the City of Vienna.

1928 'Zur Methodenfrage der Denkpsychologie' (unpublished). Doctoral dissertation submitted to the Philosophical Faculty of the University of Vienna.

1931 'Die Gedächtnispflege unter dem Gesichtspunkt der Selbsttätigkeit', *Die Quelle* (Vienna) 81, pp. 607–619.

1932 'Pädagogische Zeitschriftenschau', *Die Quelle* (Vienna) 82, pp. 301–303; 580–582; 646–647; 712–713; 778–781; 846–849; 930–931.

1933 'Ein Kriterium des empirischen Charakters theoretischer Systeme', a letter to the editor, *Erkenntnis* 3, pp. 426–427.

1934 *Logik der Forschung*, Julius Springer Verlag, Vienna (with the imprint '1935').

1935 ' "Induktionslogik" und "Hypothesenwahrscheinlichkeit" ', *Erkenntnis* 5, pp. 170–172.

1938 'A Set of Independent Axioms for Probability', *Mind* 47, pp. 275–277.

1940 'What is Dialectic?', *Mind* 49, pp. 403–426.

1944 'The Poverty of Historicism, I', *Economica* 11, pp. 86–103.
'The Poverty of Historicism. II. A Criticism of Historicist Methods', *Economica* 11, pp. 119–137.

1945 'The Poverty of Historicism, III', *Economica* 12, pp. 69–89.
The Open Society and Its Enemies, vol. I, *The Spell of Plato*, Routledge & Sons, London.
The Open Society and Its Enemies, vol. II, *The High Tide of Prophecy: Hegel, Marx, and the Aftermath*, Routledge & Sons London.
'Research and the University: A Statement by a Group of Teachers in the University of New Zealand', 'The Caxton Press (Christchurch, New Zealand); written in cooperation with R.S. Allan, J.C. Eccles, H.G. Forder, J. Packer and H.N. Parton.

1946 'Why are the Calculuses of Logic and Arithmetic Applicable to Reality?', in *Aristotelian Society, Supplementary Volume XX: Logic and Reality*, Harrison & Sons, London, pp. 40–60.

1947 'New Foundations for Logic', *Mind* 56, pp. 193–235.
'Logic Without Assumptions', PAS XLVII, pp. 251–292.
'Functional Logic without Axioms or Primitive Rules of Inference', *Koninklijke Nederlandsche Akademie van Wetenschappen, Proceedings of the Section of Sciences* (Amsterdam) 50, pp. 1214–1224, and *Indagationes Mathematicae* 9, pp. 561–571.

1948 'On the Theory of Deduction, Part I, Derivation and its Generalizations', *Koninklijke Nederlandsche Akademie van Wetenschappen, Proceedings of the Section of Sciences* (Amsterdam) 51, pp. 173–183, and *Indagationes Mathematicae* 10, pp. 44–54.
'On the Theory of Deduction, Part II. The Definitions of Classical and Intuitionist Negation', *Koninklijke Nederlandsche Akademie van Wetenschappen, Proceedings of the Section of Sciences* (Amsterdam) 51, pp. 322–331, and *Indigationes Mathematicae* 10, pp. 111–120.
'Prediction and Prophecy and their Significance for Social Theory', in *Library of the Tenth International Congress of Philosophy*, 1: *Proceedings of the Tenth International Congress of Philosophy*, edited by E.W. Beth, H.J. Pos and J.H.A. Hollak, North Holland, Amsterdam, pp. 82–91.
'The Trivialization of Mathematical Logic', in *Library of the Tenth International Congress of Philosophy*, 1: *Proceedings of the Tenth International Congress of Philosophy*, edited by E.W. Beth, H.J. Pos and J.H.A. Hollak, North Holland, Amsterdam, pp. 722–727.
'What can Logic do for Philosophy?' in *Aristotelian Society, Sup-*

plementary Volume XXII: Logical Positivism and Ethics, Harrison & Sons, London, pp. 141–154.

1949 'Naturgesetze und theoretische Systeme', in *Gesetz und Wirklichkeit*, edited by Simon Moser, Tyrolia Verlag, Innsbruck and Vienna, pp. 43–60.

1950 *The Open Society and Its Enemies*, Princeton University Press, Princeton, N.J.
'Indeterminism in Quantum Physics and in Classical Physics, Part I', BJPS 1, pp. 117–133.
'Indeterminism in Quantum Physics and in Classical Physics, Part II', BJPS 1, pp. 173–195.
De Vrije Samenleving en Haar Vijanden, F.G. Kroonder, Bussum, Holland.

1952 *The Open Society and Its Enemies* (second English edition), Routledge & Kegan Paul, London.

1953 'Language and the Body–Mind Problem', in *Proceedings of the XIth International Congress of Philosophy* 7, North Holland, Amsterdam, pp. 101–107.
'A Note on Berkeley as Precursor of Mach', BJPS 4, pp. 26–36.

1954 'Self-Reference and Meaning in Ordinary Language', *Mind* 63, pp. 162–169.

1955 'A Note on the Body–Mind Problem. Reply to Professor Wilfrid Sellars', *Analysis* 15, pp. 131–135.
'A Note on Tarski's Definition of Truth', *Mind* 64, pp. 388–391.

1956 'The Arrow of Time', *Nature* 177, p. 538.
'Irreversibility and Mechanics', *Nature* 178, p. 382.

1957 'Philosophy of Science: A Personal Report', *British Philosophy in the Mid-Century: A Cambridge Symposium*; edited by C.A. Mace, George Allen & Unwin, London, pp. 155–191.
'Irreversible Processes in Physical Theory', *Nature* 179, p. 1297.
'The Propensity Interpretation of the Calculus of Probability, and the Quantum Theory', in *Observation and Interpretation; A Symposium of Philosophers and Physicists: Proceedings of the Ninth Symposium of the Colston Research Society held in the University of Bristol, 1–4 April 1957*, edited by S. Körner in collaboration with M.H.L. Pryce, Butterworths Scientific Publications, London, pp. 65–70, 88–89.
'Irreversibility; or Entropy since 1905', BJPS 8, pp. 151–155.
The Poverty of Historicism, Routledge & Kegan Paul, London, and Beacon Press, Boston, Mass.
The Open Society and Its Enemies (third edition), Routledge & Kegan Paul, London.
'The Aim of Science', *Ratio* (Oxford) 1, pp. 24–35.
'Über die Zielsetzung der Erfahrungswissenschaft', *Ratio* (Frankfurt a.M.) 1, pp. 21–31.

Der Zauber Platons: Die offene Gesellschaft und ihre Feinde, Band I, Francke Verlag, Bern.
'Probability Magic or Knowledge out of Ignorance', *Dialectica* 11, pp. 354–372.

1958 'Irreversible Processes in Physical Theory', *Nature* 181, pp. 402–403.
'Das Problem der Nichtwiderlegbarkeit von Philosophien', *Deutsche Universitätszeitung* (Göttingen) 13, pp. 7–13.
'On the Status of Science and of Metaphysics. Two Radio Talks: (i) Kant and the Logic of Experience. (ii) The Problem of the Irrefutability of Philosophical Theories', *Ratio* (Oxford) 1, pp. 97–115.
'Über die Möglichkeit der Erfahrungswissenschaft und der Metaphysik, Zwei Rundfunkvorträge: (i) Kant und die Möglichkeit der Erfahrungswissenschaft. (ii) Über die Nichtwiderlegbarkeit philosophischer Theorien', *Ratio* (Frankfurt a.M.) 2 pp. 1–16.
Falsche Propheten: Hegel, Marx und die Folgen Die offene Gesellschaft und ihre Feinde, Band II, Francke Verlag, Bern.

1959 *The Logic of Scientific Discovery*, Hutchinson & Co., London; Basic Books, New York.
'The Propensity Interpretation of Probability', BJPS 10, pp. 25–42.
'Woran glaubt der Westen?', in *Erziehung zur Freiheit*, edited by Albert Hunold, Eugen Rentsch Verlag, Stuttgart, pp. 237–262.
'Critical Rationalism', in *Philosophy for a Time of Crisis: An Interpretation with Key Writings by Fifteen Great Modern Thinkers*, edited by Adrienne Koch, Dutton & Co., New York, pp. 262–275.

1960 'On the Sources of Knowledge and of Ignorance', *Proceedings of the British Academy* 46, pp. 39–71.

1961 'Selbstbefreiung durch das Wissen', in *Der Sinn der Geschichte*, edited by Leonhard Reinisch, C.H. Beck Verlag, Munich, 1961, pp. 100–116. (English translation 1968.)
'On the Sources of Knowledge and of Ignorance?' Annual Philosophical Lecture, Henriette Hertz Trust, British Academy, Oxford University Press, London.
'Philosophy and Physics', *Atti del XII Congresso Internazionale di Filosofia* 2, G.C. Sansoni Editore, Florence, pp. 367–374.
'Evolution and the Tree of Knowledge', Herbert Spencer Lecture, delivered on October 30 1961, in Oxford.

1962 *The Open Society and Its Enemies* (fourth English edition), Routledge & Kegan Paul, London.
The Open Society and Its Enemies, Routledge Paperbacks, Routledge & Kegan Paul, London.
'Julius Kraft 1898–1960', Ratio (Oxford) 4, pp. 2–10.
'Die Logik der Sozialwissenschaften', *Kölner Zeitschrift für Soziologie und Sozialpsychologie*, Heft 2, pp. 233–248.

1963 *Conjectures and Refutations: The Growth of Scientific Knowledge*, Routledge & Kegan Paul, London; Basic Books Inc., New York.

'Science: Problems, Aims, Responsibilities', *Federation Proceedings* (Baltimore) 22, pp. 961–972.

The Open Society and Its Enemies, Princeton University Press, Princeton, N.J.

The Open Society and Its Enemies, The Academy Library, Harper & Row, New York and Evanston.

1964 *The Poverty of Historicism*, The Academy Library, Harper & Row, New York and Evanston.

1965 'Time's Arrow and Entropy', *Nature* 207, pp. 233–234.

1966 *The Open Society and Its Enemies* (fifth English edition), Routledge Paperbacks, Routledge & Kegan Paul, London.

Logik der Forschung (second edition), J.C.B. Mohr (Paul Siebeck), Tübingen.

Of Clouds and Clocks: An Approach to the Problem of Rationality and the Freedom of Man, Washington University Press, St Louis, Missouri.

'A Theorem on Truth-Content', in *Mind, Matter and Method: Essays in Philosophy and Science in Honor of Herbert Feigl*, edited by Paul K. Feyerabend and Grover Maxwell, University of Minnesota Press, Minneapolis, Minnesota, pp. 343–353.

'Historical Explanation: An Interview with Sir Karl Popper', *University of Denver Magazine* 3, pp. 4–7.

1967 'Time's Arrow and Feeding on Negentropy', *Nature* 213, p. 320.

'La Rationalité et le statut du principe de rationalité', in *Les Fondements Philosophiques des Systèmes Economiques: Textes de Jaques Rueff et essais rédigés en son honneur 23 août 1966*, edited by Emil M. Classen, Payot, Paris, pp. 142–150.

'Zum Thema Freiheit', in *Die Philosophie und die Wissenschaften: Simon Moser zum 65. Geburtstag*, edited by Ernst Oldemeyer, Anton Hain. Meisenhem am Glan, pp. 1–12.

'Structural Information and the Arrow of Time', *Nature* 214, p. 322.

'Quantum Mechanics without "The Observer"', in *Quantum Theory and Reality*, edited by Mario Bunge, Springer Verlag, Berlin, Heidelberg, New York, pp. 7–44.

'Einstein's Influence on My View of Science: An Interview', in *Einstein: The Man and his Achievement*, edited by G.J. Whitrow, BBC, London, pp. 23–28.

1968 'Is there an 'Epistemological Problem of Perception?' in *Proceedings of the International Colloquium in the Philosophy of Science*, 3: *Problems in the Philosophy of Science*, edited by Imre Lakatos and Alan Musgrave, North Holland, Amsterdam, pp. 163–164.

'Theories, Experience, and Probabilistic Intuitions', in *Proceedings of the International Colloquium in the Philosophy of Science*, 2: *The Problem of Inductive Logic*, edited by Imre Lakatos, North Holland, Amsterdam, pp. 285–303.

BIBLIOGRAPHY

'Birkhoff and von Neumann's Interpretation of Quantum Mechanics', *Nature* 219, No. 5155, 17 Aug. pp. 682–685.

'On the Theory of the Objective Mind', in *Akten des XIV Internationalen Kongresses für Philosophie*, 1, University of Vienna, Verlag Herder, Vienna, pp. 25–53.

'Epistemology Without a Knowing Subject', in *Proceedings of the Third International Congress for Logic, Methodology and Philosophy of Science: Logic, Methodology and Philosophy of Science III*, edited by B. van Rootselaar and J.F. Staal, North Holland, Amsterdam, pp. 333–373.

'Emancipation through Knowledge', in *The Humanist Outlook*, edited by A.J. Ayer, Pemberton., London, pp. 281–296.

1969 *Logik der Forschung* (third edition), J.C.B. Mohr (Paul Siebeck), Tübingen.

Conjectures and Refutations, The Growth of Scientific Knowledge (third edition), Routledge & Kegan Paul, London.

'A Pluralist Approach to the Philosophy of History', in *Roads to Freedom: Essays in Honour of Friedrich A. von Hayek*, edited by Erich Streissler, Gottfried Haberler, Friedrich A. Lutz and Fritz Machlup, Routledge & Kegan Paul, London, pp. 181–200.

'The Aim of Science', in *Contemporary Philosophy: A Survey*, edited by Raymond Klibansky, III: *Metaphysics, Phenomenology, Language and Structure*, La Nuova Italia Editrice, Florence, pp. 129–142.

'Die Logik der Sozialwissenschaften', in *Der Positivismusstreit in der deutschen Soziologie*, edited by H. Maus and F. Fürstenberg, Hermann Luchterhand Verlag, Neuwied and Berlin, pp. 103–123.

1970 'Plato, *Timaeus* 54E–55A', *The Classical Review* XX, pp. 4–5.

'A Realist View of Logic, Physics, and History', in *Physics, Logic and History*, edited by Wolfgang Yourgrau and Allen D. Breck, Plenum Press, New York and London, pp. 1–30, and 35–37.

1971 'Revolution oder Reform?', in *Revolution oder Reform? Herbert Marcuse und Karl Popper – Eine Konfrontation*, edited by Franz Stark, Kösel-Verlag, Munich, pp. 3, 9–10, 22–29, 34–39, 41.

'Conjectural Knowledge: My Solution of the Problem of Induction', *Revue Internationale de Philosophie* 25 fasc. 1–2, No. 95–96, pp. 167–197.

'Conversation with Karl Popper', in *Modern British Philosophy* by Bryan Magee, Secker & Warburg, London, pp. 66–82.

'Particle Annihilation and the Argument of Einstein, Podolsky, and Rosen', in *Perspectives in Quantum Theory: Essays in Honor of Alfred Landé*, edited by Wolfgang Yourgrau and Alwyn van der Merwe. MIT Press, Cambridge, Mass., and London, pp. 182–198.

1972 *Objective Knowledge: An Evolutionary Approach*, Clarendon Press, Oxford.

'On Reason and the Open Society: A Conversation', *Encounter* 38, No. 5, pp. 13–18.

BIBLIOGRAPHY

1973 'Indeterminism is Not Enough', *Encounter* 40, No. 4, pp. 20–26.
Die offene Gesellschaft und ihre Feinde, vols I and II, third edition, Francke Verlag, Bern and Munich.

1974 'Autobiography of Karl Popper', in *The Philosophy of Karl Popper*, in *The Library of Living Philosophers*, edited by P.A. Schilpp, vol. I, Open Court, La Salle, pp. 3–181.
'Replies to my Critics', in *The Philosophy of Karl Popper*, in *The Library of Living Philosophers*, edited by P.A. Schilpp, vol. II, Open Court, La Salle, pp. 961–1197.
'Scientific Reduction and the Essential Incompleteness of All Science', *in Studies in the Philosophy of Biology*, edited by F.J. Ayala and T. Dobzhansky, Macmillan, London, pp. 259–284; also University of California Press, Berkeley.
'Normal Science and Its Dangers', in *Criticism and the Growth of Knowledge*, edited by Imre Lakatos and Alan Musgrave, Cambridge University Press, Cambridge, pp. 51–58.

1975 'How I See Philosophy', in *The Owl of Minerva. Philosophers on Philosophy*, edited by C.T. Bontempo and S.J. Odell, McGraw-Hill, New York, pp. 41–55.
'The Rationality of Scientific Revolutions', in *Problems of Scientific Revolution. Progress and Obstacles to Progress in the Sciences, The Herbert Spencer Lectures 1973*, edited by Rom Harré, Clarendon Press, Oxford, pp. 72–101.
'Wissenschaft und Kritik', in *Idee und Wirklichkeit: 30 Jahre Europäisches Forum, Alpbach*, Springer Verlag, Vienna and New York, pp. 65–75.

1976 *Logik der Forschung* (sixth revised impression). J.C.B. Mohr (Paul Siebeck), Tübingen.
'The Logic of the Social Sciences', in T.W. Adorno *et al. The Positivist Dispute in German Sociology*, Heinemann London, pp. 87–104.
'Reason or Revolution?', in T.W. Adorno *et al. The Positivist Dispute in German Sociology*, Heinemann, London, pp. 288–300.
'A Note on Verisimilitude', BJPS 27, pp. 147–159.
'The Myth of the Framework', in *The Abdication of Philosophy. Philosophy and the Public Good. Essays in Honor of Paul Arthur Schilpp*, edited by Eugene Freeman, Open Court, La Salle, pp. 23–48.
The Poverty of Historicism (ninth impression), Routledge & Kegan Paul, London.
Conjectures and Refutations (sixth impression), Routledge & Kegan Paul, London.
'On Reason and Open Society', in *Revolution or Reform? A Confrontation*, edited by A.T. Ferguson, New University Press, Chicago.

1977 'The Death of Theories and of Ideologies', in *La Reflection sur la mort*, 2, Symposium International de Philosophie 'PLETHON', Athens, pp. 296–328.
'Some Remarks on Panpsychism and Epiphenomenalism', *Dialectica*

31, pp. 177–186. *The Logic of Scientific Discovery* (ninth impression) Hutchinson, London.

The Self and Its Brain: An Argument for Interactionism with John C. Eccles. Springer International, Berlin, Heidelberg, London, New York.

The Open Society and Its Enemies (twelfth impression), Routledge & Kegan Paul, London.

1978 'On the Possibility of an Infinite Past: A Reply to Whitrow', BJPS 29, pp. 47–8.

'Natural Selection and the Emergence of Mind', *Dialectica* 32, pp. 339–355.

'Bemerkungen über die Frankfurter Schule', in *Gespräche mit Herbert Marcuse*, Suhrkamp Verlag, Frankfurt am Main pp. 130–134.

1979 *Objective Knowledge: An Evolutionary Approach* (fifth (revised) impression). Clarendon Press, Oxford. (This contains a new Appendix 2.)

'Is it True What She Says About Tarski?', *Philosophy* 54, p. 98.

'Die Wechselwirkung und die Wirklichkeit der Welt 3', in *Wissen und Macht*, edited by O. Molden, Verlag Fritz Molden, Vienna, Munich, Zürich, Innsbruck, pp. 108–116.

'Three Worlds', *Michigan Quarterly Review* 18, No. 1, pp. 1–23.

'Epistemology and Industrialization', *Ordo* 30, pp. 3–20.

'Ich weiss, dass ich fast nichts weiss, und kaum das', *Uni Report*, Universität Frankfurt 12, no. 9, pp. 3f.

Ausgangspunkte, Meine Intellektuelle Entwicklung, Hoffman & Campe, Hamburg.

'Creative Self-Criticism in Science and in Art', *Encounter* 53, pp. 10–14.

Die beiden Grundprobleme der Erkenntnistheorie, edited by Troels Eggers Hansen, J.C.B. Mohr (Paul Siebeck), Tübingen.

The Growth of Scientific Knowledge, Vittorio Klosterman, Frankfurt am Main.

'Uber die sogenannten Quellen der menschlichen Erkenntnis', *Das Fenster* 25, pp. 2527–2529.

1980 *The Logic of Scientific Discovery* (tenth impression (revised)), Hutchinson, London.

'Wissen und Nichtwissen', in *Verleihung der Ehrendoktorwürde an Sir Karl Popper*, Pressestelle der Universität, Frankfurt am Main.

'Three Worlds', in *The Tanner Lectures on Human Values*, vol. 1, edited by Sterling M. McMurrin, University of Utah Press, Salt Lake City, and Cambridge University Press, Cambridge, pp. 141–167.

The Open Society and Its Enemies, vols I and II (thirteenth impression), Routledge & Kegan Paul, London.

Det öppna samhället och dess fiender, vol. I, Akademilitteratur, Stockholm.

1981 'An Experiment to Interpret E.P.R. Action-at-a-Distance: The

Possible Detection of Real De Broglie Waves' (with A. Garuccio and J.-P. Vigier), Epistemological *Letters* 30th Issue.
'Wissenschaft: Wissen und Nichtwissen', *Weltwoche Magazin* no. 33, pp. 10–12.
'Uber den Zusammenprall von Kulturen', in *25 Jahre Staatsvertrag*, Osterreichischer Bundesverlag, Vienna, pp. 118–122.
'Joseph Henry Woodger,' BJPS 32, pp. 382–330.
'The Present Significance of Two Arguments of Henri Poincaré', *Methodology and Science* 14, pp. 260–264.
Foreword to *Cosmology, Physics and Philosophy*, by Benjamin Gal-Or, Springer Verlag, New York.

1982 *The Open Universe: An Argument for Indeterminism. From the Postscript to the Logic of Scientific Discovery*, edited by W.W. Bartley III, Hutchinson, London; Rowman & Littlefield, Totowa, N.J.
Quantum Theory and the Schism in Physics. From the Postscript to the Logic of Scientific Discovery, edited by W.W. Bartley III, Hutchinson of London; Rowman & Littlefield, Totowa, N.J.
Logik der Forschung. (seventh impression), revised and enlarged, with six new Appendices, J.C.B. Mohr (Paul Siebeck), Tübingen.
Ausgangspunkte: Meine Intellektuelle Entwicklung (second revised edition with augmented bibliography), Hoffman & Campe, Hamburg.
'Proposal for a Simplified New Variant of the Experiment of Einstein, Podolsky and Rosen', in *Physik, Philosophie und Politik* (Festschrift for C.F. von Weizsäcker's 70th birthday), edited by Klaus Michael Meyer-Abich, Carl Hanser Verlag, Munich, pp. 310–313.
Offene Gesellschaft – offenes Universum. Discussions between Franz Kreuzer and K.R. Popper; (1979, 1981, 1982), and a lecture by K.R. Popper; edited by Franz Kreuzer, Franz Deuticke, Vienna,
'The Place of Mind in Nature' in *Mind in Nature* (Nobel Conference XVIII, Gustavus Adolphus College), edited by Richard Q. Elvee, Harper & Row, San Francisco, pp. 31–59.
'Duldsamkeit und Intellektuelle Verantwortlichkeit', in *Toleranz*, edited by Peter Stuhlmacher and Luise Abramowski, Atempto Verlag, Tübingen University Press, pp. 173–185.
'A Critical Note on the Greatest Days of Quantum Theory', *Foundations of Physics* 12, no. 10, pp. 971–976.

1983 *The Logic of Scientific Discovery* (eleventh impression). Hutchinson, London.
Realism and the Aim of Science. From the Postscript to the Logic of Scientific Discovery, edited by W.W. Bartley III, Hutchinson, London, Rowman & Littlefield, Totowa. N.J.
'Is Determinism Self-Refuting?' *Mind* 92, pp. 103–104
'Bücher und Gedanken', *Anzeiger des Osterreichischen Buchhandels* 118.
'A Proof of the Impossibility of Inductive Probability', published with David Miller, *Nature* 302, pp. 687–688.

A Pocket Popper, Selection from Popper's writings, edited, with an Introduction, by David Miller, Fontana Paperbacks, London and Glasgow.

'The Critical Attitude in Medicine: The Need for a New Ethics', in collaboration with Professor Neil McIntyre. *British Medical Journal*, 287, pp. 1919–1923.

1984 *Logik der Forschung* (eighth edition) (50 Jahre *Logik der Forschung*), with a New Appendix, J.C.B. Mohr (Paul Siebeck). Tübingen.

Auf der Suche nach einer besseren Welt, Lectures and Essays compiled over 30 years, Piper Verlag, Munich.

'The Impossibility of Inductive Probability: Popper and Miller Reply', *Nature*, 310 pp. 433–434.

'Against Induction: One of Many Arguments', in *Rationality in Science and Politics*, edited by Gunnar Andersson, Reidel, Dordrecht, pp. 245–247.

'Evolutionary Epistemology', in *Evolutionary Theory: Paths into the Future*, edited by J.W. Pollard, Wiley, Chichester and New York, pp. 239–255.

'A Critical Note on the Greatest Days of Quantum Theory', in *Quantum, Space and Time – The Quest Continues, Studies and Essays in Honour of Louis de Broglie, Paul Dirac and Eugene Wigner*, edited by Asim O. Barut, Alwyn van der Merwe and Jean-Pierre Vigier, Cambridge University Press.

'Critical Remarks on the Knowledge of Lower and Higher Organisms, the So-called Sensory Motor Systems', in *Sensory Motor Integration in the Nervous System*, edited by O. Creutzfeldt, R.F. Schmidt and W.D. Willis, Springer Verlag, Berlin, pp. 19–31.

'Festvortrag: 40 Jahre Naturwissenschaft', in *Der Beitrag: Europas Erbe und Auftrag, Europäisches Forum Alpbach 1984*, edited by Otto Molden, Österreichisches College, Vienna.

1985 'Realism in Quantum Mechanics and a New Version of the EPR Experiment', *Open Questions in Quantum Physics*, edited by G. Tarozzi and A. van der Merwe, Reidel, Dordrecht, Holland, pp. 3–25.

Popper Selections, edited by David Miller, Princeton University Press, Princeton, N.J.

Die Zukunft ist offen. Das Altenberger Gespräch. Mit den Texten des Wiener Symposiums, by K.R. Popper and Konrad Lorenz, edited by Franz Kreuzer (also containing contributions by others), Piper Verlag, Munich, Zurich.

'The Non-Existence of Probabilistic Inductive Support', in *Foundations of Logic and Linguistics: Problems and their Solutions*, edited by Georg Dorn and Paul Weingartner, Plenum Press. New York and London, pp. 303–318.

'Has Inductive Probability been Proved Impossible? Popper and Miller Reply', *Nature* 315, p. 461.

'Towards a Local Explanatory Theory of the Einstein–Podolsky–Rosen–Bohm Experiment' (with Thomas D. Angelidis), in *Sym-*

posium on the Foundations of Modern Physics, edited by P. Lahti and P. Mittelstaedt, World Scientific Publishing Co., pp. 37–49.

'Realism and Quantum Theory', in *Determinism in Physics. Proceedings of the Second International Meeting on Epistemology*, edited by Eftichios Bitsakis and Nikos Tambakis, Gutenberg Publishing Company, Athens, pp. 11–29.

'Festvortrag: 40 Jahre Naturwissenschaft', in *Der Beitrag: Europas Erbe und Auftrag, Europäisches Forum Alpbach 1984*, edited by Otto Molden, Österreichisches College, Vienna.

1986 *Offene Gesellschaft – offenes Universum Discussions between Franz Kreuzer and K.R. Popper*, Serie Piper, Munich.

'Realism and a Proposal for a Simplified New Variant of the EPR-Experiment' in *Foundations of Physics*, a selection of papers contributed to the Physics Section of the 7th International Congress of Logic, Methodology and Philosophy of Science, edited by Paul Weingartner and Georg Dorn, Hölder-Pichler-Tempsky, Vienna, pp. 227–249.

1987 'Bell's Theorem: A Note on Locality', in *Microphysical Reality and Quantum Formalism*, edited by G. Tarozzi and A. van der Merwe, Reidel, Dordrecht, pp. 413–417.

Das Ich und sein Gehirn, with John C. Eccles, sixth edition (first paperback), R. Piper & Co., Munich.

'Why Probabilistic Support Is Not Inductive', with D.W. Miller, *Philosophical Transactions of the Royal Society*, A 321, No. 1562, pp. 569–596.

'Die erkenntnistheoretische Position der Evolutionären Erkenntnistheorie', in *Die Evolutionäre Erkenntnistheorie: Bedingungen, Lösungen, Kontroversen*, edited by Rupert Riedl and Franz M. Wuketis, Verlag Paul Parey, Berlin and Hamburg.

Letter to the Editor about Hegel and Hitler. *The Salisbury Review*, July 1987.

'Zur Theorie der Demokratie', *Der Spiegel*, 3 Aug., Hamburg.

'Popper versus Copenhagen, letter in reply to Collett and Loudon', *Nature* 328, 20.8.1987.

Objekive Erkenntnis: Ein Evolutionärer Entwurf (fifth impression), Hoffmann & Campe, Hamburg.

'Toleration and Intellectual Responsibility', in *On Toleration*, edited by Susan Mendus and David Edwards, Clarendon Press, Oxford.

'Campbell on the Evolutionary Theory of Knowledge', in *Evolutionary Epistemology, Rationality, and the Sociology of Knowledge*, edited by G. Radnitzky and W.W. Bartley III, Open Court, La Salle, pp. 115–120.

'Natural Selection and the Emergence of Mind', in *Evolutionary Epistemology, Rationality, and the Sociology of Knowledge*, edited by G. Radnitzky and W.W. Bartley III, Open Court, La Salle, pp. 139–155.

1988 'Popper on Democracy. *The Open Society and Its Enemies*

Revisited', *The Economist*, 23 April, pp. 25–28. (Title not chosen by the author.)

'Bermerkungen zu Theorie und Praxis des demokratischen Staates'. Lecture given in Munich, 9 June, published by Bank Hofmann AG, Zürich.

1989 *Quantum Theory and the Schism in Physics, From the Postscript to the Logic of Scientific Discovery*, edited by W.W. Bartley III, Unwin Hyman, London.

'Zwei Bedeutungen von Falsifizierbarkeit', in *Handlexikon zur Wissenschaftstheorie*, edited by Helmut Seiffert and Gerard Radnitzky, Ehrenwirt GmbH Verlag, Munich, pp. 82–86.

Conjectures and Refutations, fifth edition (revised and corrected), Routledge, London, (Eleventh impression.)

'Popper on Schrödinger', *Nature* 342, 23 Nov.

'On a Little Known Chapter of Mediterranean History', *Catalònia*, No. 15, pp. 31–37. Centre Unesco de Catalunya, Barcelona.

'Creative Self-Criticism in Science and in Art', *Diogenes*, 145. Casal-'ini Libri, Fiesole, pp. 36–45.

Das Ich und sein Gehirn, with John C. Eccles, (ninth edition), R. Piper & Co., Munich.

The Open Society and Its Enemies, I, Routledge, London. (Eighth reprint of the fifth (revised 1966) edition.)

The Poverty of Historicism (thirteenth impression), Ark paperbacks (an imprint of Routledge & Kegan Paul), London and New York.

1990 *A World of Propensities*, Thoemmes, Bristol. Two lectures, revised and extended: (1) 'A World of Propensities: Two New Views of Causality', delivered at the 1988 World Congress of Philosophy at Brighton, and (2) 'Towards an Evolutionary Theory of Knowledge', delivered at the London School of Economics on June 1989.

'Pyrite and the Origin of Life', *Nature* 344, No. 6265, p. 387. 29 March.

'Progenote or Protogenote?' with Dr. Günter Wächtershäuser. *Science*, 250/4984 ('Letters'), 23 Nov., p. 1070.

1991 'Kepler: Seine Metaphysik des Sonnensystems und seine empirische Kritik', in *Wege der Vernunft, Festschrift zum 70. Geburtstag von Hans Albert*, J.C.B. Mohr (Paul Siebeck), Tübingen.

'Révolutions scientifiques et révolutions idéologiques', Introduction to *Karl Popper: Science et Philosophie*, edited by Renée Bouveresse and Hervé Barreau, Librairie Philosophique J. Vrin, Paris.

The Open Society and Its Enemies, I, Routledge, London. (Ninth reprint of the fifth (revised 1966) edition.)

The Poverty of Historicism (fourteenth impression), Routledge, London and New York.

'Ich weiss, dass ich nichts weiss – und kaum das': Karl Popper im Gespräch über Politik, Physik und Philosophie, Ullstein GmbH, Berlin. (Two interviews with *Die Welt*, in 1987 and 1990.)

1992 'How the Moon Might Throw Some of Her Light upon the Two Ways of Parmenides', *Classical Quarterly*, 86, pp. 12–19.

1993 'A Discussion in the Mind–Body Problem', with B. Lindhal and P. Arhem, *Theoretical Medicine*, 14, pp. 167–180.

1994 *Alles Leben ist problemlösen. Über Erkenntnis, Geschichte und Politik*, Piper Verlag, Munich.
Knowledge and the Mind–Body Problem: In Defence of Interaction, edited by M.A. Notturno, Routledge, London.
The Myth of the Framework, Routledge, London.
'Una patente per fare TV', *Reset*, September.

CRITICAL LITERATURE

Studies of the cultural context

Achinstein, P. and Barker S., *The Legacy of Logical Positivism*, Johns Hopkins University Press, Baltimore, 1969.

Agassi, J. and Jarvie I. (eds), *Rationality: The Critical View*, Nijhoff, Dordrecht, 1987.

Andersson, G., *Kritik und Wissenschaftsgeschichte. Kuhns, Lakatos' und Feyerabends Kritik des kritischen Rationalismus*, J.C.B. Mohr (Paul Siebeck), Tübingen, 1988.

Baldini, M., *Teoria e storia della scienza*, Armando, Rome, 1975.

Barone, F., *Il neopositivismo logico*, 2 vols, Laterza, Rome and Bari, 1977.

—— *Immagini filosofiche della scienza*, Laterza, Rome and Bari, 1985.

Brown, H.I., *Perception, Theory and Commitment: The New Philosophy of Science*, University of Chicago Press, Chicago, 1977.

Corvi R., *I fraintendimenti della ragione. Saggio su P.K. Feyerabend*, Vita e Pensiero, Milan, 1992.

Egidi R., *Il linguaggio delle teorie scientifiche: esperienza ed ipotesi nell'epistemologia contemporanea*, Guida, Naples, 1979.

Feyerabend, P., Cohen R.S. and Wartofsky, M.W. (eds), *Essays in Memory of Imre Lakatos*, Reidel, Dordrecht, 1976.

Focher, F., *I quatro autori di Popper*, Angeli, Milan, 1982.

Gillies, D., *Philosophy of Science in the Twentieth Century: Four Central Themes*, Blackwell, Oxford, 1993.

Giorello, G., 'Filosofia della scienza e storia della scienza nella cultura di lingua inglese', in L. Geymonat (ed.), *Storia del pensiero filosofico e scientifico*, Garzanti, Milan, 1976, vol. 7, pp. 190–298.

Hacking, I., *Scientific Revolutions*, Oxford University Press, Oxford, 1981.

Haller, R., *Studien zur österreichischen Philosophie*, Rodopi, Amsterdam, 1979.

Hanson, N.R., *Patterns of Discovery*, Cambridge University Press, Cambridge, 1958.

Hempel, C.G., *Aspects of Scientific Explanation*, The Free Press, London and New York, 1965.

Howson, C. (ed.), *Methods of Appraisal in the Physical Sciences*, Cambridge University Press, Cambridge, 1976.

Jacob, P., *De Vienne à Cambridge*, Gallimard, Paris, 1980.

—— *L'Empirisme logique, ses antécedents, ses critiques*, Editions de Minuit, Paris, 1980.

Kraft, V., 'Popper and the Vienna Circle', in P.A. Schilpp (ed.), *The Philosophy of Karl Popper*, Open Court, La Salle, 1974, vol. 1, pp. 105–204.

Lakatos, I. and Musgrave, A. (ed.), *Criticism and the Growth of Knowledge*, Cambridge University Press, Cambridge, 1974.

Losee, J., *A Historical Introduction to the Philosophy of Science*, Oxford University Press, Oxford, 1972.

Malherbe, J.F., *La Philosophie de Karl Popper et le positivisme logique*, PUF, Paris, 1979.

Minazzi, F., *Il flauto di Popper. Saggio critico sulla 'New Philosophy of Science' e la sua interpretazione di Galileo*, Angeli, Milan, 1995.

Nordhofen, E., *Philosophen des 20. Jahrhunderts in Portraits*, Athenäum Verlag, Königstein, 1980.

Nyiri, J.C. (ed.), *Austrian Philosophy: Studies and Texts*, Philosophia Verlag, Munich, 1981.

Oldroyd, D.R., *The Arch of Knowledge: an Introduction to the History of the Philosophy and Methodology of Science*, Methuen, London, 1986.

Polanyi, M., *Personal Knowledge*, Routledge & Kegan Paul, London, 1958.

—— *The Tacit Dimension*, Routledge & Kegan Paul, London, 1967.

Radnitzky, G. and Andersson, G. (eds), *Progress and Rationality in Science*, Reidel, Dordrecht, 1978.

—— and —— (eds), *The Structure and Development of Science*, Reidel, Dordrecht, 1979.

Restaino, F., 'L'epistemologia post-positivistica', in G. Fornero (ed.), *La filosofia contemporanea*, UTET, Turin, 1991, pp. 789–830.

Stockman, N., *Antipositivist Theories of Science: Critical Rationalism, Critical Theory and Scientific Realism*, Reidel, Dordrecht, 1983.

Toulmin, S., *Foresight and Understanding*, Hutchinson, London, 1961.

Vozza, M., *Rilevanze. Epistemologia ed ermeneutica*, Laterza, Rome, 1982.

Watkins, J., *Science and Scepticism*, Hutchinson, London, 1984.

Worrall, J., 'Philosophy, Logic and Scientific Method at the LSE. Popper's Influence on the School of Economics', *LSE Magazine*, June 1982.

General studies of Popper's thought

Various authors, *La sfida di Popper*, Armando, Rome, 1981.

Ackermann, R., *The Philosophy of Karl Popper*, University of Massachusetts Press, Amherst, 1976.

Alcaro, M., *La crociata anti-empirista*, Angeli, Milan, 1981.

Alt, J.A., *Karl R. Popper*, Campus Verlag, Frankfurt a.M., 1992.

Antiseri, D., *Karl R. Popper. Epistemologia e società aperta*, Armando, Rome, 1972.

—— 'Epistemologia e politica in Karl Popper', *Studi urbinati* 48 (1974), nos 1–2, pp. 265–282.

—— *Regole della democrazia e logica della ricerca*, Rome, 1977.

—— 'Popper', in A. Bausola (ed.), *Questioni di storiografia filosofica*, La Scuola, Brescia, 1978, vol. 5, pp. 457–494.

—— 'Karl Raimund Popper', in A. Negri (ed.), *Novecento filosofico e scientifico*, Marzorati, Milan, 1991, vol. 3, pp. 487–505.

Artigas, M., *Karl Popper. Búsqueda sin término*, EMESA, Madrid, 1980.

Bartley, W.W., 'The Philosophy of Karl Popper, Part I: Biology and Evolutionary Epistemology', *Philosophia* 6 (1976), pp. 463–494; Part II: Consciousness and Physics', *Philosophia* 7 (1978), pp. 675–716; 'Part III: Rationality, Criticism and Logic', *Philosophia* 11 (1982), pp. 121–221.

Baudouin, J., *Karl Popper*, PUF, Paris, 1989.

Baum, W. and Gonzales, K.E., *Karl R. Popper*, Morgenbuch, Berlin, 1994.

Bouveresse, R. and Barreau, H. (eds), *Karl Popper: science et philosophie*, Vrin, Paris, 1991.

Boyer, A., *Introduction à la lecture de Karl Popper*, Presses de l'École Normale Supérieure, Paris, 1994.

Brescia, G., *Epistemologia ed ermeneutica nel pensiero di Karl Popper*, Schena, Fasano, 1986.

Bunge, M. (ed.), *The Critical Approach to Science and Philosophy. In Honour of Karl Popper*, The Free Press, London and New York, 1964.

Burke, T.E., *The Philosophy of Popper*, Manchester University Press, Manchester, 1983.

Buzzoni, M., *Conoscenza e realtà in K.R. Popper*, Angeli, Milan, 1982.

—— *La persona fra natura e cultura*, Studium, Rome, 1984.

Corvi, R., 'Critica della ragione incerta. In ricordo di Karl Popper (1902–1994)', *Vita e Pensiero* 78/1 (1995), pp. 48–60.

Döring, E., *Karl R. Popper. Einführung ins Leben und Werk*, Hoffmann & Campe, Hamburg, 1987; Parerga, Bonn, 1992.

Eidlin, F. (ed.), *Newsletter for Those Interested in the Philosophy of Karl Popper*, University of Guelph, Guelph (Ont.), vol. 1, 1983.

Falanga, M., 'Sulla filosofia di Karl Popper', *Rivista critica di storia della filosofia* 34 (1979), pp. 177–206.

Geier W., *Karl Popper*, Rowohlt, Reinbek, 1994.

Gumnion, H., *Karl Popper*, Rowohlt, Reinbek, 1980.

Handjaras, L. and Marinotti, A., *Epistemologia, logica e realtà. Una introduzione a K. Popper e a W.V. Quine*, La Nuova Italia, Florence, 1983.

Hosnik, A. (ed.), *Caminos de apertura. El pensamiento de Karl R. Popper*, Trillas, Mexico City, 1991.

Hülsman, H., *Die Anonimität von Dialektik im Reden über Dialektik. Zur Philosophie K. Poppers*, Scriptor, Kronberg, 1975.

Kekes, J., 'Popper in Perspective', *Metaphilosophy* 8 (1977), pp. 36–61.

Lentini, L. and Fornero, G., 'Popper', in G. Fornero, *La filosofia contemporanea*, UTET, Turin, 1991, pp. 585–678.

Levinson, P. (ed.), *In Pursuit of Truth. Essays on the Philosophy of Karl Popper on the Occasion of his 80th Birthday*, Humanities Press, Atlantic Highlands, 1982.

Lieberson, J., 'Karl Popper', *Social Research* 49 (1982), pp. 68–115.

Lunghi, S., *Introduzione al pensiero di Karl R. Popper*, Le Monier, Florence, 1979.

Magee, B., *Popper*, Fontana, London, 1977.

Malherbe, J.F., *La Philosophie de Karl Popper et le positivisme logique*, PUF, Paris, 1976, second edition 1979.

Mellor, D.H., 'The Popper Phenomenon', *Philosophy* 52 (1977), pp. 195–202.

Müller, K., Stadler, F. and Wallner, F. (eds), *Versuche und Widerlegungen. Offene Probleme im Werk Karl Poppers*, Geyer, Vienna, 1986.

Narskii, I.S., 'The Philosophy of the Late Karl Popper', *Soviet Studies in Philosophy* 18 (1979–80), no. 4, pp. 53–77.

Naydler, J., 'The Poverty of Popperism', *Thomist* 46 (1982), pp. 92–107.

Negri, A., *Il mondo della insicurezza. Dittico su Popper*, Angeli, Milan, 1983.

O'Hear, A., *Karl Popper*, Routledge & Kegan Paul, London, 1980.

Palumbo, P., *Contro la ragione pigra. Linguaggio, conoscenza e critica in Karl Popper*, Flaccovio, Palermo, 1981.

Petruzellis, N., *La crisi dello scientismo. Riflessioni su K.R. Popper, il neo-empirismo e il razionalismo critico*, Nuovo Istituto Editoriale Italiano, Milan, 1983.

Prada, M., 'Introducción al estudio de Karl Popper', *Franciscanum* 26 (1984), pp. 23–40.

Quinton, A., 'K.R. Popper', in *Encyclopedia of Philosophy*, vol. 6, New York, 1967, pp. 389–401.

Schaefer, L., *Karl R. Popper*, Beck, Munich, 1988.

Schilpp, P.A. (ed.), *The Philosophy of Karl Popper*, Open Court, La Salle, 1974, 2 vols.

Selleri, F., 'Karl Popper at Ninety: Highlights of a Lifelong Intellectual Quest', *Foundations of Physics* 21 (1991), pp. 1375–1386.

Todisco, O., *La storia della filosofia in prospettiva epistemologica. Introdu-zione alle tesi fondamentali di K.R. Popper*, Abete, Rome, 1978.

Wallner, F. (ed.), *Karl Popper. Philosophie und Wissenschaft*, Vienna 1985.

Williams, D.E., *Truth, Hope and Power: The Thought of Karl Popper*, University of Toronto Press, Toronto, 1989.

Studies of individual works

Achinstein, P., 'Review of K.R. Popper's *Conjectures and Refutations*', *BJPS* 19 (1986), pp. 159–169.

Alt, J., *Die Frühschriften Poppers: der Weg Poppers von der Pädagogik und der Psychologie zur Spätphilosophie*, Lang, Frankfurt a.M., 1982.

Bachelard, G., 'Review of *Logik der Forschung*', *Recherches Philosophiques* 5 (1935–6), p. 446.

Boutot, A., 'Le Déterminisme, est-il réfuté? Analyse de la critique poppér-ienne du déterminisme scientifique dans *The Open Universe*', *Revue de Métaphysique et de Morale* 93 (1988), pp. 489–512.

Carnap, R., 'Review of *Logik der Forschung*', in *Erkenntnis* 5 (1935), pp. 290–294.

Douglas, R., 'Popper and Eccles' Psychophysical Interaction Thesis Exam-ined', *Grazer philosophische Studien* 23 (1985), pp. 129–153.

Feyerabend, P.K., 'Popper's Objective Knowledge', *Inquiry* 17 (1974), pp. 475–507.

—— 'Trivializing Knowledge. A Review of Popper's *Postscript*', *Inquiry* 29 (1986), pp. 93–119.

Flach, 'Der Kritizismus als Triebkraft der Entwicklung des modernen Empirismus', *Philosophische Rundshau* 28 (1981), nos. 1–2, pp. 84–100.

Geymonat, L., 'Review of *Logik der Forschung*', *Rivista di Filosofia* 27 (1936), pp. 261–265.

Gomez Tutor, J.I., *Das Induktions- und Abgrenzungsproblem in den Frühschriften von Karl R. Popper*, Lang, Frankfurt a.M., 1988.

Gröbl, E., *Geltung und Gegenstand. Zur Metaphysik im Frühwerk Karl R. Poppers*, Campus Verlag, Frankfurt a.M., 1983.

Gullo, L., 'Popper e lo storicismo', *Verifiche* 4 (1975), pp. 328–343.

Hatmangadi, J., 'The Realism of Popper and Russell', *Philosophy of Social Science* 15 (1985), pp. 461–486.

Klemke, E.D., 'Karl Popper, Objective Knowledge, and the Third World', *Philosophia* 9 (1979–80), pp. 45–62.

Mackie, J.L., 'Failures in Criticism: Popper and his Commentators', BJPS 29 (1978), pp. 363–387.

Miller, D., 'Popper's Qualitative Theory of Verisimilitude', BJPS 25 (1974), pp. 166–177.

Mondadori, M., 'Probabilità e contenuto semantico nella Logica della scoperta scientifica di Karl. R. Popper', *Lingua e stile* 6/2 (1971), pp. 317–333.

Neurath, O., 'Pseudorationalismus der Falsifikation', *Erkenntnis* 5 (1935), pp. 353–365.

Oetjens, H., *Sprache, Logik, Wirklichkeit. Der Zusammenhang von Theorie und Erfahrung in K.R. Poppers Logik der Forschung*, Frommann-Holzbog, Stuttgart, 1975.

Reichenbach, H., 'Über Induktion und Wahrscheinlichkeit. Bemerkungen zu Karl Poppers *Logik der Forschung*', *Erkenntnis* 5 (1935), pp. 264–284.

Schurz, G. and Dorn, G., 'Why Popper's Basic Statements Are Not Falsifiable. Some Paradoxes in Popper's *Logic of Scientific Discovery*', *Zeitschrift für allgemeine Wissenschaftstheorie* 19 (1988), pp. 124–143.

Staflen, M., 'Popper's Postscript', *Philosophia Reformata* 48 (1983), pp. 50–65; 49 (1984), pp. 71–91.

Stotz, G., *Person und Gehirn. Historische und neurophysiologische Aspekte zur Theorie des Ich bei Popper/Eccles*, Olms, 1988, pp. xiv–344.

Stove, D.C., 'Critical Notice on Popper's *Logic of Scientific Discovery*', *Australasian Journal of Philosophy* 38 (1960), pp. 173–187.

Stuermann, W.E., 'Review of *The Logic of Scientific Discovery*', *Filosofia* (1960), pp. 637–645.

Tonini, S.E., 'Lettura dei dialoghi Popper–Eccles', *La Nuova Critica* (1981), nos 59–60, pp. 143–149.

Toulmin, S.E., 'Review of *The Logic of Scientific Discovery*', *L'Industria*, (1959), pp. 360–366.

Warnock, G.J., 'Review of *The Logic of Scientific Discovery*', *Mind* 69 (1960), pp. 99–101.

Wettersten, J.R., 'The Road through Würzburg, Vienna and Göttingen', *Philosophy of Social Science* 15 (1985), pp. 487–505.

Zahar, E., 'The Popper–Lakatos Controversy in the Light of *Die beiden Grundprobleme der Erkenntnistheorie*', BJPS 34 (1983), pp. 149–171.

Studies on epistemology and the theory of knowledge

Various authors, *Le piú recenti epistemologie: Popper–Hempel, Proceedings of the XVIII Convention of Philosophy Lecturers, Padua, 1973*, Gregoriana, Padua, 1974.

Various authors, *Methodologies: Bayesian and Popperian*, Reidel, Dordrecht, 1975.

Agassi, J., *Science in Flux*, Reidel, Dordrecht, 1975.

—— 'Science in Flux: Footnotes to Popper', in R.S. Cohen and M.W. Wartofsky (eds), *Boston Studies in the Philosophy of Science*, vol. 3, Dordrecht, 1968.

—— 'The Novelty of Popper's Philosophy of Science', *International Philosophical Quarterly* 8 (1968), pp. 442–463.

Albert, H., 'Der kritische Rationalismus Karl Raimund Poppers', *Archiv für Rechts- und Sozialphilosophie* 46 (1960), pp. 391–415.

—— 'The Myth of Total Reason' (1964), in T.W. Adorno *et al.*, *The Positivist Dispute in German Sociology*, Heinemann, London, 1976.

—— *Treatise on Critical Reason* (1968), Princeton University Press, Princeton, 1985.

—— *Plaidoyer für kritischen Rationalismus*, Piper Verlag, Munich, 1971.

Alt, J., *Vom Ende der Utopie in der Erkenntnistheorie. Poppers evolutionäre Erkenntnistheorie und ihre praktische Konsequenzen*, Gruppe Athenaeum, Königstein, 1980.

Antiseri, D., 'Il ruolo della metafisica nella scoperta scientifica e nella storia della scienza', *Rivista di Filosofia Neo-scolastica* 74 (1982), pp. 68–108.

Baldini, M., 'La dimensione ideologica dell'epistemologia di Karl R. Popper', *Sapienza* 27 (1974), pp. 129–154.

—— 'Le riflessioni epistemologiche di Karl R. Popper', *Sapienza* 28 (1975), pp. 405–446.

Bartley, W.W., 'Theories of Demarcation between Science and Metaphysics', in I. Lakatos and A. Musgrave (eds), *Problems in the Philosophy of Science*, North Holland, Amsterdam, 1968.

Bayertz, K. and Schleistein, J., *Mythologie der 'kritischen Vernunft'. Zur Kritik der Erkenntnis- und Geschichtstheorie Karl Poppers*, Pahl-Rugenstein, Cologne, 1977.

Bernardini, S., *Logica della conoscenza scientifica*, Lignori, Naples, 1980.

Bouveresse, R., *Karl Popper ou le rationalisme critique*, Vrin, Paris, 1981.

—— (ed.), *Karl Popper et la science d'aujourd'hui. Actes du colloque de Cérisy 1981*, Aubier, Paris, 1989.

Bouveresse, R. and Barreau, H. (eds), *Karl Popper: science et philosophie*, Vrin, Paris, 1991.

Boyer, A., *Karl Popper, une épistémologie laïque?*, Presses de l'Ecole Normale Supérieure, Paris, 1978.

Boyer, M., Sanchez de Zavala, V. and Schwartz, P. (eds), *Ensayos de filosofía de la ciencia. En torno a la obra de Sir Karl Popper*, Burgos Symposium, 22–25 September 1968, Editorial Tecnos, Madrid, 1970.

Braun, G., 'Von Popper zu Lakatos. Das Abgrenzungsproblem zwischen Wissenschaft und Pseudo-wissenschaft', *Conceptus* 28–30 (1977), pp. 217–242.

Campbell, D., 'Evolutionary Epistemology', in G. Radnitzky and W.W. Bartley (eds), *Evolutionary Epistemology, Rationality, and the Sociology of Knowledge*, Open Court, La Salle, 1987.

Capecci, A., 'Scienza e razionalità. Osservazioni sul "principio di falsificazione" ', in *Atti del XVIII Convegno di assistenti universitari di filosofia*, Gregoriana, Padua, 1974, pp. 315–323.

Castrodera, C., 'De la epistemología popperiana a la epistemología darwinista', *Revista de Filosofía* 5 (1992), pp. 329–350.

Coniglione, F., *La scienza impossibile. Dal popperismo alla critica del razionalismo*, Il Mulino, Bologna, 1978.

Currie, G., 'Popper's Evolutionary Epistemology: A Critique', *Synthèse* 37 (1978), pp. 413–431.

Daros, W.R., 'Realismo crítico y conocimiento en el pensamiento de Carlos Popper', *Pensamiento* 46 (1990), no. 182, pp. 179–200.

De Carvalho, M.C., *Karl Poppers Philosophie der wissenschaftlichen und der vorwissenschaftlichen Erfahrung*, Lang, Berne, 1982.

Dinis, A., 'Popper on Metaphysics and Induction', *Epistemologia* 10 (1987), no. 2, pp. 285–301.

Dombrowsky, D.A., 'Popper's World 3 and Plato', *Diotima* 12 (1984), pp. 186–192.

Dottarelli, L., *Popper e il 'gioco della scienza'*, Erre Emme Edizioni, Rome, 1992.

Dumouchel, P., 'Une Théorie darwinienne de la connaissance', *Horizons Philosophiques* 2 (1991–2), pp. 131–153.

Echevarria, J.R., *El critério de falsibilidad en la epistemología de Karl Popper*, G. del Toro, Madrid, 1970.

Feyerabend, P., *Against Method*, New Left Books, London, 1975.

Flor, J.R., 'Karl Raimund Poppers kritischer Rationalismus', in A. Hügli and P. Lübcke (eds), *Philosophie im 20. Jahrhundert*, vol. 2, Rowohlt, Reinbek, 1993, pp. 473–498.

Frascolla, P., *Tre modelli di razionalità. Popper, Carnap e la probabilità inductiva*, ETS, 1991.

Gallo, M., *La fatica della ragione. Il problema dell'oggettività nel pensiero di K.R. Popper*, Loffredo, Naples, 1990.

García Norro, J.J., 'El cuadruple problema de la inducción. Crítica de la solución popperiana del problema de Hume', *Revista de Filosofía* 3 (1990), pp. 5–21.

Gilroy, J.D., 'A Critique of Popper's World 3 Theory', *Modern Schoolman* 62 (1984–85), pp. 185–200.

Giorello, G., 'Il falsificazionismo di Popper', in L. Geymonat (ed.), *Storia del pensiero filosofico e scientifico*, vol. 7, Garzanti, Milan, 1976, pp. 127–189.

Grattan-Guinness, I., 'What Do Theories Talk About? A Critique of Popperian Fallibilism', *Fundamenta Scientiae* 7 (1986), pp. 177–221.

Grünbaum, A., 'Is the Method of Bold Conjectures and Attempted Refutations Justifiably the Method of Science?', BJPS 28 (1976), pp. 105–136.

—— 'Popper versus Inductivism', in G. Radnitzky and G. Andersson (eds), Progress and Rationality in Science, Reidel, Dordrecht, 1978, pp. 117–142.

—— 'Is Freudian Psychoanalytic Theory Pseudo-Scientific by Karl Popper's Criterion of Demarcation?', American Philosophical Quarterly 16 (1979), pp. 131–141.

Haack, E., 'Epistemology with a Knowing Subject', Review of Metaphysics 33 (1979–80), pp. 309–335.

Henke, W., Kritik des kritischen Rationalismus, J.C.B. Mohr (Paul Siebeck), Tübingen, 1974.

Hooker, C.A., 'Formalist Rationality. The Limitations of Popper's Theory of Reason', Metaphilosophy 12 (1981), pp. 247–266.

Howson, C., 'Popper, Prior Probabilities and Inductive Inferences', BJPS 38 (1987), pp. 207–224.

Hübner, K., 'Some Critical Comments on Current Popperianism on the Basis of a Theory of System Sets', in G. Radnitzky and G. Andersson (eds), Progress and Rationality in Science, Reidel, Dordrecht, 1978, pp. 279–289.

Jeffrey, R.C., 'Probability and Falsification: Critique of the Popperian Program', Synthèse 30 (1975), pp. 95–117.

Johannson, I., A Critique of Karl Popper's Methodology, Scandinavian University Books, Stockholm, 1975.

Jones, G. and Perry, C., 'Popper, Induction and Falsification', Erkenntnis 18 (1982), pp. 97–104.

Koertge, N., 'The Methodological Status of Popper's Rationality Principle', Theory and Decision 10 (1979), pp. 83–95.

Krige, J., 'Popper's Epistemology and the Autonomy of Science', Social Studies of Science 8 (1978), pp. 287–307.

—— 'A Critique of Popper's Conception of the Relationship between Logic, Psychology and a Critical Epistemology', Inquiry 21 (1978), pp. 313–335.

Krips, H., 'Popper, Propensity and Quantum Theory', BJPS 35 (1984), pp. 253–274.

Kuhn, T.S., The Structure of Scientific Revolutions, University of Chicago Press, Chicago, 1962.

Lafleur, G., 'Vérisimilarité et méthodologie poppérienne', Dialogue (New York) 28 (1989), no. 3, pp. 365–390.

Lakatos, I., 'Criticism and the Methodology of Scientific Research Programmes', PAS 69 (1968–9), pp. 149–186.

—— 'Changes in the Problem of Inductive Logic', in his, Philosophical Papers, vol. 2: Mathematics, Science and Epistemology, ed. by J. Worrall and G. Currie, Cambridge University Press, Cambridge, 1978.

—— 'Popper on Demarcation and Induction', in his, Philosophical Papers, vol. 1: The Methodology of Scientific Research Programmes, ed. by J. Worrall and G. Currie, Cambridge University Press, Cambridge, 1978.

Largeault, J., 'Critique du rationalisme critique', Archives de Philosophie 48 (1985), pp. 129–142.

Laudan, L., 'Two Dogmas of Methodology', *Philosophy of Science* 43 (1976), pp. 585–597.

—— *Progress and Its Problems: Towards a Theory of Scientific Growth*, Routledge & Kegan Paul, London, 1977.

Ledermann, E.K., 'Popper's Objective Knowledge and the Human Image', *Exploration in Knowledge* 5 (1988), pp. 48–51.

Lentini, L., 'Popper e il problema della demarcazione', in S. Natoli (ed.), *La scienza e la critica del linguaggio*, Marsilio, Venice, 1980.

Leser, N., *Die Gedankenwelt Sir Karl Poppers. Kritischer Rationalismus in Dialog*, Winter, Heidelberg, 1991.

Martinez, Gonzales, *Ciencia y dogmatismo. El problema de la objectividad en Karl R. Popper*, Ediciones Catédra, Madrid, 1980.

Miller, D., 'Karl Popper's Contributions to Logic and Philosophy of Science', *Foundations of Physics* 21 (1991), pp. 1369–1373.

Moravia, S., 'Successo e verità. L'epistemologia critica di K. Popper', *Nuova Corrente* 53 (1970), pp. 219–279.

—— 'Il mito del realismo. Per una critica dell'epistemologia popperiana', *Bolletino di Storia della Filosofia* 4 (1976), pp. 71–84.

Morpurgo-Tagliabue, G., 'Il contro-Popper e la nostalgia dell'induzione', *Verifiche* 11 (1982), pp. 161–197.

Musgrave, A., 'Method or Madness?', in P. Feyerabend, R.S. Cohen and M.W. Wartofsky (eds), *Essays in Memory of Imre Lakatos*, Reidel, Dordrecht, 1976, pp. 457–492.

Nola, R., 'The Status of Popper's Theory of Scientific Methodology', BJPS 38 (1987), pp. 441–480.

Notturno, M., *Objectivity, Rationality and the Third Realm*, Nijhoff, Dordrecht, 1985.

Nuzzaci, F., *Karl Popper. Un epistemologo fallibilista*, Glaux, Naples, 1975.

Obermaier, O., *Poppers 'kritischer Rationalismus': eine Auseinandersetzung über die Reichweite seiner Philosophie*, Vögel, Munich, 1980.

Parrini, P., *Una filosofia senza dogmi*, Il Mulino, Bologna, 1980.

Pera, M., 'La logica della scoperta scientifica in Karl Raimund Popper', *Atti della Accademia delle Scienze in Torino* 106 (1972), no. 2, pp. 635–720.

—— 'Logica della scoperta e ontologia del terzo mondo in K.R. Popper', *Atti della Accademia delle Scienze in Torino* 107 (1973), no. 2, pp. 595–640.

—— *Popper e la scienza su palafitte*, Laterza, Rome and Bari, 1980.

Pozzato, P., 'Prospettive dell'epistemologia popperiana', *Verifiche* 16 (1987), pp. 177–190.

Quillot, R., 'Indeterminisme et interactionisme chez Popper', *Archives de Philosophie* 48 (1985), pp. 109–127.

Radnitzky, G., 'From Justifying a Theory to Comparing Theories and Selecting Questions. Popper's Alternative to Foundationalism and Scepticism', *Revue Internationale de Philosophie* 34 (1980), pp. 179–228.

—— 'Popper as a Turning Point in the Philosophy of Science', in P. Levinson (ed.), *In Pursuit of Truth: Essays on the Philosophy of Karl Popper on the Occasion of His 80th Birthday*, Humanities Press, New York, 1982, pp. 64–82.

—— 'Popperian Philosophy of Science as an Antidote against Anarchism', in P. Feyerabend, R.S. Cohen and M. Wartofsky (eds), *Essays in Memory of Imre Lakatos*, Reidel, Dordrecht, 1976, 506–546.

—— 'Réflexions sur Popper', *Archives de Philosophie* 48 (1985), pp. 79–108.

Reeder, H. and Langsdorf, L., 'A Phenomenological Exploration of Popper's World 3', in (various), *The Horizons of Continental Philosophy*, Kluwer Academic, Dordrecht, 1988, pp. 93–129.

Reichberg, G., 'Popper en question. Quelques critiques sur la croissance du savoir, I–II', *Revue Thomiste* 85 (1985), pp. 38–68, pp. 431–456.

Rescher, N., *A Useful Inheritance: Evolutionary Aspects of the Theory of Knowledge*, Rowman & Littlefield, Savage, 1990, pp. 15–38.

Riverso, E., 'I problemi della ricerca scientifica in K. Popper', *Rassegna di scienze filosofiche* (1961), pp. 240–265.

Rosa, R., 'Chance in Classical Physics. Popper's Manmade Indeterminism', *Epistemologia* 6 (1983), pp. 125–131.

Rossi, A., *Popper e la filosofia della scienza*, Sansoni, Florence, 1975.

Rudder, C., 'The Falsification Fallacy', *Studies in Philosophy and Education* 12 (1993), pp. 179–199.

Ruiz Velasco, N., 'Karl Popper. Racionalismo crítico, metafísica y metodología de lo inverificable', *Tópicos* 1 (1991), no. 1, pp. 99–135.

Salamun, K. (ed.), *Karl R. Popper und die Philosophie des kritischen Rationalismus. Zum 85. Geburtstag von Karl Popper*, Rodopi, Amsterdam, 1989.

Salmon, W.C., 'The Justification of Inductive Rules of Inference', in I. Lakatos (ed.), *The Problems of Inductive Logic*, North Holland, Amsterdam, 1968, pp. 24–43.

Schäfer L., 'Über die Diskrepanz zwischen Methodologie und Metaphysik bei Popper', *Studium Generale* 23 (1970), pp. 856–877.

Schneider, W.L., *Objectives Verstehen. Rekonstruktion eines Paradigmas: Gadamer, Popper, Toulmin, Luhmann*, Westdeutscher Verlag, Opladen, 1991.

Schramm, A., 'Objektive Erkenntnis und Methodologie', *Conceptus* 11 (1977), nos. 28–30, pp. 377–392.

Schurz, G., 'Karl Popper und das Induktionsproblem', in M. Seller and F. Stadler (eds), *Heinrich Gomperz, Karl Popper und die Österreichische Philosophie*, Rodopi, Amsterdam, 1994, pp. 147–161.

Schurz, G. and Weingartner, P., 'Verisimilitude Defined by Relevant Consequence-Elements. A New Reconstruction of Popper's Original Idea', in T. Kuipers (ed.), *What Is Closer to Truth?*, Rodopi, Amsterdam, 1987, pp. 47–77.

Simkin, C., *Popper's Views on Natural and Social Science*, Brill, Leiden, 1993.

Spinner, H., 'Ist der kritische Rationalismus am Ende?', *Analyse & Kritik* 2 (1980), pp. 99–126.

Ströker E., 'Konventionalistische Argumente in Poppers Wissenschaftsphilosophie', *Erkenntnis* 21 (1984), pp. 385–403.

Tarca, L., 'Problemi del razionalismo popperiano', in S. Natoli (ed.), *La scienza e la critica del linguaggio*, Marsilio, Venice, 1980, pp. 41–75.

Tilley, N., 'Popper and Prescriptive Methodology', *Metaphilosophy* 24 (1993), pp. 155–166.
Todisco, O., 'La crisi dei fundamenti e la risposta del razionalismo fallibilista di K.R. Popper', *Miscellanea Francescana* 84 (1984), pp. 47–114.
Turney, P., 'A Note on Popper's Equation of Simplicity with Falsifiability', BJPS 42 (1991), pp. 105–109.
Volpe, G., 'Intuizione e interpretazione nell'epistemologia dell'ultimo Popper', *Discipline filosofiche* 1 (1991), pp. 25–49.
—— 'Realtà, spiegazione causale e ontologia nella teoria dei tre mondi di Karl Popper', *Annali di Discipline filosofiche dell'Università di Bologna* 9 (1987–8), pp. 67–90.
Wallner, F. (ed.), *Karl Popper – Philosophie und Wissenschaft*, Braumüller, Vienna, 1985.
Waterhouse, J., 'Popper and Metaphysical Scepticism', *The Philosophical Forum* 15 (1983–4), pp. 365–391.
Watkins, J., 'The Popperian Approach to Scientific Knowledge', in G. Radnitzky and G. Andersson (eds), *Progress and Rationality in Science*, Reidel, Dordrecht, 1978, pp. 23–43.
Weinheimer, H., *Rationalität und Begründung. Das Grundlagenproblem in der Philosophie Karl Poppers*, Bouvier, Bonn, 1986.
Weinke, K., 'Der Kritische Rationalismus', *Zeitschrift für philosophische Forschung* 27 (1973), pp. 551–568.
Wellmer, A., *Methodologie als Erkenntnistheorie zur Wissenschaftslehre Karl R. Poppers*, Suhrkamp, Frankfurt a.M., 1967.
Wettersten, J.R., 'Traditional Rationality versus a Tradition of Criticism. A Criticism of Popper's Theory of the Objectivity of Science', *Erkenntnis* 12 (1978), pp. 329–338.
Worrall, J., 'The Popperian Approach to Scientific Knowledge', in G. Radnitzky and G. Andersson (eds), *Progress and Rationality in Science*, Reidel, Dordrecht, 1978, pp. 23–43.
Wuketits, F.M., *Concepts and Approaches in Evolutionary Epistemology: Towards an Evolutionary Theory of Knowledge*, Reidel, Dordrecht, 1984.

Studies on political philosophy and the human sciences

Adorno, T.W. *et al.* (1969), *The Positivist Dispute in German Sociology*, Heinemann, London, 1976.
Albrecht, R., *Sozialtechnologie und ganzheitliche Sozialphilosophie. Zu Karl R. Poppers Kritik der ganzheitliche Sozialphilosophie*, Bouvier, Bonn, 1979.
Alcaro, M., *Filosofia democratica. Scienza e potere nel pensiero di J. Dewey, B. Russell, K. Popper*, Dedalo, Bari, 1986.
Antiseri, D., 'La filosofia politica di Karl Popper', *Rivista di filosofia neoscolastica* 67 (1975), pp. 201–223.
Bagnulo, R., 'Metodo scientifico e metodo democratico in Karl Popper', *Fenomenologia e società* 4 (1981), pp. 189–217.
Bambrough, R. (ed.), *Plato, Popper and Politics: Some Contributions to a Modern Controversy*, Barnes & Noble, New York, 1967.

BIBLIOGRAPHY

Baudouin, J., *La Philosophie politique de Karl Popper*, PUF, Paris 1994.

Bausola, A., 'Neopositivismo e scienze umane nel pensiero di Karl Popper', in his, *Indagini di storia della filosofia*, Vita e Pensiero, Milan, 1969, pp. 64–114.

Bellino, F., *Ragione e morale in Karl R. Popper. Nichilismo, relativismo e fallibilismo etico*, Edizioni Levante, Bari, 1982.

Bobbio, N., 'Società chiusa e società aperta', *Il Ponte*, 1946, pp. 1039–1046.

Boniolo, G., *Questioni di filosofia e di metodologia delle scienze sociali*, Borla, Rome, 1990.

Buzzoni, M., 'Popper e l'oggettività delle scienze storiche', *Contributo* 5 (1981), pp. 3–20.

Carr, E.H., *What Is History?*, Macmillan, London, 1962.

Cipolla, C., *Dopo Popper*, Borla, Rome, 1990.

Clark, D., 'Karl Popper's Solution to the "Problem of Human Freedom" ', *Modern Schoolman* 61 (1983–4), pp. 117–130.

Cornforth, M., *The Open Philosophy and the Open Society: A Reply to Dr Popper's Refutations of Marxism*, Lawrence & Wishart, London, 1968.

Corvi, R., 'Popper: il buon profeta', *Humanitas* 48 (1993), pp. 403–427.

Cotroneo, G., *Popper e la società aperta*, SugarCo, Milan, 1981.

Cubeddu, R., 'Karl Raimund Popper: una fondazione epistemologica al liberalismo', *Il pensiero politico* 10 (1977), pp. 253–267.

—— 'La teoria della spiegazione storica in Popper', *Rivista di Filosofia* 70 (1979), pp. 236–268.

Curi, U., 'Sulla 'democrazia di conflitto' di Popper e Feyerabend', *Centauro* (1983), no. 8, pp. 122–144.

Currie, G. and Musgrave, A (eds), *Popper and the Human Sciences*, Nijhoff, Dordrecht, 1985.

De Marchi, W. (ed.), *The Popperian Legacy in Economics*, Cambridge University Press, Cambridge, 1988.

De Vries, G.J., *Anthistenes Redivivus: Popper's Attack on Plato*, Amsterdam, 1952.

Euchner, W., 'Conflits de méthodes dans la sociologie allemande', *Archives de Philosophie* 33 (1970), pp. 177–221.

Finocchiaro, M., 'Methodological Criticism and Critical Methodology. An Analysis of Popper's Critique of Marxian Social Science', *Zeitschrift für allgemeine Wissenschaftslehre* 10 (1979), pp. 363–374.

Fleck, C., 'Sieg der "Offene Gesellschaft"?', in M. Seller and F. Stadler (eds), *Heinrich Gomperz, Karl Popper und die Österreichische Philosophie*, Rodopi, Amsterdam, 1994, pp. 201–222.

Flew, A., 'Popper and Historical Necessities', *Philosophy* 65 (1990), pp. 53–64.

Freeman, M., 'Sociology and Utopia: Some Reflections on the Social Philosophy of Karl Popper', BJPS 26 (1975), pp. 20–34.

Gallic, W.B., 'Popper and the Critical Philosophy of History', in M. Bunge (ed.), *The Critical Approach to Science and Philosophy. In Honour of Sir Karl Popper*, The Free Press, London and New York, 1964, pp. 410–422.

Gendin, A.M., 'Societal Prognosis and Popper's Interpretation', *Soviet Studies in Philosophy* 8 (1969), pp. 148–168.

Gray, J.N., 'The Liberalism of Karl Popper', *Government and Opposition* 11 (1976), pp. 337–355.

Hands, D., 'Karl Popper and Economic Methodology. A New Look', *Economics and Philosophy* 1 (1985), pp. 83–99.

Heine, W., *Methodologischer Individualismus*, Königshausen und Neumann, Würzburg, 1983.

Howson, C., 'Some Further Reflections on the Popper–Miller "Disproof" of Probabilistic Induction', *Australasian Journal of Philosophy* 68 (1990), pp. 221–228.

Jacobs, S., *Science and British Liberalism: Locke, Bentham, Mill and Popper*, Avebury, Aldershot, 1991.

James, R., *Return to Reason: Popper's Thought in Public Life*, Pen Books, Shepton Mallet, 1980.

Joly, R., 'Karl Popper critique de Platon', *Réseaux* 1981, nos. 39–40, pp. 87–103.

Koertge, N., 'Popper's Metaphysical Research Program for the Human Sciences', *Inquiry* 18 (1975), pp. 437–462.

Largeault, J., 'Popper, épistémologie et pensée politique', in his, *Enigmes et controverses*, Aubier, Paris, 1980, pp. 138–154.

Lührs, G., Sarrazin, T., Spreer, F. and Tietzel, M. (eds), *Kritischer Rationalismus und Sozialdemokratie*, Dietz Nachf., Berlin, 1975.

Marcuse, H., 'Karl Popper and the Problem of Historical Law', in his, *Studies in Critical Philosophy*, Beacon Press, Boston, 1972, pp. 191–208.

Messmer, B., *Die Grundlagen von Poppers Sozialphilosophie*, Lang, Berne, 1982.

Moldofsky, 'The Open Society: Hayek vs Popper?', *Newsletters for Those Interested in the Philosophy of Karl Popper* 3/3–4 (1987–8), pp. 25–35.

Montaleone, C., *Scienze umane e metodologia. Weber, Popper, Durkheim*, Cisalpino-La Goliardica, Milan, 1975.

—— *Filosofia e politica in Popper*, Guida, Naples, 1979.

Nadeau, R., 'Popper et la méthodologie économique. Un profond malentendu', *Revue de Synthèse* 214 (1993), pp. 61–85.

Parekh, B., *Contemporary Political Thinkers*, Robertson, Oxford, 1982, pp. 124–153.

Parlej, P., 'History, Historicism, Narratives: Identity in the Philosophy of History of Karl Popper', *International Studies in Philosophy* 23 (1991), pp. 31–46.

Passmore, J., 'The Poverty of Historicism Revisited', *History and Theory* 24 (1975), pp. 30–47.

Pellicani, L., 'I nemici della società aperta', in various, *La sfida di Popper*, Armando, Rome, 1981.

Perkinson, H., *The Possibility of Error: An Approach to Education*, McKay Company, New York, 1971.

Perona, A.J., *Entre el liberalismo y la social democracia. Popper y la 'sociedad abierta'*, Anthropos, Barcelona, 1993.

Petroni, A.M. (ed.), *Karl Popper: il pensiero politico*, Le Monnier, Florence, 1981.

BIBLIOGRAPHY

Possenti, V., 'La società aperta nel pensiero politico del '900 (Bergson, Popper e Maritain)', *Rivista di Filosofia neo-scolastica* 76 (1984), pp. 269–291.

Radnitzky, G. and Bartley, W.W. (eds), *Evolutionary Epistemology, Rationality and the Sociology of Knowledge*, Open Court, La Salle, 1987.

Rossi, P., 'Karl Popper e la critica neopositivistica dello storicismo', *Rivista di Filosofia* 48 (1957), pp. 46–73.

Ruelland, J.G., *De l'épistémologie à la politique. La philosophie de l'histoire de Karl R. Popper*, PUF, Paris, 1991.

Sassower, R., 'Economics according to Popper', *Philosophy of the Social Sciences* 18 (1988), pp. 383–386.

Schmid, M., 'The Idea of Rationality and its Relationship to Social Science. Comments on Popper's Philosophy of the Social Sciences', *Inquiry* 31 (1988), pp. 451–469.

Schupp, F., *Poppers Methodologie der Geschichtswissenschaft. Historische Erklärung und Interpretation*, Bouvier, Bonn, 1975.

Schwarzburg, D., *Abstraktes Denken und verwissenschaftliche Gesellschaft. Zum Theorie–Praxis–Verhältnis bei Weber, Habermas, Popper und Feyerabend*, Materialis Verlag, Frankfurt a.M., 1990.

Sciarra, E., *L'epistemologia delle scienze storico-sociali nel pensiero di Karl Popper*, University of Abruzzi, Chieti, 1981.

Shaw, P.D., 'Popper, Historicism and the Remaking of Society', *Philosophy of the Social Sciences* 1 (1971), pp. 299–308.

Skagestad, P., *Making Sense of History: The Philosophy of Popper and Collingwood*, Universitetsforlaget, Oslo, 1975.

Spinner, H., *Popper und die Politik. Rekonstruktion und Kritik der Sozial-, Polit- und Geschichtsphilosophie des kritischen Rationalismus, I: Geschlossenheitsprobleme*, Dietz, Berlin, 1978.

Suchting, W., 'Marx, Popper and "Historicism"', *Inquiry* 15 (1972), pp. 235–266.

Urbach, P., 'Is Any of Popper's Arguments against Historicism Valid?', BJPS 29 (1978), pp. 117–130.

Van Eikema Hommes, H., 'The Relevance of Popper's Scientific Method for Legal Theory', *Rechtstheorie* 14 (1983), pp. 459–471.

Wild, J., *Plato's Modern Enemies and the Theory of Natural Law*, University of Chicago Press, Chicago, 1953.

Wilkins, B.T., *Has History Any Meaning? A Critique of Popper's Philosophy of History*, Hassocks/Cornell Univerity Press/The Harvester Press, Ithaca, 1978.

Studies on particular themes

Andersson, G., 'The Problem of Verisimilitude', in G. Radnitzky and G. Andersson (eds), *Progress and Rationality in Science*, Reidel, Dordrecht, 1978.

Bamford, G., 'Popper's Explications of Ad Hocness: Circularity, Empirical Content and Scientific Practice', BJPS 44 (1993), pp. 335–355.

Barnhardt, J.E., *The Study of Religion and Its Meaning: New Exploration in the Light of Karl Popper and Émile Durkheim*, Mouton, The Hague, 1977.

Berkson, W. and Wettersten, J.R., *Learning from Error: Karl Popper's Psychology of Learning*, Open Court, La Salle, 1984.

Blaukopf, K., 'Logik der Musikforschung: Karl Poppers methodischer Beitrag', in M. Seller and F. Stadler (eds), *Heinrich Gomperz, Karl Popper und die Österreichische Philosophie*, Rodopi, Amsterdam, 1994, pp. 147–161.

Buzzoni, M., 'Filosofia e storiografia filosofica nell'interpretazione popperiana dei presocratici', *Bolletino della Società filosofica italiana*, (1985), no. 126, pp. 28–43.

Carnap, R., 'Popper on the Demarcation between Science and Metaphysics', in P.A. Schilpp (ed.), *The Philosophy of R. Carnap*, Open Court, La Salle, 1963, pp. 877–882.

—— 'Popper on Probability and Induction', in P.A. Schilpp (ed.), *The Philosophy of R. Carnap*, Open Court, La Salle, 1963, pp. 995–998.

Carr, B., 'Popper's Third World', *The Philosophical Quarterly* 27 (1977), pp. 214–226.

Dorn ,G.J.W., 'Popper's Law of the Excess of the Probability of the Conditional Probability', *Conceptus* 26 (1992–93), pp. 3–61.

Faludi, A., *Critical Rationalism and Planning Methodology*, Pion, London, 1986.

Farr J., 'Popper's Hermeneutics', *Philosophy of the Social Sciences* 13 (1983), pp. 157–176.

Ferraris Favaro L., 'Oltre Popper. Per un'etica fallibilista, ma non relativista', *Filosofia e Teologia* 5 (1991), pp. 207–220.

Harris, J.H., 'Popper's Definition of Verisimilitude', BJPS 25 (1978), pp. 160–166.

Hochkeppel, W., 'Wider den Modernismus in der Kunst. Karl Poppers Materialien zu einer Ästhetik', in M. Seller and F. Stadler (eds), *Heinrich Gomperz, Karl Popper und die Österreichische Philosophie*, Rodopi, Amsterdam, 1994, pp. 147–161.

Jammer, M., 'Sir Karl Popper and His Philosophy of Physics', *Foundations of Physics* 21 (1991), pp. 1357–1368.

Janoska, G., 'Popper und das Problem der Metaphysik', *Kant-Studien* 58 (1967), pp. 158–172.

Kirk, G.S., 'Popper on Science and Presocratics', *Mind* 69 (1960), pp. 318–339.

Kulka, T., 'Art and Science: An Outline of Popperian Aesthetics', *British Journal of Aesthetics* 29 (1989), no. 3, pp. 197–212.

—— 'The Logical Structure of Aesthetic Value Judgements. An Outline of a Popperian Aesthetics' [Hebrew text with a summary in English], *Iyyun* 38 (1989).

Lakatos, I., 'Necessity, Kneale and Popper', in his, *Philosophical Papers*, vol. 2: *Mathematics, Science and Epistemology*, edited by J. Worrall and G. Currie, Cambridge University Press, Cambridge, 1978, pp. 121–127.

—— 'On Popperian Historiography', in his, *Philosophical Papers*, vol. 2: *Mathematics, Science and Epistemology*, Cambridge University Press, Cambridge, 1978, pp. 201–210.

Langsdorf, L. and Reeder, H., 'A Phenomenological Exploration of Popper's "World 3"', in H.J. Silverman (ed.), *The Horizons of Continental Philosophy*, Kluwer, Dordrecht, 1988, pp. 93–129.

Largeault, J., 'Popper, objectivité et troisième monde', in his, *Enigmes et controverses*, Aubier, Paris, 1980, pp. 64–80.

Lorenzetti, L.M. and Antonietti, A., *Il gatto in gondola. Conoscenza/persona, educazione/società nella prospettiva di K.R. Popper e oltre*, UNICOPLI, Milan, 1987.

Mackie, J.L., 'Failure in Criticism: Popper and His Commentators', BJPS 29 (1978), pp. 363–375.

Miller, D.W., 'Popper's Qualitative Theory of Verisimilitude', BJPS 25 (1974), pp. 166–177.

—— 'Propensity: Popper or Peirce?', BJPS 26 (1975), pp. 123–132.

—— 'Verisimilitude Deflated', BJPS 27 (1976), pp. 363–380.

Milotti, A., 'Appunti sulla fortuna di Popper in Italia. Sviluppi e contrasti', *Nuova antologia* 118 (1983), no. 2147, pp. 412–423.

Mondadori, M., 'Probabilità e contenuto semantico nella logica della scoperta scientifica di K. Popper', *Lingua e stile* 6 (1971), pp. 317–333.

Montaleone, C., 'A proposito di dialettica, metodo scientifico, sociologia', *Rivista di Filosofia* 1 (1971), pp. 44–68.

Neumaier, O., 'Popper und die Frühgeschichte der Leib-Seele-Problematik', *Conceptus* 21 (1987), nos. 53–54, pp. 247–266.

Newton-Smith, W.H. and Tianji Jiang (eds), *Popper in China*, Routledge, London, 1992.

Nola, R., 'Some Observations on a Popperian Experiment Concerning Observation', *Journal for General Philosophy of Science* 21 (1990), pp. 329–346.

Petrovic, A.G., 'Les sciences biologiques et biomédicales face à la méthodologie poppérienne', in R. Bouveresse and H. Barreau (eds), *Karl Popper: science et philosophie*, Vrin, Paris, 1991, pp. 217–249.

Raymond, P., 'Matérialisme historique ou matérialisme biologique? A propos de Karl R. Popper', *Pensée*, 1979, no. 203, pp. 20–40.

Rizzacasa, A., 'Epistemologia, arte e storia dell'arte. Un'ipotesi interpretiva da K.R. Popper e E.H. Gombrich', *Filosofia e società* 5 (1979), no. 22, pp. 41–70.

Rosier, M., 'Rationalité universelle et raisons singulières', *Revue de Synthèse* 114 (1993), pp. 33–59.

Rossi, A., 'Il "Methodenstreit" tra la scuola analitica di Popper e la scuola dialettica di Francoforte', *La nuova critica* 23 (1969–70), pp. 113–124.

Rossi, P.A., 'Predizione e retrodizione in storia. Note sul modello Popper–Hempel', *Verifiche* 7 (1978), pp. 21–35.

Ruse, M., 'Karl Popper's Philosophy of Biology', *Philosophy of Science* 44 (1977), pp. 638–661.

Sachs, M., 'Popper and Reality', *Synthèse* 33 (1976–7), pp. 355–369.

Santinello, G., 'Principi di storiografia filosofica nell'interpretazione dei presocratici di K.R. Popper', *Bolletino di storia della filosofia* 3 (1975), pp. 142–164.

Scheibe, E., 'Popper and Quantum Logic', BJPS 25 (1974), pp. 319–328.

Schneider, C., 'Two Interpretations of Objective Probability: On the

Ambiguity of Popper's Conception of Propensities', *Philosophia Naturalis* 31 (1994), pp. 107–131.

Tichy, P., 'On Popper's Definition of Verisimilitude', BJPS 25 (1974), pp. 155–160.

—— 'Verisimilitude Redefined', BJPS 27 (1976), pp. 25–42.

—— 'Verisimilitude Revisited', *Synthèse* 74 (1978), pp. 175–196.

Tournier, F., 'Un retournement dans la philosophie de la biologie de Karl R. Popper', *Philosophiques* 18 (1991), pp. 61–94.

Watkins, J., 'Corroboration and the Problem of Content-Comparison', in G. Radnitzky and G. Andersson (eds), *Progress and Rationality in Science*, Reidel, Dordrecht, 1978, pp. 339–378.

Williams, D.E., 'Masons, Evangelists and Heretics in Karl Popper's Cathedral', *Queen's Quarterly* 91 (1984), pp. 679–692.

Witschel, G., *Wertvorstellung im Werk Karl R. Poppers*, Bouvier, Bonn, 1977.

Zwirn, D. and Zwirn, H., 'L'Argument de Popper et Miller contre la justification probabiliste de l'induction', in P. Jacob (ed.), *L'Âge de la science*, Odile Jacob, Paris, 1989, pp. 59–81.

Studies of Popper in relation to other authors

Antiseri, D., 'Sulla teoria storiografica di Popper ed Hempel', *Proteus* 2 (1970), pp. 69–118.

—— 'Epistemologia evoluzionistica da Mach a Popper', *Nuova Civiltà delle Macchine* 4 (1986), pp. 52–66.

Antonietti, A., *Cervello, mente e cultura. L'interazionismo di J.C. Eccles (e K.R. Popper)*, Angeli, Milan, 1986.

Bartley, W.W., 'Non-justificationism: Popper versus Wittgenstein', in P. Weingartner and J. Czermak (eds), *Epistemology and Philosophy of Science*, Hölder-Pichler-Tempsky, Vienna, 1983, pp. 255–261.

Bayertz, K., 'Wissenschaftsentwicklung als Evolution? Evolutionäre Konzeptionen wissenschaftlichen Wandels bei Ernst Mach, Karl Popper und Stephen Toulmin', *Zeitschrift für allgemeine Wissenschaftstheorie* 18 (1987), pp. 61–91.

Carettini, G.P., 'Peirce, Holmes, Popper', in U. Eco and T.A. Sebeok (eds), *The Sign of Three*, Indiana University Press, Bloomington, 1988, pp. 135–153.

Casarin Donadon, E., 'La teoria linguistica di Karl Bühler e sua influenza sull'epistemologia di Karl Popper', *Sapienza* 40 (1987), pp. 421–434.

Chauvire, C., 'Vérifier ou falsifier. De Peirce à Popper', *Les Etudes Philosophiques* (1981), no. 3, pp. 257–278.

Cipolla, C., *Dopo Popper*, Borla, Rome, 1990.

Coppola, B., 'Due prospettive storiche ed epistemologiche: Kuhn e Popper', *Annali della Facoltà di Lettere e Filosofia dell'Università di Napoli* 22 (1979–80), pp. 363–390.

Cotroneo, G., 'La critica dell'"evidenza" in Popper e Perelman', *Discorsi* 2/1 (1982), pp. 92–109.

Dahrendorf, R., 'Remarks on the Discussion of the Papers by Karl R.

Popper and Theodor W. Adorno', in T.W. Adorno et al., The Positivist Dispute in German Sociology, Heinemann, London, 1976, pp. 123–130.

D'Amico, R., 'Karl Popper and the Frankfurt School', Telos 86 (1990–1), pp. 33–48.

De Coorebyter, V., 'Hypothèse auxiliaire et petition de principe: entre Popper et Feyerabend', in V. De Coorebyter (ed.), Rhétorique de la science, PUF, Paris, 1994, pp. 91–116.

Dederer, A., 'Schopenhauer und Popper', Schopenhauer Jahrbuch 59 (1978), pp. 77–89.

Dombrowski, D., 'Rorty and Popper on the Footnotes to Plato', Dialogos 22 (1987), no. 49, pp. 135–145.

Donagan, A., 'Historical Explanation: the Popper–Hempel Theory Reconsidered', History and Theory 4 (1964), pp. 3–26.

Englader, J.L., Pour l'incertain. L'apport de Popper à Marx, Syllepse, Périscope, Paris, 1990.

Fernandes, S., Foundations of Objective Knowledge: The Relationship of Popper's Theory of Knowledge to That of Kant's, Reidel, Dordrecht, 1985.

Fistetti, F., Neurath contro Popper. Otto Neurath riscoperto, Dedalo, Bari, 1985.

Galeazzi, U., 'Scienza e ragione strumentale nella scuola di Francoforte e in K. Popper', Proteus 5 (1974), no. 13, pp. 97–122.

Geymonat, L., Riflessioni critiche su Kuhn e Popper, Dedalo, Bari, 1983.

Giannaras, A., Platon und K.R. Popper. Zur Kritik der politischen Philosophie Platons, Φιλοσοφία 3 (1973), pp. 208–223.

Gomez Tutor, J.J., 'Die Interpretation des kantischen Apriorismus in Poppers Frühwerk', Studi Kantiani 2 (1989), pp. 97–116.

Gozzi, G., 'Dialettica e razionalismo critico. Analisi del dibattito epistemologico tra Popper e la scuola di Francoforte', Il Mulino 23 (1974), no. 231, pp. 66–92.

Haack, S. and Kolenda, K., 'Two Fallibilists in Search of the Truth [Peirce and Popper]', PAS, supp. vol. 51 (1977), pp. 63–104.

Habermas, J., 'The Analytical Theory of Science and Dialectics', in T. Adorno et al., The Positivist Dispute in German Sociology, Heinemann, London 1976, pp. 131–162.

Habermehl, H., Historizismus und kritischer Rationalismus. Einwände gegen Poppers Kritik an Comte, Marx und Platon, Alber, Freiburg, 1980.

Hahn, R., Die Theorie der Erfahrung bei Popper und Kant. Zur Kritik des kritischen Rationalismus am Transzendentalen Apriori, Alber, Freiburg, 1982.

Hudelson, R., 'Popper's Critique of Marx', Philosophical Studies (Dordrecht), 37 (1980), pp. 236–268.

Idan, A., 'Political Criticism in History: Popper and Althusser', Manuscrito 9 (1986), no. 2, pp. 25–37.

Jansohn, H., 'Zur Kritik der unkritischen Kritik. Ein Vergleich zwischen T.W. Adorno und K.R. Popper', Zeitschrift für philosophische Forschung 29 (1975), pp. 544–561.

Juffras, A., 'Popper and Dewey on Rationality', *Journal of Critical Analysis* 4 (1972), no. 3, pp. 96–103.

Klemke, E.D., 'Popper's Criticism of Wittgenstein's *Tractatus*', *Midwest Studies in Philosophy* 6 (1982), pp. 239–261.

Koertge, N., 'Towards a New Theory of Scientific Inquiry', in G. Radnitzky and G. Andersson (eds), *Progress and Rationality in Science*, Reidel, Dordrecht, 1978, pp. 253–278.

Lacharite, N., 'Le Développement des sciences est-il un procès normé? Faut-il choisir entre Kuhn, Feyerabend et Popper?', *Dialogue* 17 (1978), pp. 616–633.

Largeault, J., 'Réglements de comptes entre épistémologues', in his, *Enigmes et controverses*, Aubier, Paris, 1980, pp. 121–137.

Levinson, R.B., *In Defence of Plato*, Cambridge University Press, Cambridge, 1957.

Michalos, A., *The Popper-Carnap Controversy*, Nijhoff, The Hague, 1971.

Munz, P., 'Popper and Wittgenstein', in M. Bunge (ed.), *The Critical Approach to Science and Philosophy. In Honour of Karl Popper*, The Free Press, London and New York, 1964.

—— 'Transformation in Philosophy through the Teaching Methods of Wittgenstein and Popper', *Proceedings of the Tenth International Conference on the Unity of the Sciences*, New York, 1982, vol. 2, pp. 1235–1265.

—— *Our Knowledge of the Growth of Knowledge: Popper or Wittgenstein?*, Routledge, London, 1985.

Pera M., 'La scienza a una dimensione? Un esame delle epistemologie di G. Bachelard e K. Popper', *Nuova Corrente*, (1974), no. 64, 287–338.

Philippoussis, J., 'Popper's Sceptic Tendencies in Relation to Plato's Aporia', in L.C. Bargeliotes (ed.), *Scepticism: Interdisciplinary Approaches*, Ministry of Culture, Athens, distributed by Vrin, Paris, 1990, pp. 265–283.

Pollak, G., *Fortschritt und Kritik. Von Popper zu Feyerabend*, Fink, Munich, 1987.

Quintanilla, M., 'Popper y Piaget. Dos perspectivas para la teoría de la ciencia', *Teorema* 3 (1973), pp. 5–23.

Radnitzky, G., 'Philosophie und Wissenschaftstheorie zwischen Wittgenstein und Popper', *Conceptus* 11 (1977), pp. 249–281.

—— 'Contemporary Philosophical Discussion as Debates between Early Wittgensteinians, Popper and Later Wittgensteinians', *Manuscrito* 2 (1978–9), no. 2, pp. 67–117.

—— 'Analytic Philosophy as the Confrontation between Wittgensteinians and Popper', in J. Agassi and R.S. Cohen (eds), *Scientific Philosophy Today: Essays in Honor of M. Bunge*, Reidel, Dordrecht, 1982, pp. 239–286.

—— *Entre Wittgenstein et Popper. Détours vers la découverte: le vrai, le faux, l'hypothèse*, Vrin, Paris, 1987.

Ray, L.S., 'Critical Theory and Positivism: Popper and the Frankfurt School', *Philosophy of the Social Sciences* 9 (1979), pp. 149–173.

Ruelland, J.G., 'La controverse Habermas–Popper', *La Petite Revue de Philosophie* 2 (1980), pp. 105–135.

Scoppolini, S., *Popper contra Hegel. Per una critica della critica*, Olmi, Macerata, 1985.

Seller, M. and Stadler F. (eds), *Heinrich Gomperz, Karl Popper und die Österreichische Philosophie*, Rodopi, Amsterdam, 1994.

Stadler, F., 'Heinrich Gomperz und Karl Popper im Kontext des logischen Empirismus', in M. Seller and F. Stadler (eds), *Heinrich Gomperz, Karl Popper und die Österreichische Philosophie*, Rodopi, Amsterdam, 1994, pp. 1–29.

Stegmüller, W., 'Normale Wissenschaft und wissenschaftliche Revolutionen. Kritische Betrachtungen zur Kontroverse zwischen Karl Popper und Thomas S. Kuhn', *Wissenschaft und Weltbild* 29 (1976), nos. 3–4, pp. 169–180.

Stove, D., *Popper and After: Four Modern Irrationalists*, Pergamon Press, Oxford, 1982.

Toben, G.F., *Peirce's Fallibilism and Popper's Falsification Theory*, Peace Books, Edenhorpe, 1986.

Urbach, P., 'Francis Bacon as a Precursor to Popper', BJPS 33 (1982), pp. 113–132.

Valdré, L., 'Giustificazioni ermeneutiche a una lettura parallela Popper–Bachelard', *Protagora* 24 (1984), no. 5, pp. 115–123.

Vernon, R., 'The "Great Society" and the "Open Society": Liberalism in Hayek and Popper', *Canadian Journal of Political Science* 9 (1976), pp. 261–276.

Vidanovic, D., 'Rationalism or Empiricism: Chomsky or Popper?', *Synthesis Philosophica* (Zagreb), 2 (1987), no. 3, pp. 179–188.

Vigliani, A., 'Karl Popper e John Eccles: il problema del rapporto mente–corpo tra filosofia e scienza', *Filosofia* 34 (1983), pp. 87–144.

Volpe, G., 'Perchè non siamo cervelli in una vasca: Putnam, Popper e il realismo', *Rivista di Filosofia* 82 (1991), pp. 369–397.

Wagner, H., 'Poppers Deutung von Kants Kritik der reinen Vernunft', *Kant-Studien* 67 (1976), pp. 425–441.

Watkins, J., 'Hume, Carnap, Popper', in I. Lakatos (ed.), *The Problems of Inductive Logic*, North Holland, Amsterdam, 1968, pp. 271–282.

Worrall, J., 'The Ways in Which the Methodology of Scientific Research Programmes Improves on Popper's Methodology', in G. Radnitzky and G. Andersson (eds), *Progress and Rationality in Science*, Reidel, Dordrecht, 1978, pp. 45–70.

Yearley, S., 'Imputing Intentionality: Popper, Demarcation and Darwin, Freud and Marx', *Studies in the History and Philosophy of Science* (London), 16 (1985), pp. 337–350.

Yulina, N., 'On Popper's Implicit Hegelianism', *Philosophia Naturalis* 21 (1984), pp. 652–661.

NAME INDEX

207